THIS IS OUR HOUSE

Popular Cultural Studies

Series editors: Justin O'Connor and Derek Wynne.
Series sub-editor: Maggy Taylor.

The editors are, respectively, Director and Research Director of the Manchester Institute for Popular Culture where this series is based. The Manchester Institute for Popular Culture, at The Manchester Metropolitan University, England, was set up in order to promote theoretical and empirical research in the area of contemporary popular culture, both within the academy and in conjunction with local, national and international agencies. The Institute is a postgraduate research centre engaged in comparative research projects around aspects of consumption and regulation of popular culture in the city. The Institute also runs a number of postgraduate research programmes, with a particular emphasis on ethnographic work. The series intends to reflect all aspects of the Institute's activities including its relationship with interested academics throughout the world. Current theoretical debates within the field of popular culture will be explored within an empirical context. Much of the research is undertaken by young researchers actively involved in their chosen fields of study, allowing an awareness of the issues and an attentiveness to actual developments often lacking in standard academic writings on the subject. The series will also reflect the working methods of the Institute, emphasising a collective research effort and the regular presentation of work-in-progress to the Institute's research seminars. The series hopes, therefore, both to push foward the debates around the regulation and consumption of popular culture, urban regeneration and postmodern social theory whilst introducing an ethnographic and contextual basis for such debates.

This is Our House

House music, cultural spaces and
technologies

Hillegonda C. Rietveld

Ashgate

ARENA

Aldershot • Brookfield USA • Singapore • Sydney

Published by

Ashgate Publishing Limited
Gower House
Croft Road
Aldershot
Hants GU11 3HR
England

Ashgate Publishing Company
Old Post Road
Brookfield
Vermont 05036
USA

British Library Cataloguing in Publication Data
This is our house : house music, cultural spaces and
  technologies. - (Popular cultural studies)
  1.Rock music 2.Rock music - Social aspects
  I.Rietveld, Hillegonda C.
  306.4'84

Library of Congress Cataloging-in-Publication Data
Rietveld, Hillegonda C.
  This is our house : house music, cultural spaces, and technologies
  / Hillegonda C. Rietveld.
    p. cm.
  Revision of the author's thesis (Ph. D.)--1995.
  Includes bibliographical references, videography and
  discography.
    ISBN 1-85742-242-2 (hardback), -- ISBN 1-85742-243-0 (paperback)
    1. House music--History and criticism. I. Title.
  ML3528.5.R54 1998
  781.64--dc21   97-46173
                                                                   CIP

ISBN 1 85742 242 2 (Hardback)
ISBN 1 85742 243 0 (Paperback)

Printed and bound by Athenaeum Press, Ltd.,
Gateshead, Tyne & Wear.

Contents

Part IV — Epilogue

Part V — Sources

Part VI — Appendices

Acknowledgements

First and foremost, I am grateful to Steve Redhead and the Unit for Law and Popular Culture, later the Manchester Institute for Popular Culture, at The Manchester Metropolitan University, for giving me full academic encouragement and facilitating financial support to initiate the research for and to complete this particular thesis and book. The Law Department of Manchester Metropolitan University has been especially helpful in financing my research trips to both the USA and the Netherlands.

For supervision I thank Steve Redhead, Kate McGowan and Derek Wynne at Manchester Metropolitan University. In addition, I thank Hans Mommaas of the University of Tilburg (Katholieke Universiteit Brabant) for advice on ethnographic methodology; the latter was made possible through funding by the Erasmus student exchange scheme. In addition, I thank Dave Wall for his kind suggestions as external examiner and David Huxley for taking on the task of independent internal examiner to the PhD version of this project.

Many thanks to Maggy Taylor at the Manchester Institute for Popular Culture for the effort with which she has sub-edited this text and processed it into a camera ready product. In addition I thank Ted Dave, Maud Hand, Karim Reed, Lisa Blackman and Sue Dinsmore for reading the script and for their useful comments.

Cheers to Tod Fath for the cover photograph. It was taken in the middle of the crowd at the Haçienda, Manchester, UK, during its acid house hay day. That time and place formed the main inspiration for the start of this research.

This project would not have been possible without the hospitality of Wendy Blatt, Evie Camp, Cath Carroll, Sarah Champion, Kevin

Elliott, Romanna de Flores, Vince Lawrence, Marina Kraaijeveld, Reinier Rietveld, Kristen TuTu, and Russell Vaught.

Essential support was also given by Rob Gretton, Jon Savage, Richard Haynes, Kate Butler, Dominic Sagar, Mark van Harmelen, Penny Henry, Pam Sehmar, Jamie Gibson, Helen Lucey and Oliver Taylor.

In addition, I thank the Department of Media and Communications at Goldsmiths' College for their substantial financial aid towards the (only) commercial fee demanded by its publishers Leo Song and Fiction Song to clear the copyright for quotations from the lyrics of *Can You Feel It?* (*in our house*) by Mr Fingers Inc., featuring Chuck Roberts (Desire, 1988). Also a thank you to the above publishers for keeping the clearing fee for the above song within an affordable range in the context of a 'dog-eats-dog' music publishing industry.

For all the kind advice and lengthy conversations, my respects to Marcel Bakker; Neil Barker at King Bee Records (Manchester); Ardy Beesemer; Glenn Berry; Burt 'Non-Stop' Blanchard; Rob Bright at Vinyl Exchange (Manchester); Evie Camp; Sarah Champion; Phil Cheeseman; Paul Cons; Tyree Cooper; Stuart Cosgrove; David Davies; Paul Davies; Jon Dasilva; Down Town Records (London); Mike E-Block; Fast Eddie; Glenn and Brendan; Derek Carter, Mark Farina and Spencer Kincy at Gramophone (Chicago); Kenny Grogan, Russ and Greg at Manchester Underground (Manchester); Andre Halmon; Alan Haughton; David Hesmondhalgh; Sheila Henderson; Steve 'Silk' Hurley; Linda Hyneman of the MCPS; Steve Jones of the IASPM; Maurice Joshua; Princess Julia; Robert Hamilton; Jeff Horsley; Mark Kamins; Ted Langebach; Peter Larwood; Scott Lash; Rick Lenoir; Lu; Jazzy M; Joe Marshall; Antonio Melechi; Jon McCready; Gary McLarnan; Mark McLean; the nice man on the phone at Midtown Records (Rotterdam); Mikey Midi; Mark Moore; Mixmaster Morris; Lutgard Mutsaers; Justin O'Connor; the hospitable folks at Outland Records (Amsterdam); Michael Paoletta; Graeme Park; To Pereira; Mike Pickering; Bob Pieck; DJ Pierre; Quinten at Boudisque (Amsterdam); Steve Redhead; Reinier Rietveld; Andrew Robinson; Pete Robinson; Frank Rodrigo; Richard Rogers; Dave Rofe; Joe Shanahan; Larry Sherman; Earl Smith Jr. ('Spanky'); Joe Smooth; E Smoove; Will Sogolov; Larry Sturn; Oliver Taylor; Rogan Taylor; David Toop; Tutu; Russell Vaught; Alain C. Verhave; the inspiring sales person at Vinylmania (New York City); Erik van Vliet; Gary Wallace; Pete Walsh; Pete Waterman; Rik Zwaan; as well as hundreds of other important and nice persons whom I communicated with on the topic of house music at dance parties and clubs, in DJ booths, in record shops, in car parks, at airports, on beaches, at music business and academic conferences, in recording studios, in offices and in their own homes.

When working on this book, Dr Hillegonda Rietveld was initially a research assistant and PhD student with the Unit for Law and Popular Culture at The Manchester Metropolitan University. During the finishing stages, she worked as a temporary lecturer for the Department of Media and Communications at Goldsmiths' College, London. Currently, she is a section reviewer for the year's work in Critical and Cultural Theory.

This book is dedicated to
my mother, my brother and my father.

Hillegonda C. Rietveld

Part I
Introduction

1   House is a feeling

Aesthetics is born as a discourse of the body
[Terry Eagleton, 1990].[1]

Perhaps it is time to study discourses not only in terms of their expressive value or formal transformations, but according to their modes of existence. The modes of circulation, valorization, attribution, and appropriation of discourses vary with each culture and are modified within each [Foucault, 1984].[2]

In autumn 1983 I stood on stage in front of about two thousand euphoric men in New York gay club Paradise Garage. My Roland TR 808 drumbox[3] was pounding out its repetitive beats, triggering the Pro 1 synth to produce a relentless syncopated bassline. I was vaguely aware that the non-techno part of our musical trio felt a bit disconcerted, since the bass was in a different key than the saxophone. No problem, I thought, and with the confidence of a spaced out person and a grin to match, I attempted to tune my synthesizer to the singer's voice which in its turn increasingly lost its melodic stability due to the lack of a supportive bass. Melody effaced, bass run amok and rhythm foregrounded, our dance tune, *Love Tempo* (Factory Records, 1983), radical enough for those times, entered a new world. The crowd, in a similar state of mind as the mad woman behind the keyboards, went wild; wide open eyes and happy smiles were highlighted by UV light. The rest of my band

1 {p.13} Reference type or page number of citation is indicated between brackets { }.
2 {p.117}
3 Explanations for technical terms related to musical equipment can be found in Chapter 6, which deals with production technologies.

3

wasn't that sure; the next day I had a bad hangover.

Even though some vinyl releases from Chicago indicated that there had been other producers, such as Mr Fingers, who were proud of their danceable 'mistakes',[4] it took another five years before a pulsing dance track with a chaotic bass line gained international success when Phuture released *Acid Trax* (Trax, 1987). American house music had entered the British charts in 1986, but it was the notion of acid house that inspired an explosion of dance parties in Britain which put house music firmly on the map in 1988.

As with most products in popular culture, the formal qualities of house music are recognisable, yet ephemeral and always changing, depending on who is producing and using it at what place and what time. One could, for instance, point out that house music has the format of a repetitive 4/4 beat, roughly between 120 and 140 bpm;[5] that house music could be defined by the use of certain types of production and consumption technologies; that house music may be described as a functional type of dance music produced specifically for the use by DJs; and also that house music has often been designed to take the dancing crowd out of this world. However, as with most cultural productions, the format and meaning of the genre of house music does change within various social and cultural contexts. There is not one 'real and true' form of house music, even though some conservative social elements would like to divide the world between those who enjoy 'real' house music and those who are deemed to be ignorant of 'good taste'. Chuck Roberts, speaking on the Fingers Inc track *Can You Feel It* (Desire, 1988) could not have explained it better: '... once you enter into my house it then becomes our house and our house music ... This is our house' [Heard and Roberts, 1988].[6]

And so arose the thesis for my PhD [Rietveld, 1995], which makes up the bulk of this book: to inquire into the way that house music has been developed and reinterpreted in three different social and cultural locations, Chicago in the USA, England and the Netherlands. In doing so, I was able to map some of the power structures and discourses which surround house music and which have given shape to its formal structures and sensibilities, as well as to its procedures and technologies of production and consumption. I also wanted to see if across these different localities there were any similarities in

---

4 For the concept of 'mistakes' and examples of these in music recording, see Chapter 6, in the section on creative process in relation to house music and computer generated music.

5 beats per minute — some versions can be faster.

6 {music recording}

4

the specific techniques of house DJs. The latter should not be confused with any DJ in someone's home. With 'house DJ', I mean a DJ who produces a sound track for a dance event which contains house music or who uses a particular musical aesthetic which hopefully will become clear as you read the fragmented and sometimes contradictory stories surrounding this dance music. Of course, nothing will explain this aesthetic better than a couple of nights out dancing at several house music related events:

> You see, house is a feeling and no-one can understand really
> unless their feet moved onto the sound of our house.
> Can — you — feel — it? [Heard and Roberts, 1988].[7]

I hope that reading about the discursive field of house music as a supplement to your dancing activities will add to a deeper pleasure of house music. Even if you don't feel like going out for a dance, this study can be seen as an example of how ethnography can work from the inside out,[8] rather than as a supposedly scientific method of imposing a theoretical 'straight jacket' upon an object of study. If anything, theory has been sampled to fit some of the rhythms and moods of this subject.[9] I see this type of methodology as a nomadic tactic [Deleuze and Guattari, 1986], whereby the available arsenal of contemporary critical cultural theory has been utilised as a type of 'tool-kit' [Plant, 1992].[10]

As a starting point for this book a comparative ethnographic research project was set up in order to see if local 'modes of existence'[11] [Foucault, 1984] were of any significant influence on the development of the notion of house music. The research took place mainly in Chicago, New York, Rotterdam, Amsterdam, Manchester and London, although other European places were visited as well in the context of this project. A history of events could be traced in the process of analysis. Even though house music has often been represented as a 'global' or 'international' type of dance music,[12]

---

7 {music recording}

8 See Appendix A.

9 This is in analogy to a basic rule in electronic dance music production: 'if you can use it, sample it'.

10 {p. 148}

11 {p. 117}

12 The term 'global' needs to be qualified to indicate mainly urbanised parts of Western Europe, the USA, parts of Latin America, South Africa, Australia and Japan, as well as parts of the world which function as holiday resorts for the folks from the aforementioned areas.

5

local differences were of significance in the interpretation and production of house music. Within each locality there had been various contributions of cultural discourses which were specific to the cultural history of its users.

In Chicago and New York during the 80s, where the term was coined, its main users were African-American and Latino. This meant that African-American musical traditions such as gospel, soul, jazz and funk as well as Latino salsa music had informed the musical structures and sensibilities of house music. For example, its gospel elements, which influenced the vocal parts, added notions of community, love and hope for 'better days'.[13] In addition, in these cities house music developed out of a resourceful and competitive disco scene, where people played with sexual identities. In this context, 'gay' identity and its discourses had been crucial to the hedonistic meanings and sensual formats of house music which articulated sexual desire. These aesthetic and moral sensibilities informed a choice of records to be played at dance events, resulting in a mixture of imports (such as Italian disco, German trance, English electronic pop and HiNRG) and American records (like disco and soul). Out of this melting pot the structural aspects of house music were formulated, which initially started out as DIY DJ tracks. The availability of a local record pressing plant made it possible for this music to be heard by a crowd outside of its immediate cultural and social environment; it could be exported in its raw form without the aesthetic and moral interference as a 'mainstream' pop music industry. Many of the bigger house parties and clubs in Chicago were taking place away from residential areas in deserted nineteenth century industrial spaces. In this way public surveillance was kept to a minimum. If they were not licensed as clubs, some of these spaces were squats. Parties and clubs suffered some interference by police which, combined with the close down of local dance music station WBMX in 1987, resulted in a partial destruction of the local house music scene in Chicago. In the 90s, house music labelled as deep house was still produced in Chicago, mainly for a market outside of that area. An extended version of this American adventure can be found in Chapter 2.

Chapter 3 looks at the use and development of house music in England. Elements of the formal aspects of house music were

---

13 The phrase 'better days' is one which is often heard in both the lyrics of gospel as well as of African-American house music and garage.

6

employed in the production of English pop music since 1986. Around that time house music was imported from the USA and sometimes played on local radio stations or in clubs where the main soundtrack consisted of electro and funk. A combination of factors created the right environment for a hedonistic and yet communally loving fast paced dance music such as house to explode in its popularity. In 1987 there was a malaise in British club land where a new format was sought. During the 80s more English people spent their holidays abroad than ever before and brought back ideas from the Balearic islands of how to play music in clubs as well as the notion that clubs do not, as British legislation dictates, have to close at 2 am. Other souvenirs were taken back home as well. For example, in 'gay' clubs at Spanish holiday resort Ibiza, the entactogenic[14] drug ecstasy had gained popularity and its use in a dance club environment was imported back to places like London and Manchester. People on ecstasy and other dance drugs do not wish to go home when they are not ready to do so. Empty industrial spaces such as warehouses, docks and airports as well as empty agricultural fields were available for parties and alleviated the opening restrictions which were made on clubs. House music became the soundtrack for dance marathons which often took place in an unlegislated environment. The latter provided a space for acid house parties which, in England, were called raves from 1989 onwards. By the end of the summer of 1988 a moral panic was created through sensationalist attention by the English tabloid press. As a result, acid house parties became a national phenomenon and in the process the consumption and production of house music increased significantly. The sense of community, which can be found in American house records, fitted the idea of being pitched against a society which legislated against parties as well as the fact that people under the influence of the drug ecstasy wanted to be 'nice' to their fellow human beings.[15] Due to its national success (rather than being confined to the use by one specific social and cultural group) the English production of house music has taken on many different directions depending on the type of musical scene the producer belongs to. Not only dance club music, but also

---

14 Increasing an awareness of tactile sensations; for more on this subject see Chapter 7.

15 An example of a changed meaning of a song as a result of change of context of consumption is *Promised Land* by Joe Smooth (DJ International, 1987), which in Chicago made a comment on the local active policy of ethnic segregation but in England, for some people, it was no more than a happy song, while for others it signified a sense of hope and community for a mass of party people in the face of the illegality of their leisure time pursuits.

7

rave music was produced, which articulated the specific sensibilities of a rave party for teenagers. Since African-Caribbean culture has been influencing English music and dance culture since the 60s, it is not surprising to see that some of its musical formats, such as MC talk-overs during DJ sets, can be found in English productions of house related dance music. Due to the powerful position in pop journalism which the English had acquired on an international level, the format of raves was exported elsewhere, such as the USA and the Netherlands. Because of the particular way in which the British night time economy had been legislated, the consumption of house music had had some significant interference from governmental authorities. One example of this was legislation against paid parties, in the form of the Entertainments (Increased Penalties) Act, 1990. Another example is the Criminal Justice and Public Order Act, 1994, which contains an attempt to legislate against free parties which provide the amplification of 'repetitive' beats in certain public and private spaces. In addition, some dance clubs had problems in keeping their licenses, due to negative reactions by police, who were worried about drug (ab)use at house music related events. At the time of writing, in 1996, various forms of house music related events were still popular in England. In Manchester, for example, house music could still be heard in many bars and shops and in London there were various radio stations which were dedicated to house music. The music press was even announcing a 'return' of house, indicating an increased popularity during the mid-90s.

Chapter 4 deals with house music in the Netherlands, where there had been a tendency to follow English youth and pop cultures, due to the availability of British music publications. In addition, English people who attempted to escape draconian British legislation with regards to their leisure and cultural pursuits exiled themselves to Amsterdam and introduced the format of house parties in empty industrial spaces in the docklands at the end of the summer in 1988. The *avant garde* elites had already had some experience with house parties a year earlier. However, it was not until the end of 1988 that house music, which often included English productions, started to gain pop chart popularity. By the early 90s, it had established itself on a national level as a musical format, which was enjoyed by middle class bohemians as well as by football loving youth which were also known as 'gabbers'. In the Netherlands, European sensibilities were added to its productions, such as those which can be found within a tradition of Belgian electronic body music or within that of electronic trance, which was initially developed in Germany. One noticeable form of Dutch house music was gabberhouse[16] (which could also be described as techno) in which notions of love seem to have been replaced by those of hate and where the soulful sensuality which can be found in American house music have been replaced by an industrial aggression not only by means of significantly speeding up the pace of the music to 160 bpm and higher, but also through a different choice of sounds and textures. The consumption of house music experienced some problems with Dutch authorities. In 1988 and 1989 this took the form of interference by the police, who were influenced by the panic that acid house parties and the use of ecstasy had caused amongst their colleagues in England. When they realised that valuable police time was wasted on what seemed to be a relatively harmless form of entertainment, their reaction mellowed. In 1992 the Horeca, which represents caterers for the entertainment industry, made a futile demand on the government to stop house parties because of loss of income. As in England, the change in leisure time pursuits towards house music related events, for example, has affected the traditional leisure industry negatively. At times when negative images of house parties were generated in the public domain, city councils had been reluctant to grant the necessary licence applications. Since 1993, Evangelical activists were in moral uproar about Dutch house parties, mainly because of the hellish imagery used in the context of gabberhouse. Since the early 90s, the Dutch house music scene set its own agenda as a cultural entity within a 'global' context.

As the research for my thesis developed, it became apparent that the DJ is a central figure in the production and consumption of house music. Chapter 5 discusses the role of the (house) DJ, which is to provide a sound track for the dance night and to put the right tunes in the right place at the right time. The DJ is thereby in the position of an entertainer and author, who utilises records as building blocks, which are used whole or partially, with or without musical additions provided by the DJ and sometimes by extra musicians or an MC. It also became clear that the house DJ has a different technique than DJs within other musical genres. This technique, the 'slow mix', has its roots in a methodology developed by New York disco DJs. Therefore, even though house music as entertainment for the dance floor has embraced a wide spectrum of musical influences from

---

[16] a.k.a. gabba house.

9

African-American, Latino and European twentieth century traditions in popular dance music, its structural or grammatical rules and codes have been developed within an avant-garde New York disco environment.

Chapter 6 discusses similarities in the use of production technologies of house music, despite the local differences in musical traditions. The relative affordability of electronic instruments has been a crucial factor in the plethora of DIY dance music products which have flooded the (relatively) independent dance market. The use of samplers has brought about a crisis for legislation of copyright in the definition of the author and therefore of the owner of royalties. Due to the radical intertextuality which can be achieved using samplers, a sense of loss of grounding can have an effect of bliss on the listener. Another consequence of the use of samplers is that any type of musical source material can be either 'plundered' or 'honoured'; how this is interpreted depends on one's place in cultural history and one's social position. The feeling of control over one's cultural production is a source of a great sense of pleasure and power. A desire to either merge with, create or master 'the (structural) other' of one's sense of identity could, in theory, be gratified within the virtual 'magic' of electronic sound manipulation.

Some of the similarities in the spaces and technologies of consumption and the discourses that surround house music are encountered in Chapter 7. House music is produced for the dance floor and is 'listened' to by the body. An environment which is conducive to this type of consumption follows from this requirement and at the same time invites the production of dance music which fits this type of space. In this type of space, music is amplified to the extent that it can be physically felt, while the visual field is distorted. The result is that the music is foregrounded as a tactile entity. Dance drugs can enhance these aspects of a house music event. A filtering system is set up at the peripheries of dance spaces which exclude elements which would have a negative effect on the strong sense of community which can be achieved whilst consuming house music. Negative elements can at times include people who like to fight rather than to love; after all, house music defines notions of communal and sexual love, with the exception of gabber house which, as mentioned earlier, often gathers its dancing community around articulations of images of a hellish underworld. At other times unwelcome elements can be agents of public surveillance such as newspaper journalists and police. In contrast, those who work for media which report within the realm of house music (such as specialist press)[17] are by definition present within the group of participants. One could propose that part of the consumption of house music takes place as a process of disappearance from the surveying eye of the outsider. In addition to the attempt to disappear from the outside 'eye' or gaze there is also a disappearance from the 'I' and the 'eye' of 'the self' whilst consuming house music on the dance floor. The dancer loses a sense of alienation during the abandonment to the relentless groove, which according to some Shamanic ideas, can make the dancer lose his or her bearings. Thereby the mastering gaze (of the potential observer) dissolves within the dancing group. As subjectivity disintegrates, a sense of 'the (objectified) other' disappears as well. Hereby a temporary carnivalesque community is forged, whose celebrations of disappearance can seem to the observing outsider to be rather spectacular and which to the participant is nothing less than being part of 'our house'[18] [Heard and Roberts, 1988].

---

[17] See Appendix C.
[18] {music recording}

Part II
A definition of love

2 The house that Jack built

We must make allowance for the complex and unstable process whereby discourse can be both an instrument and an effect of power, but also a hindrance, a stumbling-block, a point of resistance and a starting point for an opposing strategy [Foucault, 1981].[19]

Well, this is the house that Jack built, I can tell you that [Sherman, 1992].[20]

Introduction

The first quote, taken from Foucault's *The History of Sexuality* [Foucault, 1981], was written in the context of 'gay' politics. It describes how a discourse which belongs to a body of knowledge that defines what is 'normal' sexual behaviour can exclude groups of people who are described as 'not normal'. The Chicago-produced dance music described in this chapter, and which acquired the tag 'house music', has come into existence in a space created by such an exclusion in a society which is both racist and homophobic; the production and consumption of this music has generated a sense of community, of belonging, thereby creating its own definitions of 'normality'.[21] Although during the 80s Chicago produced its own identifiable dance sound and party scene with a name tag, 'the house

---

[19] {p. 101}
[20] {interview}
[21] Also compare the practice of voguing [Ninja, 1994].

15

that Jack built' has never been an isolated musical community. Rather, it is part of a type of musical scene, which Will Straw has carefully defined as follows:

> A musical scene, in contrast (to a musical community), is that cultural space in which a range of musical practices coexist, interacting with each other within a variety of processes of differentiation, and according to widely varying trajectories of change and cross-fertilization [Straw, 1991].[22]

The specific historical and social context of the cultural tapestry of Chicago has led to a musical scene which has produced a dance music with recognisable local characteristics, while at the same time this music is part of a wider international flow of (musical) communication.

The term 'house music' was first used in Chicago in the late 70s. In order to inquire into a 'root' meaning of this signifier, ethnographic research was undertaken in Chicago in the summer of 1992. This chapter will inquire into the way that the concept of 'house', its name and the discourses that surround it, has come into being in a local historical and geographical sense. In doing so, it has been possible to produce a description of its 'original' setting and of some of the local power structures that were part of the conception of house music. The year 1987 seems to have been a dramatic turning point for the development of this musical genre within its original geographical and social boundaries. Therefore, two questions will be considered. How were the European derivatives received and consumed in 1992 and what does the original social set with its own traditions do now 'the party is over'?

Chicago house scene

According to Frankie Knuckles, when he arrived in 1977 in Chicago there were mostly drinking places with jukeboxes; perhaps the city had about two or three clubs that employed DJs at the time [Knuckles, 1990]. Given this situation, and Knuckles' experience in the mushrooming underground 'gay' discos in the hip city of New York, he became resident DJ in Chicago dance club The Warehouse in 1977

---

22 {p. 373}

16

[Knuckles, 1990], after his New York DJ colleague Larry Levan did not take the job [Martin, 1992]. There he gained a large audience. He had access to a lot of records shipped from New York. He also had a specific style of playing records that set him apart from the few other local DJs. Rather than playing one record after the next, he would mix Philadelphia soul music, New York club music, Euro-disco and sound effects such as a running train in order to create a sound-track for the entire night [Cosgrove, 1988]. According to Berry this is in line with a traditional African-American jazz attitude that plays with past and present forms of sounds in order to create a new form each time, thereby paying homage to a tradition and to a line of cultural ancestors [Berry, 1992]. His audience favoured an up-tempo type of disco, at around 124 bpm. He also restructured old and new disco favourites to make it fit his 'dance floor', his audience. He would use his own rhythm makers and drum machines and would totally re-edit a song. The new rhythm added would be 'beefier': meaning, with bass in a louder volume [Knuckles, 1990].23 For example, the theme song for The Warehouse, *Let No Man Putasunder* by First Choice (Salsoul, 1983) was cut up and restructured with success. These tracks were created specifically for The Warehouse and played on a reel-to-reel tape recorder, a method which he still employed in 1994.24 This style, the layering of sounds by the DJ and the special restructuring of songs is what was first termed house music in the phrase 'this could be played in the "house"',25 meaning in The Warehouse club [Tong, 1990]. Another explanation for the occurrence of the word 'house' and certainly for its staying power is that a 'house' is also a group of partying people. For instance in voguing26 competitions one belongs to a 'house' [Ninja, 1994], which is illustrated in, for example, the lyrics of Jack and Jill, *Work It Girlfriend*, (Strictly Rhythm, 1993), where it is stated that one wins 'prizes in (...) the houses'. A club can also be a 'house', like in the term 'burn the house down' which can be found on many dance records as early as The Trammps, *Disco*

---

23 {transcript}
24 I have witnessed him working as a DJ several times, both in New York and in the UK; the last time I saw this was in March 1994 at Soak in the Corn Exchange in Leeds.
25 {transcript}
26 'Voguing' is a type of dance which enacts the posing by photo models [Ninja, 1994]. The striking of poses is done in a fluent and almost acrobatic manner, whereby any role model can be taken for the outfit and pose, from film star to business man. This type of competitive dancing stems from the New York African-American 'gay' scene. See for example the film *Paris is Burning* (ICA, 1991).

Inferno (Atlantic, 1977).[27] Whatever the roots of 'house' were, the term became a marketing tool for the dance music styles that developed in Chicago.

The dance club The Warehouse is worth mentioning in some greater detail since it seems that its atmosphere, attitude and music, as well as its setting in the urban layout, were seminal to many later house music parties in one way or another. It was away from any mainstream leisure area of Chicago, and its management policies and audience showed an attitude which enhanced its special and underground character. The entertainment was specifically aimed at young homosexuals, male and female, who were mostly from an African-American and Latino background. The management allowed for an inter-racial gathering which was quite unusual in Chicago. Like a New York underground dance club it provided the punters with non-alcoholic drinks ('Juice Bar') and snacks ('munchies'), which according to Frankie Knuckles was never done before in Chicago; up till then, clubbers used to go out to drink until 2 am. In terms of space, Frankie Knuckles has described it as:

> ... a three storey building (which) sits in the western part of the Loop. Now the Loop in Chicago is the main down town area and the western part is more of an industrial loft area and at that time it was pretty desolate and there was really not that much around there, so it was like the perfect place for if anyone wanted to take a loft and (...) build a night club then it was a perfect area to do it. Now it, it's like prime you know, it's prime real estate now, I mean there are major high-rises over there and all those lofts have been turned into apartments, but, the building itself was a three storey building, it was about nine thousand square feet. At that particular time it was a pretty big club (...) for Chicago you know with three different floors. The dance floor was like in the center floor and then there was like the lounge area (...) on the upper floor [Knuckles, 1990].[28]

The upper floor had a trap door that let one down to the centre dance floor; the action of having to go down the steps enhanced its underground 'feel'. Apparently, the heat of the dancing bodies would

---

27 This track can also be found on the movie sound track for the film that celebrated disco music and its culture, *Saturday Night Fever* (RSO, 1977).
28 {transcript}

rise up. The rather low entry fee of four dollars meant that one did not have to be rich to go there. Elsewhere, Frankie Knuckles said:

It wasn't a polished atmosphere, the lighting was real simplistic, but the sound system was *intense* and it was about what you heard as opposed to what you saw. Comfortably, the place held about 600, but coming and going we did about two thousand to two and a half thousand people. The crowds came in shifts[29] [Garratt, 1986].

The dancers were 'Jacking', while at times holding on to the drain pipes that led diagonally across the walls [Walters, 1989]. To 'Jack' is a term specific for the type of sexualised dance movements made to the music. People were interpreting the music and moved to and fro, up and down, wheeling their bodies around and against the rhythms, mostly in couples but also on their own. The dancing crowd were in the club from midnight on Saturday until Sunday noon, losing themselves in an ecstatic, frenzied dance. Hodge and Kress remark in *Social Semiotics* that: 'Night is a special time (...) They are times when social syntagms lose their force ...'[30] [Hodge and Kress, 1988], whereby: '... the availability of these oppositional practices is mapped on to social time and space, organised into a system of domains'[31] [Hodge and Kress, 1988].

One could therefore claim that in this isolated twelve hour frenzy of the night in the middle of the weekend new identities could be forged that were not necessarily there to be sustained throughout the rest of the week. The dance, the music, even the club itself were built for that moment in the weekend, to disappear once it had occurred.[32] However, the sense of community and of a shared 'conspiracy' it created, as well as the force of that experience, could give one a greater confidence in a private identity constructed outside a 'mainstream'. Marshall Jefferson, producer of *The House Anthem* (Trax Records, 1986) exclaimed to an English journalist in 1986 that:

You'll leave there a changed person. You might go and seek religion afterwards! You'll love it. It's gonna be hot, it's gonna be

---

[29] {p. 21}
[30] {p. 73}
[31] {p. 78}
[32] See Chapter 7.

sweaty, and it's gonna be great![33] [Garratt, 1986].

This was not a political movement with manifestos in print. It was an ephemeral cultural event which was experienced through the movements of the body, its sexuality and its emotional reserves.

The contents of the lyrics of Chicago house music were often sexually explicit. There was also a celebration of purely being alive in these hedonistic frenzied dance gatherings. Perhaps one could claim that religious sentiments, as can be found in the gospel impulse [Berry, 1992], were translated into sex talk, thereby drawing the crowd of dancers even closer together in a sense of community as though they were attending a religious gathering. Jamie Principle, for example, was very much responsible for setting such a trend. He was a vocalist who worked together with Frankie Knuckles when the latter had left The Warehouse to work at The Powerplant. This club catered for a 'mixed' crowd, meaning a mix of sexualities. Jamie used to sing to tracks for Frankie, which were specially created for his audience. At first Frankie Knuckles was bothered about the sexual explicitness of Jamie's lyrics:

> (He) fantasized about what he wants to do and he wants to say stuff like that. He set the groundwork for that you know, then all of a sudden different little cult records started coming up like *Sensuous Black Woman* and *Sweet Pussy Pauline* and these different little house records have you know, heavy house rhythms underneath it and all this sexual whatever going on the top of it[34] [Knuckles, 1990].

A tradition of 'sleazy' tracks with highly sexualised lyrics has established itself on the house scene. In night clubs which cater to dancers who enjoyed experimenting with their sense of sexuality, these often melancholic tracks, driven by deep rolling bass sounds and filled with sentiments of desire and lust, fitted perfectly. *Feelin' Sleazy* by Fingers Inc. (Jack Trax, 1988) as well as Liz Torres' *When You Hold Me*, vocalised by Master C&J, and *What You Make Me Feel* (Jack Trax, 1987), as well as the much later *French Kiss* by Lil Louis (FFRR, 1989) are just a few of many examples.

Often the lyrics of Chicago house music portrayed a sense of hope

---

33 {p. 20}
34 {transcript}

for the community as well, much in the way that gospel lyrics do [Berry, 1992]. Many of the American singers of the house music genre such as Shawn Christopher, Daryl Pandy, Keith Nunally or Robert Owens, were trained in gospel church choirs. As Marshall Jefferson put it: (House) is more like a feeling that runs through, like old time religion in the way that people just get happy and screamin'[35] [Garratt, 1986].

For a group of mainly urban African-American youths, who liked to transcend the oppressing boundaries of a racist, homophobic and sexist world, these parties and clubs were a haven, a night time church if you like, where a sense of wholeness could be regained.[36] The social structure of Chicago lends itself especially well to the development of a distinct style within one social group; people from Chicago I spoke to confirmed that this city has an active policy of segregation [Blanchard, 1992; Smooth, 1992; Cooper, 1992; Joshua, 1992; Lash, 1992]. The house scene was a closed one, which mainly involved people from the African-American communities who liked to live on the edge of being sexually adventurous, where 'it's hip to be gay'[37] [DJ Pierre, 1992]. In this specific cultural space, an idiosyncratic language in dance music developed which is now called house music.

It may be suggested that in the sense that 'it was hip to be gay', African-Americans created their own 'bohemia', on the margin of the 'mainstream' African-American community, which had a different taste in music and entertainment [O'Connor, 1993]. Within the African-American cultural tradition, blues was seen to be for an older generation and R&B was too slow in tempo for this hedonist night club crowd; rap was originally created by and for non-'gay' New Yorkers and go-go was specific for the big bands of Washington. The notion of 'bohemia' is interesting in itself. While it cannot be identical to youth, often the two groups do overlap [Mailer, 1959]. In the case of the emergence of house music, this bohemia was based on a re-definition of sexual identities within the African-American community. Although this redefinition is critical, it has been argued elsewhere that this 'bohemia' kept close links to the African-American community at large through the church and its gospel influence [Berry, 1992; Thomas, 1989].

In the early 80s loft parties developed within this particular African-

---

[35] {p. 20}
[36] See Chapter 7.
[37] {interview}

21

American scene or cultural space. 'Mad' dance gatherings in people's houses and in derelict areas proliferated, inspired by a style of presenting dance music which DJs like Frankie Knuckles, Ron Hardy or Farley 'Jackmaster Funk' had developed to a sophisticated form. Maurice of I-D Productions said it was 'the best club scene, ever was possible'[38] [Joshua, 1992]. DJ Pierre commented on this subject:

> Yeah, like, a few years ago it used to be like huge. Man, we had our own type of dress, we thought house music, we thought, 'That's just a way of life man!' We used to walk around ... Parties — oh! 48-hour marathon parties at Ron Hardy's ... a whole weekend straight, non-stop[39] [DJ Pierre, 1992].

The regular parties had resident DJs and had names like The Loft, The Playground, The Sowers, The First Impression or Joe Smooth's East Hollywood. This party scene reached a peak between 1984 and 1986.

A problem for Chicago club DJs was the lack of availability of dance music [Moulton, 1975]. This was partly alleviated by the development and availability of relatively cheap Japanese electronic instruments around 1982.[40] Records heard on the radio or at the parties could be reinterpreted, recorded, pressed to vinyl and played at one's own party. Hereby the ephemeral DIY sensibility of house music is stressed; rather than being occupied with a sense of purism, the production of house music is about what is at that moment the most effective on the dance floor to make people lose themselves,[41] within the restrictions of the available means, economically, technically and in the sense of skill. An example of this is On & On by First Choice (Salsoul, 1979), which was re-recorded by Jessie Saunders and Vince Lawrence. Released in 1983 on Trax Records, this became the first house track which was commercially available [Lawrence, 1992].[42] Tracks were tools for DJs to be able to boost their performance. There was hardly any song structure to them; they consisted of mainly a

---

38 {interview}
39 {interview}
40 See Chapter 6.
41 See Chapter 7.
42 With many people in Chicago wanting to claim to have been the first house protagonist, it is difficult to verify reports. Phil Cheeseman claims that Jessie Saunders' Project Z Factor was first, but not on Trax Records, with either Fantasy or I Like To Do It In A Fast Car (Mitchball, 1993). According to Adonis, Jessie Saunders 'bootlegged' Jamie Principle's Waiting On Your Angel by re-recording it for Larry Sherman's label Precision [Cheeseman, 1993].

drum-machine[43] generated rhythm track, a simple yet powerful bass-line, some keyboards based on Latin-American rhythms (mainly Salsa) and, when released commercially, perhaps a sparse gospel based vocal. The drum-machine was especially useful, since it could play a steady tempo without changing the speed or needing a break which would be necessary for a real drummer. Using a drum-machine on a record made the job of mixing two records together much easier for the disco and house DJ, since this requires a consistent beat.[44] Within European forms of disco similar technologies were employed, as opposed to New York club music which preferred the sound of real drummers; therefore it was this material that gained popularity in Chicago [Berry, 1992]. Avant-garde electronic dance music such as Kraftwerk, Depeche Mode or Quando Quango and European disco such as *Dirty Talk* by Klein & MBO (Baby Records, 1983) were therefore employed within the mix. However, European voices were not liked by the African-American house audience, so it was the instrumentals of Euro-disco tracks which became important [Berry, 1992]. As the competition between the DJs increased so did the urge to be different. E Smoove, who has been a DJ since 1982, said that they 'all made tracks to play at parties, to be one above the rest'[45] [Smoove, 1992]. In this way the aesthetic of house became more strictly defined.

According to Frankie Knuckles, it was *Baby Wants to Ride* by Jamie Principle (Trax Records, 1984), which broke the concept of house music to a larger audience. Jamie had become a popular vocalist within the house scene of Chicago; he was paid fifteen hundred to two thousand dollars for performing just one or two songs in a club. Some years after *Baby Wants to Ride* had been written, Frankie sent a copy of it to his colleague of yesteryear[46] Larry Levan who at that time DJed in the New York underground dance club Paradise Garage. According to Frankie Knuckles:

> Larry flipped over it and started playing it at the Garage (...) and everyone that went to the Garage was like demanding this record. (...) New York City made it, you know[47] [Knuckles, 1990].

---

[43] A drum machine is a sequencer with pre-recorded drum sounds, which can be sequenced by a programmer.
[44] See Chapter 5.
[45] {interview}
[46] In the early 70s they both worked at the Continental Baths in New York [Smith Jr., 1992].
[47] {transcript}

Presided over by DJ Larry Levan, the club Paradise Garage had been responsible for its own brand of club music.[48] Slower and more soulful, this was a sound track for a more upmarket 'gay' crowd in New York, where people cared just a little bit more about their appearance than the wild crowds in Chicago's The Warehouse. However, some of the music which was played at 'the garage', otherwise known as garage music, did cross over with what was played at house events in Chicago and vice versa. While the speed of the records danced to in New York was slower than in Chicago, there was also, for example, a sharing of a love for Italian disco records, although those were ultimately more popular in Chicago. As a member of an electronic dance outfit, I had first hand experience of the atmosphere in this huge club, in which my band performed three times in 1983. It had a custom built Richard Lund sound system [Harvey, 1983] and catered for 'gays' mainly from African-American and Latino-American backgrounds. The crowd was frantic (on stimulants like cocaine and ecstasy),[49] not like anything seen in England before 1988, which leaves one wondering about the frenzy at the Chicago parties, which was relatively more intense. In this atmosphere, Chicago house crossed to a New York 'gay' crowd, where, in 1994, its form still has its male homosexual connotations.

The music became more widely known to the outer world around 1986, when a host of Chicago house artists presented their work at the New York annual music business conference, the New Music Seminar or NMS. Artists from the Chicago label DJ International were especially well represented. This larger independent Chicago dance label hosted a special party during the NMS in New York's Better Days club. With the attention of English press which this event attracted, Americans in a wider sense began to gain interest, which meant that Chicago house finally got some radio outside of Chicago. This kind of exposure is necessary to get out of one's isolation, to make a form of music available to a wider audience. An indication of its local popularity is that in 1986 Farley 'Jackmaster' Funk attracted 2000 people at La Mirage on both Friday and Saturday nights, while both Ron Hardy and Frankie Knuckles attracted capacity crowds [Garratt, 1986] at The Music Box and The Powerplant respectively.

Given this information, one is forced to consider the racial

---

48 'Club' is one of the purposefully indefinable terms for dance music in the underground dance clubs of New York. It is, in many ways, related to the initial ideas of both house and garage music, which articulate sensibilities from the African-American and 'gay' communities.
49 See Chapter 7.

segregation at work in Chicago and elsewhere, which disadvantages non-'whites' as well as homosexuals who would like to have a greater success in their artistic endeavours. This particular sound track had to wait for the attention of Europeans, and in particular of the English, for it to have a wider popular and therefore financial success. As an aesthetic, house music started as an effect of the positive power of a sense of community and a particular style of musical presentation that was specific for a dance floor, not radio listening, although this medium was important. However, it was also the effect of the negative power of racial and sexual segregation. Perhaps by seeing its existence as a pure act of 'bohemia' would be to romanticise its political context. In an act of desire for 'the other', bohemian young 'white' Europeans and in particular the English, were keen to buy in on the sense of strength of resistance (as well as the musical energetic novelty) that this underground and its music showed.

In the Chicago outside of this scene, no-one wanted to know about it and most people there are still ignorant of its existence. If anything, as the house scene briefly appeared from its underground existence, it was eventually perceived as 'trouble'. For example, in 1987, residents of neighbourhoods which accommodated some of the dance parties started to complain about loud youths leaving rubbish like chicken bones on their lawns. This happened to some of the parties which Detroit based Derek May and Kevin Saunders gave in Chicago [Blanchard, 1992]. Although for a while the Chicago authorities seemed to have ignored the illegal tapping of electricity from street lighting and the cutting off of electricity by rival party organisers [Elliott, 1992], this time the police put a ban on after-hours parties. It also withheld late night licences from house music related clubs [Blanchard, 1992]. DJ Pierre argued that it was not only official harassment which stopped house parties from continuing:

It was more than the police though. Like one of the radio stations, (102.7) WBMX,[50] went off the air.[51] That stopped, 'cause (inaudible — sic) used to play a lot of house music, and he was really the only house jock that played the type of music that we liked, right. So, when that went off, that was the end of that.

[50] This was the radio station which featured Farley Jackmaster Funk and the Hot Mix 5 with Mickey Oliver, Ralphy Rosario, Mario Diaz, Julian Perez and Steve Silk Hurley every day after midnight [Cheeseman, 1993a].
[51] In 1988 [Martin, 1992]. {p.11}

Frankie Knuckles moved to New York, that destroyed it. (...) (Ron Hardy) self-destructed, you know, between drugs and other things, you know[52] [DJ Pierre, 1992].

After 1987 without a party scene the development of Chicago house music became stagnant since there was hardly a party scene to support its development.

Although the house party scene in Chicago was stifled, in 1988 house music became an institution in the mainly 'white' heterosexual club world in Europe, especially in England, Holland, Germany, Belgium and Italy. In Europe this musical form gradually lost its African-American sensibilities. Categories like rave, techno and trance house mainly share with house a use of similar technologies, DJ techniques, the characteristic of a 4/4 beat at 125 bpm or over as well as their places of consumption. At times European house music styles seem like sparse pastiches of what in Chicago was based in a long lived African-American cultural history. In Europe the term house music has acquired a different meaning, where its own sensibilities have been added, such as its legacy of electronic avant garde. European house music styles have been exported back to the United States in the shape of German and Dutch hardcore super speedy tracks, which the Americans call techno-rave. There, European-American youth went wild at Euro-styled rave parties in the suburbs of the larger American cities such as Washington, New York, Los Angeles and Chicago.

Ethnography on the Chicago house scene in 1992

One may wonder what happened after the party was over for the early house scene in Chicago. The original pioneers have moved on. Some of the party-professionals left town for a career elsewhere. Frankie Knuckles returned to New York:

... because I felt I had done everything that I could do here. And I hate the fact that in Chicago, so many people are stuck in a time warp. You have to know when it is time to move on[53] [Martin, 1992].

---

52 {interview}
53 {p. 12}

26

In 1992 he presided over 'gay' club the Roxy, which was originally designed to be an ice ring. There, male strippers and elaborately dressed transvestites on platforms keep the crowd visually entertained, while Knuckles moved the mostly male mixed race crowd along with a steady beat which grows more hectic over a time span of eight hours.[54] *Acid Tracks* collaborator DJ Pierre works as a producer in Manhattan for the prolific underground dance label Strictly Underground, where in 1992 he also had a brief spell as A&R person. Chicago singer Robert Owens, who used to collaborate with Mr Fingers and Fingers Inc., left New York to live in London. Others, who were less successful have just drifted away from the scene and have returned to their jobs which, according to most interviewees and reports, were in places like the post-office or supermarket. Although Chicago clubland was not as severely hit by the AIDS virus as New York City, it still took its toll when, for instance, the legendary DJ Ron Hardy fell ill around 1987 and died in 1992. However, once again in a kind of isolation, the Chicago dance music scene kept working hard on their sensual brand of escapist music. The older generation of musicians and DJs who stayed on have their own studios, production companies or record labels, making the music that moves the dance floors in the New York underground and the 'cooler' European clubs. Also, a new set of DJs is busy setting up parties and club nights. Research visits took place during the summer of 1992 and give an idea of the setting in which the current deep house is produced.

A first place to visit was Larry Sherman's independent pressing plant and distribution company. As I walked into the messy office, Sherman greeted me in an 'American' self-assured yet mumbly manner, which was barely audible over the noise of worn out rattling air conditioners: 'Welcome to the house that Jack built'[55] [Sherman, 1992]. The plant was a grimy place in a desolate area on the south side of the city, just past the Sox stadium. The pressing plant has been in existence throughout the 70s and 80s. Initially it was financed by the earnings which Jewish-American Larry Sherman once received when he used to be a successful teenage pop musician. The notorious 'snap, crackle and pop'[56] effects [Walters, 1989] on some of Chicago's dance records are the result of the recycling of old vinyl as raw

---

[54] Ten years before it had been the 'hot bed' of the electro scene; see Chapter 5.
[55] {interview}
[56] {p. 60}

material.[57] Record labels which have used Larry's pressing plant can be recognised by the simplicity of the mono-coloured label. Larry Sherman has dealt with many small record labels. Amongst these was his own legendary Trax Records, which in 1990 metamorphosed into Saber Records. Sherman said he changed the name because he got bored with Trax [Sherman, 1992], although an administrative reason seems more likely, since the name Trax Records is good business. Its reputation is synonymous with underground credibility, whilst at the same time having produced many of the early house classics such as Marshall Jefferson's *The House Anthem* (Trax, 1986) and Phuture's *Acid Tracks* (Trax, 1987).

It transpired later during my two visits to Chicago, that there were many others who either claimed to be responsible for the beginning of Chicago house music, or alternatively they knew of someone who was. Yet, although unwilling at first, Larry Sherman could at least lay a claim on having had a major part in the process (and thereby being 'Jack') due to what seemed a cynical drive to make money. The release of *On & On* by Trax Records had been part of a bet, whereby Larry told musicians Vince Lawrence and Jesse Saunders that 'this shit'[58] would never sell and that he would give his car, a Corvette, away if it sold more than he had expected [Sherman, 1992; Lawrence, 1992]. Since *On & On* did sell, he lost his car, which Vince eventually wrapped around a lamp-post at a speed of 70 mph in a crash when he was making record deliveries, for which he was banned from driving for eight years. This detail has been included to show the kind of 'randomness' that can ultimately affect a culture, even though at the same time (as shown above) these events never occur in a vacuum. Larry Sherman overcame his loss by earning a lot of money from house music tracks which musicians and DJs would give him. As the controversial manager of Trax Records, he owns the rights to many of the original house classics, which is still a sore point amongst the local dance community. Pete Waterman, part of the British pop music writer team Stock, Aiken and Waterman, has claimed that in 1985 he was able to pick up 'bootlegs'[59] from the plant which he used as inspiration for his own production work [Waterman, 1992]. At the time of their success in England, many of Trax's artists were unaware of this. DJ Pierre explained that he did not know of the

---

57 As witnessed at the pressing plant of Larry Sherman during my visit to Chicago in 1992.
58 {various interviews}
59 {interview}

success of *Acid Tracks* straight away:

> Well, we were aware of it, but probably not as exactly when it happened, because you know, we were with Trax Records and he didn't want us to think our record was going too well. (...) We never knew what was going on outside of Chicago, but by the time we found it was big in London, it probably had been playing in London for a little while[60] [DJ Pierre, 1992].

In the context of Sherman's business practices, Frankie Knuckles has referred to him as 'Byron Sherman'[61] [Martin 1992]. Yet, despite the financial heartbreak his ruthless business tactics may have caused, it is hard to imagine how house music could have developed in Chicago and into a bigger market place without the presence of a local independent pressing plant which was willing to exploit a local music scene.

In 1992 Vince Lawrence was still doing A&R[62] and production work for Larry Sherman through Bang! Productions, which was run by both Evie Camp and Vince Lawrence. The latter is mainly concerned with the dance music production of the company and is one of the early creators of Chicago house music. Apart from co-producing *On & On* (Trax Records, 1983), he worked with Marshall Jefferson on the Virgo Project (Trax Records, 1985) and also rewrote the lyrics for the classic *Love Can't Turn Around*, which was recorded by Farley 'Jackmaster' Funk (DJ International, 1986) and which was contested with JM Silk's *I Can't Turn Around* (RCA/Victor, 1986).[63] By 1986, he said, he got bored with making house 'tracks'. Around that time, his band, the Bang! Orchestra had been signed by semi-major record company Geffen, who then found out to their horror that Evie, the lead singer, was a European-American of the palest shade in skin colour and who looked like a punk with long bleached and bright pink hair [Camp, 1992]. In their (mistaken) search for authentic 'black' house music, the 'perfect' vocal sound turned out to have been created by a 'white' heterosexual woman. Since the late 80s Vince Lawrence has been producing what he describes as 'house music to

---

60 {interview}
61 {p. 12}
62 'A&R' is short for Artist and Repertoire; it is a record business word for a talent scout.
63 Part of the Chicago dance music mythology is the story of how producer-DJs Steve Silk Hurley and Farley fell out over who had the rights to these similar songs, while ultimately 70s soul singer and song writer Isaac Hayes had made the song which had inspired both versions.

29

fuck by'[64] [Lawrence, 1992], which is a type of R&B with a slow dominant groove of around 100 bpm. A main source of income for Bang! Productions has been advertising work,[65] which is directed at an African-American audience. In 1992, latter day stars like Daryl Pandy (who sang the 1986 international house success *Love Can't Turn Around)* popped by to do the odd money spinning vocal for the advertising tunes. This type of independent income has given the company financial space to experiment with recreational dance music; new talent is nurtured by the production team and every spare moment is used in their studio to produce new tunes. The work space and guest sleeping place was situated in a windowless basement 'loft'. At one end Evie has a practice space for live performance in which she rehearses her European-American all-women group Jezebel's Church. On the other side is the recording studio space. While I was there for a continuous ten days, there was always someone there, hanging around or doing some recording, which made the place feel like it was caught in a 24 hour warp. Vince works in a maniacal manner, which does not allow for a biological clock. Somehow, in between a million phone calls that follow a pattern of 'what's up; chillin'; just hangin'; don't heat me',[66] he finds time to produce and write. The lack of daylight did have an averse effect on the sense of well being of the team, so they have moved their studios to ground floor place since.

The other legendary, as well as locally controversial record label, which played an important part in the promotion of house music, is DJ International. The owner is Rocky Jones who, as has been described above, took his 'stable' of artists to the NMS in 1986, thereby exposing house music to the rest of the world. When I went to visit the company, their city centre headquarters looked like a maze of offices and rooms. Across the wide avenue, which points straight into the skyscraper centre of Chicago, is the new The Warehouse club. Since the club is long and narrow on all three floors, it is locally known as a 'highway lane'[67] [Elliott, 1992]. Artists on the label use the club to try out their new ideas. The club's name is a homage to the old The Warehouse club. Thursdays and Saturdays, when its audience is dominantly heterosexual African-American, were acknowledged to

---

64 {interview}
65 Advertising is big business in Chicago.
66 As observed during the time of the interview as well as during my one week stay later on in 1992 (see Appendix A).
67 {interview}

be the nearest to what the old Chicago dance scene used to be like; hot, sweaty and into the groove. Yet when I visited the place, it seemed that in comparison with the English rave parties of 1988 and 1989 it was not as intense, even though it was wilder than an average disco. Like at English house events, people danced on raised floors, addressing themselves to the dancers on the floor. The body dancing, especially when performed by a couple, was very agile and creative. I left quite soon, when I discovered that unlike the English house scene the men were out to find a woman to spend the night with. Being a woman on my own, as well as the only 'white' person in this heterosexually orientated club, I ended up being harassed in a persistent possessive manner which would not occur at a house party in England. What seemed to be different in this particular club to the English house scene, was that there was no noticeable amount of dancers on dance drugs such as ecstasy.[68]

In The Warehouse I talked with the gentle and soft spoken Joe Smooth, who was still connected with DJ International and who manages the club. Joe Smooth wrote, performed and sang the classic deep house anthem *Promised Land* (DJ International, 1987), which crossed the boundaries of the Chicago scene and became popular in New York as well as in England in 1988. He was working on an album, which contained a couple of classic deep house tracks. Over them he had laid positive messages, such as 'We've got to come together'[69] which is a comment on the city's active segregation policies [Smooth, 1992]. I also spoke to rappers Tyree and Fast Eddie, who were responsible for the first hybrids of hip hop and house, aptly named hip house. Examples are Fast Eddie's *Yo Yo Get Funky* (DJ International, 1988) and Tyree's *Lonely (No More)* (DJ International, 1990). Fast Eddie complained about the fact that DJ International as a company is doing very well, while he is always out of pocket [Eddie, 1992]. It has been alleged that the company offers its new artists contracts in which the copyright of their work is signed to the company, leaving a new artist with little income to look forward to [Lawrence, 1992]. However, DJ International is not an exception in Chicago, even if the practice of taking full royalties from the artist were the case.

The set-up at the more recently created I-D Productions was very different from DJ International. Here top dance producer Steve 'Silk'

---

68 See Chapters 3 and 7.
69 {interview}; during this interview Joe Smooth played me his demo tape.

31

Hurley as well as his colleagues Maurice Joshua and E Smoove put out endless productions, mixes and re-mixes. Hidden in the Chicago suburb Brookfield, their studio-complex was like a new version of Motown's music production line [Mitchell, 1990], which made E Smoove remark that it was a 'music factory'[70] [Smoove, 1992]. It was referred to as 'Little Motown'[71] and there had even been a staff outing to the original Motown complex in order to get an idea of its production methods [Halmon, 1992]. The I-D complex had 3 studios and 3 composers' rooms which were continually occupied by several people, including Hurley's sister Angie. The offices for the production company and the label were housed in the same complex. In this self sufficient environment a groove-heavy kind of dance pop was manufactured. In 1992 I-D signed a deal with the major record company Sony UK, which pleaded with the company to stop being so prolific, in case the market would become over-saturated with similar products.

Talking to Steve 'Silk' Hurley, he said that after a learning process as an underground house DJ, he feels that he has now entered the 'real' world of song production, meaning the 'mainstream' world of radio and pop dance production. He said he wanted to be seen as a songwriter/producer who could do more than just 'put beats together'. His aim was to grow up with the taste of an audience of his own age and to make 'R&B and pop special'; this way he would be able to widen his audience: 'There is a base of club party people, and that is great, but I want to reach out to the people that don't go to clubs'[72] [Hurley, 1992].

Frank Rodrigo, having been Steve's manager since 1986, boldly contributed to the conversation by saying he 'never was into house music'; in his opinion, 'doing just tracks is stifling'[73] [Rodrigo, 1992]. Rodrigo was a business man, who made the decisions over the tactics of Hurley's career. Even though Hurley remarked that he did not feel he was planning his steps, Rodrigo shook his head and made clear that Steve Hurley's status as underground DJ was only a stepping stone for bigger things; in 1992 big names such as the Pointer Sisters and Michael Jackson wanted to work with him. However, a year after my visit Little Motown stopped its operation because Rodrigo fell out with the production team over some administrative matters

[70] {interview}
[71] {various interviews}
[72] {interview}
[73] {interview}

[Elliott, 1993].

While I was at the studio complex, I also had the opportunity to speak to Maurice Joshua and E Smoove. They each had their own studio in the complex where they produced and mixed dance versions of tracks for specific club audiences. There were no doubts about their dance loyalty; their groove-heavy style of mixes underlined the fact they were still both DJs. E Smoove has always been a DJ, rather than a musician or party entrepreneur. He met up with Hurley through doing DJ mixes for the local radio. Maurice used to be a horn player before he became a DJ. Then he got into doing his own 'big huge parties'[74] [Joshua, 1992]. In two or three years, he would like to have his own club. Since the end of Little Motown, he has joined up with George Andros 'Porgy' to set up a record label and production team.

In 1992 George Andros 'Porgy' was part of Four on the Floor Productions. The other members of this production team were Gary 'Baby Jackmaster' Wallace, Larry Thompson and Rick Lenoir. The latter two are also known as LNR of the classic energetic house track *Let's Work It To The Bone* (Night Club, 1988) and the makers of the obscure jazzy deep house track *Bubbles* (Night Club, 1991). In 1991, having learned their financial lessons, they decided to become a collective, uniting their labels House-N-Effect, Tempest Records, House Jam and Night Club. Under the umbrella company name Mirage Entertainments, they shared equipment and skills as well as office and studio space which were situated in a bohemian area of derelict loft spaces, where most of Chicago's underground clubs could be found. They produced underground house such as the Black Traxx EPs, containing 'one-track-a-day-recordings'[75] [Wallace, 1992] of bass and drum patterns with an overlay of samples mostly taken from disco classics. These were popular in the early 90s amongst DJs because they were easy to use when bridging between two vocal records during a mix.[76] Their sales clearly illustrate where their support comes from. Of most records about 12,000 are sold in New York and Europe, England in particular, while only 250 copies may be sold on the local market [Wallace, 1992]. In order to get out of its musical ghetto, and to improve its financial strength Mirage Entertainments was planning to expand into R&B and hip hop, which have a larger market [Wallace, 1992] than DJs and a few dance

---

74 {interview}
75 {interview}
76 See Chapters 5 and 6.

club fanatics. When I visited, Wallace, who has a degree in musical engineering, was working on a dance re-mix of Michael Jackson's *Billy Jean* (Epic, 1983).

All of the companies described above are in touch with a larger network of distribution. Although there are complaints that European music is not widely available in the local record shops, imports are available in several specialist shops in and around Chicago. There is also an exchange of ideas in the form of DJs travelling abroad, such as Terry Hunter, who in 1992 frequently played in the massive Renaissance club in Mansfield, England. At the same time European DJs also travel to Chicago to play there, like the club tour by Manchester dance club The Haçienda in 1990, whereby a group of DJs from an English club toured some dance clubs in the USA.

People like Rick Lenoir or Maurice Joshua complained that in the early 90s there are no trend-setters in Chicago. Rick put it down to kids trying to do the same as past generations of the dance party scene over the last ten years. He argued that no-one listens to the original music which was at the root of DJ tracks any more; they only listen to the tracks themselves [Lenoir, 1992]. In addition, Maurice pointed out that there is no support from local radio since people need to pay to get air-play [Joshua, 1992]. One-time *Acid Tracks* creator Spanky said the situation is further compounded by Chicago club DJs who do not want to play music that has not involved them in some way [Smith Jr., 1992].

Despite the alleged self-protective policy of local DJ-producers, Chicago produced dance music like deep house is not easy to find in local clubs. North of the city centre, where the high rise model-architecture proudly reaches into the windy sky, there are several dance clubs that allow a sexually and racially mixed crowd on their premises. Apart from the Metro, which could be found in an affluent European-American neighbourhood on the lake coast of Lake Michigan, most of these clubs were in the post-industrial warehouse area. It was mainly the mixed but mostly African-American 'gay' nights which provided underground dance music. In 1992 most other clubs had special slots or nights for dance, although they did show a bias towards rock music, since even on a dance club night with an important local house DJ rock was either played in an adjoining bar or in the VIP[77] room.[78]

In the dominantly European-American suburbs, Germanic teeth-grinding techno was played at Euro-styled raves. Evidence of such events had been found in several record shops. It was especially striking that African-American events were hardly openly publicised and were still part of an underground. However, advertising for 'techno-raves' was to be found everywhere, especially in the rock orientated 'indie'-music shops (which usually cater for a European-American clientele) rather than in the import dance specialist shops. Names like *Absolut Citrorave* suggest legal sponsorship by alcohol suppliers, which means that this was an event with a different type of drug (and therefore atmosphere) than the early house events. Other names for raves suggest a sense of aggression like *Brain Storm, Warp Audio Attack, Monster Rave Attacking Chicago* and *Lord Michael's Mental Overdrive*, each promising '100% hardcore!'.[79]

In 1992 the deep house scene was represented by its own fanzine called *Crossfade* and in that same year in New York an underground 'gay' based club music fanzine *Underground News* was set up. However, these magazines, in addition to English specialist magazines *DJ* and *Mixmag*, were only available in one or two specialist record shops in the whole of Chicago. More accessible were columns on dance music which could be found in music business magazine *Billboard* and in local magazines such as *Chicago Music Magazine*. On the other hand, *US Rave* and *Reactor mega-magazine* were available free at most other independent vinyl selling record shops, or 'wax shops' as they are locally called in contrast to the shops selling CDs. One may therefore conclude that the rave movement, although connected with a by now 'marginalised' vinyl buying audience, was of a more overground nature than events involving the consumption of deep house. Apart from being an export product, in Chicago the latter was still an underground form of music specific for the audience of a few clubs such as The Warehouse and 'gay' club The Clubhouse as well as for the odd specialist nights in

---

[77] A 'VIP' is an abbreviation for Very Important Person; in other words, a guest of the club.
[78] The fact that I am a 'white' European female did not help my position of observation; it may be that I have been led to clubs which cater for what was assumed to be my 'kind of people'. Roller-discos in the impoverished area of South Chicago which cater for a mainly African-American and Latino audience with a mixture of garage and deep house provided by a DJ, as well as exclusively male 'gay' clubs were inaccessible for me to observe. 'Mixed' clubs were the only places which I could enter without being conspicuous or without agitating its crowd. This seems to confirm the social segregation which is at work in the Chicago area.
[79] {flyers}

other clubs. Therefore, deep house was still providing a platform for those who felt a sense of togetherness on the basis of race and sexuality as well as attitude.

As cultural events are in a permanent state of flux, the situation in the Chicago dance scene keeps changing. Since 1990, a new scene of loft parties has been growing. Like 'back in the days',[80] loft spaces have been painted black and provided with a sound system. For example, in 1992 the *Substance* loft parties, which cater for a mixed bohemian crowd,[81] were being talked about with praise. These were organised by DJs like Mark Farina, Derrick 'The Maestro' Carter and Spencer Kincy, using new insights gained from their local dance history and the stories from the English press like *Mixmag* and *DJ*. Some of the parties are kept secret, a frequent necessity to outmanoeuvre licensing problems; it can happen that one party night will move on to a sequence of three venues. A creative underground style of DJing is evolving. For example New York underground artist Ira Levi, Chicago dance musician Lidell Townsell and Northern England's soul singer Lisa Stansfield, were mixed simultaneously on all three decks if necessary. A DJ like Spencer Kincy takes a jazz attitude (as described elsewhere [Berry, 1992]) even further, overlaying a track with a fairy tale or playing some tweeting birds in the middle. The DJ mix sometimes feels rather English and manic. However, the choice of sounds and rhythms is generally more sensual than European and European-American musical products, which gives it a Chicago underground sensibility.

In New York, The Limelight, which was once a church and is now a night club, caters for mostly 'Italian' and 'Anglo' suburban youth from Brooklyn and New Jersey. Amongst other DJs, DJ Repeat plays the hardest sounds he can lay his hands on, preferably tekno from Berlin and harthouse from Frankfurt, Germany, or gabber house from Rotterdam, the Netherlands, and otherwise hardcore from Belgium.[82] I observed him as he energetically broke up the flow of the records (which are rather fragmented in themselves), spinning them backwards at breakneck speed or mixing in a random 'funny' noise.

---

80 {a figure of speech which reappears in various conversations, interviews, music recordings within an African American cultural discourse}

81 'Mixed' in terms of ethnic and cultural backgrounds as well as sexualities. Here the Californian styled European-American counter cultural avant-garde ideas of (body pierced) 'freaks' have begun to mingle with the soul and house music sensibility of Chicago dance culture.

82 Tekno, gabber, hard house and also new beat are hybrids of a mixture of European avant garde electronic dance music, Euro-disco and house, with a stress on a sense of aggression and a definition of male bonding in a heterosexual world.

Above this sound track, an MC in New York style whipped up the crowd with 'devilish' shouts. The punters seemed to be milling around, at times waving their arms, rather than dancing to a groove, which was too fast for a mortal stamina to keep up with for any great length of time. Often the go-go girls sat down in their suspended cages, dangling their legs with a sense of boredom. DJ Repeat turned around to me and enthusiastically shouted over his shoulder that he wanted to recreate the old Paradise Garage, which long since has been turned back into a parking garage.[83] One week later English DJ Graeme Park[84] played the Limelight on a Saturday night, during the New Music Seminar of 1992. He played what can only be called a 'classic garage' set[85] yet the crowd did not like his set and many left the club. From these events one may conclude that the myth of the Paradise Garage lives on, but that the interpretation of its signification, has drastically changed in time and cultural context. The same can be said for the meaning of the tag 'house', which cultural meaning has shifted according to the context of its use.

Conclusion

Using Foucault's terminology, in Chicago certain procedures have been laid down locally in its dance party environments which qualify what is included and excluded from its body of aesthetic and ethical knowledge, in the process defining what is house music and what is a house scene, incorporating the positive power of a rich tradition of African-American culture, such as gospel. This process may have started as a reaction to a sense of exclusion or negative power as an effect of racist and homophobic discourses in American society. Thereby a play with identities based on race and sexuality and perhaps a play with the notion of being 'the (bohemian) other' ultimately has created an aesthetic discourse of its own, with its own moral 'platform'.

The notion of house music became a sellable tag for a type of dance music with recognisable formal aspects. More often than not, Chicago house music has a 4/4 beat, accentuated by a regular bass drum and by an off beat open hi-hat, programmed on a drum box,

---

83 {observed in June 1992}
84 See Chapter 3.
85 {observed in June 1992}

which generally runs at a pace between 120 bpm and 135 bpm. The lyrics often refer to either a sense of community or carry explicit references to experiences of sexual intercourse. Chord structures and singing techniques seem to be derived from American gospel traditions. Other influences have been soul and contemporary European (electronic) dance music, while the traditions of funk and jazz have been crucial for the actual musical structures of house music. What follows is an inquiry into the shifts of the meanings of house music in both England and the Netherlands.

3   Rave on

England and Europe picked the ball up and took it off of Chicago, definitely[86] [Tong, 1990].

... I learned about London or the English (...) they find something, they tap into it, you know, and then they will wear it to the ground[87] [Knuckles, 1990].

But then the music reinvented itself, and then again and again until it gradually dawned on people that house wasn't just another phase of club culture, it was club culture, the continuing future of dance music. The reason? It's simple. People like to dance to house[88] [Cheeseman, 1993a].

Introduction

During the 80s, night club culture had been flowering in England [Elms, 1988; Rose, 1991]. As club culture reached a higher level of sophistication, new forms of dance music were welcomed with delight by its clientele. Different types of dance music were either used and thrown out, or stayed around alongside new styles; as journalist Robert Elms put it:

... styles hold their beat for a while, usually going to establish a

---

[86] {transcript}
[87] {transcript}
[88] {p. 3}

permanent specialist nightclub audience, or else they go mainstream and become part of the fabric of British pop[89] [Elms, 1988].

House music has followed a similar route. In the late 80s and early 90s, aspects of it have become part of the popular music idiom, while certain mutations have established themselves for different specialist audiences.

This chapter will describe how, initially in London, Manchester and Nottingham (giving Sheffield a deserved name-call as the narrative develops), the term house music entered the English popular imagination and how in 1988 it became part of an initially underground but very soon popular and exportable entertainment package called 'acid house party' or 'rave'. In this way a profile will be sketched of the English way to define house music (and thereby achieving its 'definition of love').[90] Just like rock music has changed its form since its first popularity in the 50s, since 1988 house music has mutated to suit its various culturally specific English user groups, which are varied enough to justify a separate research project. Plenty of academic discussions of English house parties, club nights and their surveillance can be found elsewhere [Henderson, forthcoming; Melechi and Redhead, 1988; McRobbie, 1994; Newcombe, 1991; Plant, 1993; Redhead and Rietveld, 1992; Redhead, 1993a; Rietveld, 1993; Thornton, 1994].[91] At this point I want to stress that, since the main research for this thesis has been conducted in England, a lot of source information for the more general chapters in this thesis on the consumption and production of house music has been gathered from an English perspective, so you can read even more on the English house scene in the more general chapters, especially the last one, which deals with spaces of consumption.

The arrival of house music in England

From around 1985, Chicago house music was available on import. In London, DJs like Mark Moore and Colin Faver were discovering house music records in the import record shops, like Spin Offs, where

---

89 (p. 37)
90 Love meaning both a self-effacing love of becoming 'one' with a community as well as meaning lust.
91 See also Chapter 7.

Jazzy M worked, and Bluebird. Around that time there was only a select group of people interested in house music [Moore, 1993]. Colin and Mark attempted to introduce this music to the audience of club night Pyramid at 'gay' club Heaven:

> ... where we played a lot of Euro-stuff, Yellow, DAF (...) and then a lot of Italian electronic disco, a lot more commercial vocally European records. We didn't play HiNRG,[92] because everywhere was playing HiNRG then; Hazel Dean and that. And we were trying to avoid Hazel Dean[93] [Moore, 1993].

This shows that, even though house music has often been compared with HiNRG because of its pace, 4/4 beat and a sensibility of an uncomplicated promiscuous sexuality based on homosexual hedonism, and even though it has produced hybrids with house music since, house music did have a separate trajectory from HiNRG. Colin had arrived at house music through the indie-music scene; in other words he was informed by a 'white' European avant garde sensibility, which had also been the cultural politics behind the electronic new wave of the late 70s[94] [Jazzy M, 1993]. Mark also adhered to an avant garde sensibility, which in his case leaned towards a camp aesthetic;[95] he therefore enjoyed using 'trash' disco as part of his set [Cheeseman, 1993b]. By playing European electro-disco and later house music, Mark and Colin were very much 'the black sheep of the gay scene'[96] [Moore, 1993]. According to Mark, the 'gay' crowds on the whole enjoyed house music, but did not get into it like the club and warehouse party crowds a couple of years later during the house music explosion of 1988. Mark adds that 'there weren't any E's[97] or anything like that'[98] in the mid-80s in the London

---

92 HiNRG is pronounced as 'high e'nergy, which is a type of fast paced 'gay' European disco at around 128 bpm with very little syncopation. It is also mentioned at the end of Chapter 5.

93 {interview}

94 For a brief elaboration on the notion of European avant garde and electronic music, see Chapter 3.

95 The camp aesthetic has a tendency to redefine established, perhaps modernist, definitions of 'good' taste in an upside down manner; kitsch and trash become desirable [Sontag, 1982]. The camp aesthetic is closely related to a (sub)culture which revolves around Westernised male homosexual communities.

96 {interview}

97 E is an abbreviation for the drug ecstasy. For a description, see Chapter 6. In American dance clubs, like New York's 'gay' club Paradise Garage, the drug ecstasy had resulted in a frenzied crowd which was conducive to its dance music.

98 {interview}

clubs [Moore, 1993], even though trend setting magazine *The Face* did publish an article on the subject in relation to the home use of the drug ecstasy in October of 1985 [Nasmyth, 1985]. However, of importance to the story of house music in England is that those people who were seminal to the future house music explosion, such as Paul Oakenfold, Danny Rampling and Jazzy M, as well as pop group The Pet Shop Boys[99] all used to go to the Pyramid.

Mark also played a set at the legendary Mud Club in London, which in 1984 presented a mixture of rare groove[100] and rockabilly to its audience. By 1986 hip hop had become enormously popular in English clubs[101] and Mark used this to warm his crowd to house music. The similarity in sound production of some of the early house music productions[102] and electro[103] like *Planet Rock* by Afrikaa Bambaataa and the Soul Sonic Force (Polydor, 1982)[104] made it possible to mix the new house sound into the old style of electro; Mark Moore explained:

> It was useful, like *Hashim* was very useful for tricking people into dancing to house, especially in the Mud Club with the home boy[105] crowd [Moore, 1993].

Yet, the 'home boys' did complain about 'that gay shit'[106] [Moore, 1993], which with a speed of more than 115 bpm was considered to be too fast to dance to or to mix with other music [Jazzy M, 1993; Tong, 1990]. For example, Mark Moore experienced the following in 1986:

I played *Strings of Life* (by Rhythim is Rhythim) and the whole of

[99] The Pet Shop Boys re-recorded the underground house music classic *It's Alright* (Parlophone, 1989), originally recorded by Sterling Void and Paris Brightledge (DJ International, 1987), with which they got to number two in the British charts. Many of their pop songs have been remixed by their favourite underground dance producers, like DJ Pierre.

[100] Rare groove was a specific London club fashion in music and clothes, which recycled the dance club culture of the seventies, such as funk, soul and the less pounding forms of disco. It reached its peak in London in 1987. Brand New Heavies is an example of a pop group which had developed in that particular scene.

[101] Also in the Netherlands, hip hop had become a dominant form of dance music. See Chapter 4.

[102] For a description of recording technologies see Chapter 6.

[103] Electronically produced hip hop; a brief description of hip hop can be found in Chapter 5. Examples can be found on compilation *Classic Electro Volume 1* (MC Mastercuts, 1994).

[104] A favourite at New York club the Funhouse. See Chapter 5.

[105] Young men who had adopted the New York Bronx-cult of hip hop electro as part of a lifestyle which also included break dancing and graffiti art.

[106] {interview}

Pyramid went crazy, although it did get widely popular (two years later) with (acid house club nights) Shoom and Spectrum. The second mix of it; it always was the second mix, not the A-side mix. And I remember playing it at the Mud club, waiting for everyone to go mad and it cleared the floor, hahaha[107] [Moore, 1993].

Apart from describing how house music was initially received in London, the above quote is also of interest because it means that as early as 1986, the use of the second mix, which is the dub-mix,[108] was more important than the A-side, which usually features more traditionally structured pop vocals with clearly defined verses, chorus and middle break. The dub-mix on the other hand is often predominantly instrumental with only a few key words strewn through its musical structure. This trend has continued, so that at the time of writing, in 1994, house music can be roughly divided on the one hand into traditional vocal club tracks such as disco and garage for mostly 'gay' dance clubs[109] and on the other hand the radically cut up dub sound of rave, trance, wild pitch, techno, hardcore, jungle and ambient as relatively new and still developing forms.[110]

In Manchester, house music entered the clubs in a similar way as in London. Most 'gay' clubs preferred HiNRG. An exception was DJ Tim Lennox, who spiced up his set of HiNRG and camp pop with house records at 'gay' night club the Number One during the mid-to late 80s. House music was also played in the 'straight' home boy environment of The Haçienda club, where on Friday nights Nude night entertained a predominantly 'working class' and 'black' crowd with mainly hip hop, reggae and funk. Between 1985 and 1987, DJs Martin Prendergast and Mike Pickering fitted house music in between their set of Paradise Garage styled club music such as the electro/garage classic *Don't Make Me Wait* by Peech Boys (Island Records, 1983) or Joyce Sims' *All and All* (Sleeping Bag, 1986), as well as streetwise electro rap, such as *Worse 'Em* by Triple M Bass (Profile, 1986), and later, *Who Is It?* by Mantronix (Ten Records, 1987). Mike Pickering had some New York acquaintances in the dance music industry who would mail him the latest in developments in

---

[107] {interview}

[108] See Chapter 6 for the concept of dub and the instrumental.

[109] In 1994, some people refer to this type of club music as 'handbag' music, which indicates a traditional, as well as ironic, image of 70s or 80s English discotheques where women and girls used to dance around their handbags.

[110] See also Chapter 4.

New York club music, which meant that since 1984 he was one step ahead of DJs in the North West of England. In 1987, after The Haçienda hosted the Chicago House Party in March, Nude night started to advertise itself as providing 'house, hip hop and funk'[111] [Rietveld, 1992a].

Another example of a seminal British house DJ could be found in Nottingham where DJ Graeme Park introduced his crowd at the Garage to house music from early 1986 onwards. He had been working at a local record shop and kept in touch with all the new imported material when he became a DJ. From disco and northern soul material[112] he changed to electro. Soon this gave way to house music, making him one of the first DJs in the Midlands to play this type of music. In contrast to his colleagues in London, he had no problem in introducing house music to his club crowd:

> I remember, going into the shop one day and they had this record by JM Silk, *Shadows of Your Love*, oh yeah, check it out, and this is wicked, really good. The first time I played it, you know, a lot of the time you play a new record, you take a few weeks for people to get into it, but straight away they were like into it, because it was fast and it fitted in with what I was doing. And then a couple of weeks later it was like, yeah we got this record by Steve Silk Hurley *Jack ·Your Body*, and I listened to it and I thought, ah this is really good. Because it has the same bass line as *Let No Man Putasunder*, First Choice, I sometimes played it, things just went mad. That was the record that made house music really take off in Nottingham[113] [Park, 1992].

The club where he worked, which briefly carried the name Kool Kat Club, has been a source of inspiration for the budding musicians and DJs in the area. Nottingham has been a landmark for house music events and sound systems, such as the legendary club night Venus at the Garage, which finished in 1993, or the travelling sound system and DJ collective DIY, which in 1994 was part of the struggle, against the then newly poposed Criminal Justice and Public Order Bill,[114] to

---

111 {filed flyer}
112 See Chapter 5.
113 {interview}
114 Further discussion of this piece of legislation can be found at a later point in this chapter.

keep travellers and open air dance parties legal.[115] Graeme has taken his set and sophisticated DJ-skills[116] to other places, such as London, as well, on which he has commented:

> Much to my surprise, I was asked to DJ at a warehouse party in London organised by Ashley, who works at Black Market.[117] He'd seen House Music working in the States, so there I was, doing exactly what I was doing in Nottingham, only everyone was standing around in their flared trousers, all the Rare Groove gear, arms folded, not into it at all. Six months later, Nicky Holloway asked me to DJ The Trip at the Astoria, playing pretty much the same thing, and everyone was going wild for it[118] [Savage, 1992].

He also had connections in the dance club scene of Sheffield in 1987. This city had been a breeding ground for many electronic dance music groups, such as The Human League and Cabaret Voltaire, since the late 70s, so its club crowds were familiar with dancing to electronic grooves. DJs Harrods and Winston Hazel were successful there with their own house music night [Park, 1992]. In 1988 Graeme met Mike Pickering at a photo session for *i-D* magazine and ended up filling in for Mike at The Haçienda during two weeks of absence that summer, because they had similar sets.[119] Since then they have teamed up together in The Haçienda to take the Nude nights into the crazed house music explosion of that year [Rietveld, 1993], which acted as a

---

[115] For a very personal account of a DIY party in 1991 (from a psychedelic sideline perspective) and for other observations made on the English rave scene around that time, see Chapter 1 in C. J. Stone's *Fierce Dancing; adventures in the underground* [Stone, 1996].

[116] In 1988, when I witnessed him play at the Haçienda club, he was one of the very few British DJs to keep three decks to mix a full sound track for the night; for instance in order to use accapellas over a groove from another record (which he got bored with by 1992 [Park, 1992]), he would need the third deck to queue up the following song.

[117] Black Market is a leading importer of American dance music in London. Their own label, Azuli, has released consistent New York club orientated dance music since 1989 and is revered by mainly African-American DJs in Chicago and New York. In order to gain a name for their label, they first pretended to be based in New York and sold their product as imports.

[118] {p. 25}

[119] The difference was that Mike played a mixture of very new and more older records and also, as with many of the early British house DJs [Cheeseman, 1993b], in 1988, he was not a smooth mixer [Park, 1992].

catalyst to his career as a DJ[120] and as a remixer.

In the second half of 1986, the first Chicago house music hits charted in the British DJ lists. By that time a particular house music style had established itself in Chicago and a steady flow of records was being produced, which meant that although a large quantity of poor quality tracks were created, the amount of interesting and innovative work had increased as well. Both Pete Tong of London Records and producer and songwriter Pete Waterman had gone to Chicago to find out what was happening. Waterman returned with 'bootlegs'[121] from Trax Records, which he used as inspiration for the Stock, Aiken and Waterman pop productions [Waterman, 1992].[122] London Records released a compilation of material from DJ International, *The Chicago House Sound* (FFRR, 1986) on its subsidiary FFRR that summer. Independent label Rhythm King also released its first compilation of Chicago house music, *Rob Olson's Chicago Jack Beat, Vol. 1* (Rhythm King, 1986), that year. The showcase organised by Chicago label DJ International at the New York New Music Seminar that summer stimulated more public interest as well.[123] In September 1986 the energetic and soaring *Love Can't Turn Around*, produced by Farley Jackmaster Funk and featuring male 'diva'[124] singer Daryl Pandy (London Records, 1986), became Number Ten in the British National Chart [Cheeseman, 1993a] and Number One in the DMC UK Dance Chart[125] [*Mixmag*, 1986]. In the same dance chart there were other Chicago 'luminaries', such as JM Silk, with *Jack Your Body* (US Underground, 1986) and also *No Way Back* by Adonis (US Trax, 1986) [*Mixmag*, 1986]. Garage act Colonel Abrahams entered this same chart with *Over and Over* (MCA, 1986). Awareness was raised in the press in September of that year with a comprehensive piece on Chicago house music by Sheryl Garratt in *The Face*. She went over to Chicago to see it for herself and told her hip and trend-

---

120 In 1994, although he has 'guested' all over the world, including Buenos Aires in Argentina ('full of amazingly beautiful wild women', according to Graeme) where he DJed with Nancy Noise, Sydney in Australia, Reykjavik in Iceland and Uruguay [Park, 1992], he still holds a residency at the Haçienda, where he presides over its Saturday night and has developed into a garage DJ, playing vocal tracks of mainly American club origin. See also near the end of Chapter 2.

121 {interview}

122 See Chapter 5.

123 See Chapter 2.

124 Daryl Pandy was, and remains, a passionate singer with a 'gay' sensibility.

125 This chart is not based on record sales, but rather on the popularity of a record on the dance floor. This is established by letting club DJs fill in chart return lists each week.

setting readership all about it [Garratt, 1986]. In January of 1987, JM Silk's *Jack Your Body*, licensed six months before for FFRR's Chicago house music compilation, hit Number One in the British National Chart [Cheeseman, 1993a], introducing the idea of jacking to a British audience. This was followed by a multitude of Chicago jack tracks, such as *Jack the Groove* by Raze (Champion, 1986), which was already popular in English clubs in the Autumn of 1986. In March 1987, the Chicago House Party toured Britain, with seminal house music artists Marshall Jefferson, Frankie Knuckles, Kevin Irving, Adonis and Fingers Inc. [Rietveld, 1992a], which made flesh of what so far had been conceived of as 'this' anonymous frenzied dance music from across the Atlantic.

Yet, there was no sign of a house or jacking craze amongst British youth. In a discussion on the state of contemporary pop music in *i-D* of April 1987, there was no sign of house music amongst the thirty five categories which were defined. This particular article stated that pop had diversified so much, that no single youth or music cult could be pin-pointed in Britain as a driving force: 'Pop is now a culture of margins around a collapsed centre'[126] [Owen, Reynolds and Jones, 1987].

In this particular text, which exemplified a general opinion within the pop/rock press, house music was like a silent absent signifier which, with hindsight, could have answered their quest for a unifying line in the development of music. The rapid movement towards dance club culture, away from the pop/rock hero motive,[127] combined with the development of electronic and computer technology[128] seemed to by-pass the attention of a rock orientated audience. Although house music was first of all the sound track for an English club culture avant garde, it was soon to become the pop music for the next generation of young people, who seemed to have no problems with the celebration of a sense of being decentred.[129] It was exactly this 'culture of margins around a collapsed centre' which was to become the unifying force that catapulted house music to become the sound track of a movement of hedonist mass gatherings.

Unlike in American cities such as Chicago, Detroit or New York, licensed radio stations in England are not as accessible to marginal cultural groups. Therefore, these groups have been forced to 'hi-jack'

---

126 (p. 50)
127 See Chapter 7.
128 See Chapter 6.
129 See Chapter 7.

the air waves in order to be able to communicate their cultural realm. In 1986, Colin Faver had a radio show on pirate radio Kiss FM, which introduced house music to a wider London audience before it actually hit the charts. Together with LWR, Kiss FM was one of the more organised pirate radio stations. Around the same time Jazzy M had started his own radio show, The Jacking Zone, on LWR. He had rolled into house music via his love for 'black' music, like soul, jazz and funk, when he was working at record shop Spin Offs [Jazzy M, 1993]. Radio stations which dare to experiment with new musical forms, because they do it for the love of music and are not tied to the corporate structures of the music industry, can be influential on the changes of musical tastes:

> These stations had enormous impact, because there was no legal station you could listen to playing black music, everybody listened to these stations. They did a whole range like jazz, reggae, r&b, hip hop and of course house. Their listening figures were like enormous, so they had a really big impact on people getting access to house music[130] [Cheeseman, 1993b].

Although house music is made for dance clubs, radio stations can inform fans of the titles and artists of tracks (which are not announced at club nights)[131] and once a new form of club music has gained popularity, to keep the club crowds updated with events.[132]

The house music shows on pirate radio stations Kiss FM and LWR, have stimulated a new generation of musicians, who might not have gone to clubs,[133] to make use of their new electronic gadgetry according to a particular aesthetic in dance music as defined by the radio DJs. This then became a two way form of communication, since listeners responded with their own ideas. For instance, young people started to send Jazzy M their own recordings, inspired by the 'different' and 'raw'[134] house sound from Chicago [Jazzy M, 1993]. The first person to send the Jacking Zone a white label was Kid

---

130 {interview}
131 See Chapter 5.
132 This also applies to the other areas which have been researched. Without Chicago's WBMX, the house dance scene was deprived of its focal point and fell apart. Radio was also influential to the house scene in that it provided the music which could not be acquired in the shops and which inspired people to make their own electronic versions of it. See Chapter 2.
133 Perhaps because they are under 18, or because they had never felt attracted to clubs until then.
134 {interview}

Bachelor of Bang The Party, with *Glad All Over* (Bostich, 1986), which became an underground hit. Others followed:

> Chicago influenced, you see, because it was so fresh and so different it was influencing young people. (...) Immediately you had a lot of smart kids, you know, what I would call Techno Kids, ... not because of the music (they were making), but because they were just into electronics and ... they were just at home, playing with their computers at the time, get a music package up on it and away they go[135/136] [Jazzy M, 1993].

The initiator of HiNRG, Ian Levine, also made an attempt at producing a house music inspired track, *On The House* by Midnight Sunrise (Nightmare Records, 1986), which did not sell a lot, since it was released 'before its time',[137] but which had a relative success on some of the club dance floors [Levine, 1990]. Elsewhere, the British began their first attempts at making dance music inspired by the house music 'invasion' from the USA. In 1987, The Haçienda's Nude night inspired percussionist Simon Topping to create, with DJ Mike Pickering, the underground Latin house track *Carino* as part of a house music production project called T-Coy (DeConstruction, 1987), which was successful in underground dance clubs on both sides of the Atlantic. A more commercial enterprise, aimed at chart success rather than at the underground house music market, was *Pump Up The Volume* by M/A/R/R/S (4AD, 1987), which was immensely popular on dance floors around the country and ended up at Number One in several British dance charts. It also caused a stir in the music business. Its prolific use of the sampler, using many recognisable parts of other songs,[138] in combination with its commercial success pushed the boundaries of British copyright law (1956 Copyright Act) as it existed at the time during a test case brought by Pete Waterman's company PWL versus record label 4AD [Bradwell, 1988].

By the end of 1987 after the release of their acid house compilation, Pete Tong's house music compilations for FFRR were running out of American artists to release:

---

[135] In 1985, before the house music 'invasion', Paul Hardcastle was the first successful 'bedroom musician' who produced an electro inspired track called *19* (Chrysalis, 1985), utilising similar technologies as the early house productions, such as a Roland drum machine and a sampler.
[136] {interview}
[137] {transcript}
[138] See Chapter 6.

... by the time we'd done our (...) third album, there wasn't really much more to plunder from Chicago, I mean ... you know, the American labels had begun to wake up to it, and so the prices had gone up (...) but the most exciting thing, by the time we got to the fourth album, (...) there was (...) the sort of technology available to sort of budding musicians in England, it had got to such a stage where, you know, the bedroom records[139] were emerging and people were doing things at home (...) but it worked, it really did work, they definitely got the hang of it enough ... I found by the time I came to the fourth album, and one of the frustrating things is, you never have them for the territory they come from, so it was quite a nice idea to try and make a record which was homegrown that you would be able to sell back to America ...[140] [Tong, 1990].

The choice of concepts in this quote may have been used in an ironic sense, yet even as humour it shows the traces of a cultural and economic form of war-like colonialism; one 'plunders' an as yet untapped commodity[141] in order to repackage and return it to the 'pillaged' area, to 'the natives' if you like, in order to 'conquer' its market or its 'territory'. FFRR's fourth compilation, *The House Sound Of London* (FFRR, 1988), featured exportable English productions such as D-Mob's *We call it Acieed* (FFRR, 1988), which blatantly celebrated the acid house party scene that had exploded in the summer of 1988, which was also known as The (second) Summer of Love.[142]

The summer of love: acid house and warehouse parties

The popularity of house music was gaining momentum at the end of 1987 and the beginning of 1988. New compilation series like Jack Trax

---

139 The terms bedroom record, bedroom musician and bedroom boffin refers to the fact that with the miniaturised computer technology one was able to set up a music recording studio at home, which usually was the bedroom of the musician/producer. See also Chapter 6.

140 {transcript}

141 Although the concept of world music is inspired by a certain kind of 'well-meaning' and sometimes patronising philanthropy, this is also informed by similar colonialist politics.

142 The first Summer of Love occurred in 1967, when acid rock and psychedelia spilled over into the Western(-ised) world from the hippie centre Haight-Ashbury in San Francisco, where the first celebrations of a sense of void and of non-specific love took place [Stevens, 1989]. See also Chapters 5 and 7 for the influence of this scene on club lighting. In addition, Chapter 7 has been informed by several theorists who would fit that era as well, such as Marcuse and McLuhan.

50

were showing a budding underground scene. Pirate radio shows Jacking Zone with Jazzy M on LWR as well as Steve Jackson's House That Jack Built on Kiss FM were spreading the sound of house music across London. Jazzy M claimed that: 'When LWR was what you call the boom, it was on half a million listeners'[143] [Cheeseman, 1993a].

However, the huge popularity of house music which took place in 1988 did not occur in isolation. For instance, the club night Delirium, which had started in 1986 at the Astoria club with DJ Morris Watson playing a mixture of hip hop, funk and house music, moved to the Thursday nights in Heaven in the middle of 1987. According to dance music journalist Phil Cheeseman, this became 'the first real house club in London'[144] [Cheeseman, 1993a]. In February 1988 Delirium organised Delirium's Deep House Convention at Leicester Square's Empire [Cheeseman, 1993a], which did not draw a lot of people and was only attended by the 'die-hards',[145] with the venue being more than half empty [Cheeseman, 1993b]. Phil Cheeseman commented in the context of the popularity of subsequent house music parties that:

> It's more than just about music, because, I think, that people who are in the industry or involved as DJs or producers or as train spotters forget that people go to clubs for reasons that are other than listening to music; it's a social thing, where the music is just a back drop[146] [Cheeseman, 1993b].

Yet, when a sound system is good enough to drive its frequencies into the body and loud enough to stifle any lengthy conversation, in addition to light effects which disorientate the visual and rational cognitive field, music can become a dominant factor. What was needed for house music to be successful was an environment like this in combination with a particular club concept with which the fickle and bored London club crowds could identify. A recreational drug such as MDMA which could open the mind to such a new concept would make its acceptance easier. At the time the ephemeral populations of dance clubs were hell-bent on escape and were ready for an idea which would fit the entrepreneurial social climate. In

---

[43] {p. 12}
[44] {interview}
[45] {interview}
[46] See Chapter 5 on the difference in reaction to electro in New York club the Funhouse and in ngland. Also see Chapter 7 on club and body technologies and the more specific way in which ouse music affects a dancing audience.

1988, the Conservatives had been in government for nine years under Prime Minister Margaret Thatcher. In this period an active form of radical capitalism had been propagated which foregrounded the entrepreneur as 'the saviour' of the nation's economy. These politics were radical in the sense that it attempted to sweep away the remains of traditional seemingly feudal social structures. However, some cultural forms which would develop from this, such as the house music parties which were to become popular in that year, were not exactly what the British Government had expected [Rietveld, 1993]. In that year, somehow the factors conducive to the success of house music within mainstream entertainment fell together in the form of a club concept that came from the hedonist atmosphere of the Spanish island and holiday resort Ibiza: new visual ideas in clothing and extremely disorientating dance floor lighting; the sudden availability of the empathy generating entactogenic drug MDMA, sold under the name ecstasy,[147] which had a quality to make its user sociable as well as susceptible to the music; warehouse parties with loud sound systems, where acid house was the main form of dance music.

Acid house had been developed in Chicago where since 1985 DJ Ron Hardy had constructed a wilder and more rhythm orientated set in dance club The Music Box than had the more paced disco-orientated Frankie Knuckles. By 1986, when a particular house music aesthetic had established itself and was produced in a steady flow, Hardy's club was used by many of the 'second generation' house music producers such as Marshall Jefferson and DJ Pierre to try out their new tracks, such as Phuture's *Acid Tracks* (Trax, 1987) [Cheeseman, 1993a].[148] The sleeve note on the Acid Tracks volume of *The House Sound Of Chicago* (FFRR, 1987) states: 'Jack is dead welcome to the weird world of trance-dance'[149] [Cosgrove, 1987].

It was this rawer sound of Chicago house music which, in combination with Detroit techno and a European tradition in electronic dance music,[150] became a source of musical inspiration in Europe. Not only the sound of acid house,[151] but also its name

147 See Chapter 7.
148 See Chapter 6 for information on the creation of this track as well as Chapter 2.
149 {sleeve note}
150 See Chapter 4 and Chapter 6. For an example of European trance which shows acid house influences, listen to the compilation *The Secret Life of Trance* (Rising High, 1993).
151 A few examples can be found on the London underground party compilation *In The Key of E* (Desire, 1988) as well as on the compilation *The House Sound Of Chicago Vol. III, Acid Tracks* (FFRR, 1987).

sparked off particular associations with psychedelia, which fitted the acid house parties which had started to develop in London. A problem occurred by the end of the summer of 1988, when the press used the same connotations in a negative sense to blow the party scene, which was about to develop, out of proportion by creating a moral panic thereby killing its initial 'innocence' of fun for its own sake.

The new club concept was imported by London DJs and their social circle from Spanish holiday resort Ibiza. For instance, in the autumn of 1987 Paul Oakenfold relived his holiday experiences with his friends after legal hours in the Project Club in Streatham [Rietveld, 1993], where he would play a mixture of the records which were being played in the fashionable clubs of Ibiza Town by DJs like Alfredo. European dance music and English pop music could be heard side by side with American house records in what was termed by the English as the Balearic mix. Since Ibiza was a stopping point for the hippie trail across Europe into Asia, psychedelic imagery in both club visuals as well as in clothing style were recycled [Rietveld, 1993]. Even the 'smiley', a yellow circle with a graphic minimalist resemblance of a smiling face which used to be popular in the early 70s, made a re-entry ('because of peace and love'[152] [Godfrey, 1988]) in the design of flyers for yet another Ibiza inspired club, Shoom.[153] This club was opened in November 1987 by Danny Rampling and presented a music track which was 'virtually all house'[154] [Cons, 1991]. Paul Cons remembered:

... Shoom took it to a very big extreme because Shoom is a very small room and they used to just pump it full of smoke because the people who came to Shoom were old hippies[155] [Cons, 1991].

It is worth noting that during the 60s, psychedelic hippie events like Ken Kesey's Acid Tests used to use plenty of disorientating visual effects as well, such as continuous strobes in smoky rooms and liquid slides [Wolfe, 1989]. Shoom was the first acid house club [Cheeseman, 1993b] and set the tone for the summer of 1988. In January, after the police had complained about the after house activities of the Project Club, Paul Oakenfold first opened a night in the Sanctuary called The

---

[152] {p. 70}

[153] This logo was adopted all through the summer to signify a 'membership' to the acid house phenomenon.

[154] {interview}

[155] {interview}

53

Future, heralding a future form of entertainment [Godfrey, 1988]. In March 1988 club night Spectrum: Heaven On Earth was started by Oakenfold in Heaven. Paul Cons observed that:

> ... it just took off overnight at Heaven. It started on a Monday with 200 people, and the next week it was 500, ... the next was 800 ..., the next 1200, the next week it was sold out, whooff ... It was all related to drug use, all related to drug use[156] [Cons, 1991].

Mark Moore remarked that despite the initial low attendance, there was 'the best atmosphere'[157] [Moore, 1993]. Therefore, he was pleased to find out that when he returned from his promotional European tour[158] for *Theme From S-Express* with his band S-Express (Torso/Rhythm King, 1988), that house music had finally 'exploded', adding (with reference to the types of drugs used at Spectrum) that he had always felt that: '... if the drug was different (from the popular 'sedative' drug cannabis, or from alcohol), they would get into it'[159] [Moore, 1993].

At the end of April, Nicky Holloway opened The Trip at The Astoria, which 'was just, you know, a road block'[160] [Moore, 1993]. Gift wrapped in the packaging of a psychedelic holiday on ecstasy, house music was finally put on the map of mass recognition. Still, the clubs may have come up with the holiday idea, but they were limited in space and ambience and were restricted by late night club licensing. A relatively new type of dance space ensured that this concept could be enjoyed relatively undisturbed on a large scale.

As the older productive industries such as steel, coal and textile have given way to an economy based on information technology as well as on tourism and entertainment [Harvey, 1989], there has been an increasing trend to use deserted workplaces for parties and night clubs, such as the legendary night club The Haçienda in Manchester Sheffield's club the Leadmill or the Music Factory, home of house music club Back To Basics, in Leeds. In London, during the 80s, late night warehouse parties had taken place in similar deserted

---

156 {interview}
157 {interview}
158 Since he has a great respect for Chicago house music, he does not see his own music as house music, but rather regards house music as a source of inspiration. Therefore, he was a bit embarrassed to find out that in Europe he had been nicknamed 'The Pope of House' [Moore, 1993] {interview}
159 {interview}
160 {interview}

industrial buildings and under railway arches. These parties were organised by diverse organisations, of which an early and, using the words of cultural writer Cynthia Rose, 'seminal'[161] example is the politicised industrial Test Department's farewell party to the GLC in 1985 [Rose, 1991].

Most of these 1980s 'raves' were organised and supervised by loose affiliations of young Britons formed into crews, posses or partnerships. Their names are deliberately flamboyant and evocative: The Mutoid Waste Company, Westworld, Family Funktion, Shake 'N' Fingerpop, General Practice, Coldcut, Soul II Soul, Starship Enterprises. They stage some events to make money, some to have fun, others to publicise ventures which range from clothing designs to illegal radio stations and political causes. But, the music being the common factor, most such events are commanded by their presiding DJs, those young men and women who supervise the sound. Or as black Britons put it - those who carry the swing[162] [Rose, 1991].

In England, immigrants from Jamaica have had a major cultural impact on the leisure pursuits of young English people since the 1960s by introducing for instance sound systems[163] and blues-parties[164] [Back, 1988]. The idea of having a large mobile sound system which can fill a large industrial space with danceable bass-centred sound most likely went beyond the wildest dreams of the humble European 'mobile disco' DJ[165] whose tradition of entertaining at weddings, pubs and school parties had started in the late 60s.

At the end of 1987, London warehouse parties, with their PA size sound systems, started to adopt house music as their sound track. Although hip hop had been very popular in the clubs, a certain amount of ill feeling had been generated amongst the London club elite by the lyrics and its following of:

... South East London kids who thought they were from the Bronx. (In contrast) at warehouse clubs and parties, everyone was

---

161 {p. 20}
162 {p. 20}
163 See Chapter 5.
164 A blues is an all-night home party, organised within the African-Caribbean community where R&B related music, such as reggae, is being played.
165 See Chapter 5.

friendly; there was no bad attitude[166] [Cheeseman, 1993a].

One of the first underground places to adopt house music in a friendly atmosphere was Hedonism in February 1988, which deeply impressed Manchester club promoter Paul Cons:

I went down there (London) in May ... I had been in New York and knew of E (the drug) earlier in the gay scene. I went to London, spent a weekend there; went to Shoom, Spectrum and some wild parties, which I think was the peak of the whole thing, not well known, they were called Hedonism. They did a series of three parties, which were all-night parties. This one was on a bank holiday Monday, that I went to. Absolutely unbelievable, there wasn't anything like it, I've never seen anything like it since. (...) a really mixed crowd (...) None of the heaviness would come into it; it was just genuine. People had discovered a new drug and were having fun with it and it was great, 'cause the music was hot and all the rest of it[167] [Cons, 1991].

In the same spring this was followed by other similar warehouse parties like regular event Rip at Clink Street near London Bridge, which started in early 1988 [Cheeseman, 1993a]. DJs such as Mr C entertained the two available dance floors. Like football, it united a crowd from various economic backgrounds, showing a mixture in race and class, which, according to one of its ex-Crass[168] affiliated organisers, had started to mingle ever since the Tottenham Riots in 1986 [Lu, 1993]. Unlike most house music parties which followed in 1988, the Rip events were continued until 1989 outside of the surveying public eye, since they made sure that the press was kept out.[169]

Another event which did not get any press during the summer of 1988 was Manchester club night Hot, which took place on Wednesday nights in The Haçienda club, organised by Paul Cons.[170] This night

---

166 {interview}
167 {interview}
168 Crass was a loosely organised group of people who had set up a commune in London, had a band with an anarcho-punk following and were involved in the organisation of political events as well as of festive party events.
169 See the end of Chapter 7 on Bey's concept of the Temporary Autonomous Zone [Bey, 1991]. For other examples, see also Chapter 4 in Sarah Thornton's book *Club Cultures* [Thornton, 1995].
170 During the summer of 1988 I was part of the Summer of Love extravaganza in Manchester as a punter.

had been inspired by the Hedonism warehouse parties and London clubs Shoom and Spectrum [Cons, 1991]. It was meant to be an Ibiza styled holiday environment to last for the summer months and included a little swimming pool, free ice bars, free whistles and special decorations. DJ Jon Dasilva played a light-hearted choice of European dance music such as More Kante's *Ye Ke Ye Ke* (Barcley Records, 1987), acid house such as Phuture's *Acid Tracks* (Trax, 1987), English house music such as *Voodoo Ray* by A Guy Called Gerald (Rham, 1988) and deep house like Joe Smooth's *Promised Land* (DJ International, 1987). He mixed this in what he gathered was the mixing style of DJ Larry Levan (famous from New York club Paradise Garage) as far as he had learned from a rare article on New York disco which had appeared in music journalist David Toop's magazine *Collusion* in 1983 [Harvey, 1983], using accapellas and sound effects of tropical rain and thunderstorms to underline the 'paragraphs'[171] of his musical text[172] [Dasilva, 1992]:

> Dasilva worked his way through the entire BBC sound effects collection and the whole club got so used to his cut and paste, they no longer stared at the roof when they heard a rainstorm[173] [McCready, 1994].

For the record selection, he was joined by DJ Mike Pickering of the Nude nights. The club's atmosphere felt like a summer breeze and attracted quite a mixture of people of different sexual persuasions and economic backgrounds.

The same club space on Friday nights in 1988 would carry quite a different atmosphere when DJs Mike Pickering and Graeme Park played a selection of Chicago acid house such as (hetero)sexually explicit *Give It To Me* by Bam Bam (Westbrook Records, 1988) and Detroit techno such as *It Is What It Is* by Rhythim Is Rhythim (Transmat, 1988) and Inner City's *Big Fun* (Ten Records, 1988), to an audience with an overwhelming majority of heterosexual young men high on amphetamines and MDMA. The club would be so full of people, that there was no space for props. Instead it was a huge dark room full of frenzied sweating bodies where it was unnoticed by most that a rain of condensation fell on the crowd [Rietveld, 1993].

---

[171] {interview}

[172] See Chapters 5, 6 and 7 on house DJ techniques.

[173] {flyer}

During the summer of 1988, as the acid house party fever escalated in London and Manchester [Garratt, 1990], events were left in relative peace. In London, at the traditional closing time for British clubs at 2 am, punters from the Trip at the Astoria would spill into the streets and block Charing Cross Road, refusing to go home. The cry 'acieed', of which a sample can be heard on dance hit *We call it Acieed* by D-Mob (FFRR, 1988), was bantered about on those occasions; despite its low amount of air play on national radio station BBC Radio One this became the first track to hit the British charts which specifically referred to the acid house scene [Thornton, 1994]. In Manchester, people spilling out of The Haçienda also found it difficult to go home straight away [Redhead and Rietveld, 1992]. The unwillingness to accept the 2 am end-of-the-night rule was caused by a combination of events. During the 80s, the British had increasingly taken their holidays abroad, mostly in Southern Europe, rather than at the British holiday resorts. There they found that Britain was on its own in patronising its pub and club clientele with licensing laws which send them home before they were finished with having fun. In addition, the drug ecstasy was relatively new and its market had not yet been polluted by inferior products, so that it yielded optimal positive effects. Its users, still on a 'buzz' when coming out of an 'acid house club', were wide-eyed, awake and eager to continue festivities, which they could do at the various warehouse parties that were offered around the city.

By the end of that summer, the first headlines started to appear in the broadsheet and tabloid press, putting the word acid house on the map of the popular imagination, with, respectively, a type of analysis which attempted some kind of dated social understanding, or showed an excess of fun in a type of sensationalist manner [Rietveld, 1993]. Through the middle of October, the latter began to change their point of view on acid house parties into a raging moral panic, representing the crowd as passive victims by feminising their casualties, for instance, by speaking of 'evil' drug pushers seducing their female victims at mass sex-and-drugs 'orgies'[174] [Melechi and Redhead, 1988]. The adverse press coverage meant that the authorities became eager to stop the blossoming house scene, while at the same time younger people were attracted by its sensational descriptions. In this context, academic researcher Sarah Thornton has stated that:

---

174 {p. 22}

Moral panics can be seen as a culmination and fulfilment of youth cultural agendas, insofar as news coverage baptizes transgression[175] [Thornton, 1994].

This instance illustrates that youth cultures are not necessarily the same as underground cultural leisure pursuits. English dance music productions related to these events were hitting the British charts [Quint, 1988], such as the dance scene inspired pop song the *Only Way Is Up* by Yazz and the Plastic Population (Big Life, 1988) and S Express' *Theme from S Express* (Rhythm King, 1988). Earlier that year Cold Cut had charted with the commercial track *Doctoring The House* (Ahead of Our Time, 1988). Many of these crossed over to the European charts, such as the Dutch.[176] The acid house scene had exploded out of all proportions and its originators were not in control of its development any more. The party scene went underground[177] in the winter to avoid the gaze of the press and authorities. The parties reappeared in the summer of 1989 outside of the surveillance of urban areas at commercially organised mass parties called raves, which at its most sensational attracted around 10,000 people at the Sunrise event [Collin and Heley, 1989; Rietveld, 1993].

Also in 1989, at the yearly rock festival in Glastonbury, a sound system was set up, which was part of the beginning of an anti-establishment rave movement [Collin, 1991; Marcus, 1993]. By 1992, nomadic young British 'travellers',[178] who attend and take part in the organisation of a British (not always official) festival circuit had also adopted the rave principle. However, their parties were free, covering the cost with a voluntary collection, as opposed to the huge commercial rave parties of 1989 and 1990, against which legislation had been passed in the form of the Entertainments (Increased Penalties) Bill, 1990. The biggest of this kind had been held near

---

[175] {p. 181}

[176] See Chapter 4.

[177] In other words, it disappeared from the centre focus of the national news channels.

[178] Although the nomadic life style of the 'traveller' stems from the hippie ideals which developed during the late 60s, the 'traveller' of the 90s is often a person rejecting as well as rejected by the economic principles of contemporary urban living. Homeless, they buy 'vehicles' such as ancient buses and vans to live in. By the same token, they have adopted the contemporary entrepreneurial principle to look after themselves whilst rejecting interference from the state. Since 1993, when it has been made near to impossible for 'travellers' to claim welfare benefits, they have come to rely even more on their own resources [Lowe and Shaw, 1993].

Castlemorton at the end of Spring 1992, where for four continuous nights and days sound systems like those of Spiral Tribe and Bedlam kept the music going [Marcus, 1993; Lowe and Shaw, 1993].[179] Since legislation had destroyed the last remains of the original free floating rave scene, commercialising and legislating its excitement out of existence, this particular dance event attracted not only around 4000 'travellers', but also more than 20,000 urban 'ravers' [Colebrook, 1992].[180] The police held Spiral Tribe responsible, but after a costly showcase trial, the sound system organisers were acquitted in 1994 [Advance Party, 1994]. However, negative attention by the authorities and the surveillance apparatus of the press was attracted again. In 1994, the new Criminal Justice and Public Order Act, 1994, has provided legislation against trespass of land, travelling in a convoy of a certain number of vehicles and the gathering 'of 100 or more (whether or not trespassers) at which amplified music is played during the night', whereby music is defined as 'wholly or predominantly characterised by the emission of repetitive beats'[181] [Aitken, 1994; Hussey, 1994; Kingston, 1994]. Hereby the legislators have attempted to define a type of house related music. The notion of 'repetitive beats' is what a person who is not part of the 'understanding' of house music related forms would use as a description of such. However, many other musical works, including those by classical composers such as Ravel's *Bolero* (EMI, 1979), could be included, as can the dancing by a group of people to the rhythm of a car alarm. In addition the concepts of 'night' and 'dance' are ill-defined in both existing and proposed British laws and seem to be motivated by an attempt to curb particular lifestyles and cultural expressions which do not belong to the 'dominant' classes, who make desperate attempts to hold on to their dispersing power.

However, after the initial moral panics which raged in the build up to the Entertainments (Increased Penalties) Bill, 1990, 'sanitised' commercial versions of legislated raves, as well as related events in clubs and leisure centres have become a normalised leisure time

---

179 See Chapter 7.
180 An estimation is that between 25,000 and 50,000 people attended this event.
181 (public information poster) This poster stems from an anti-Criminal Justice Bill collective in Nottingham and which has been designed by Linnell, who is also responsible for the public information cartoons for Manchester drugs advice centre Lifeline. More information on the way that dance parties and festivals are affected by the proposed bill (which in October of 1994 was passed by the Houses of Parliament to become the current Criminal Justice Act) has been collected and distributed by the Advance Party (PO Box 3290, London NW2 3UJ) as well as by the Freedom Network and Liberty.

activity in Britain. In 1993, the Henley Centre for Forecasting published a report on current recreational activities and the consumption of substances which affect the mood of the user, such as alcohol and ecstasy in Britain. They concluded with the following statements: 'We estimate that consumer spending on raves will be between £1 and £2 billion this year',[182] and that:

> ... raves are likely to stay on the scene for some time yet as they fit in with the Centre's long term view about the growth of out-of-home leisure options, which induce people to get actively involved. Pubs and clubs will undoubtedly suffer, but the majority of leisure sectors will also be affected due to the redirection of time and money away from other traditional leisure pursuits[183] [Veares and Woods, 1993].

Initially acid house parties, and later raves, have become formats for the consumption of house music related dance music forms which are exportable, as has been shown in both the research conducted for this thesis in Chicago[184] and in the Netherlands.[185] In Britain there is a particularly strong tradition in pop music journalism [Cheeseman, 1993b], which can be shown for instance in the amount of English publications on dance music.[186] An extensive flow of these, such as *The Face*, *i-D* and *Mixmag* are exported to places like Chicago and urban centres in the Netherlands. Therefore, it seems that Britain sets an agenda for the consumption of different music styles in the Western(ised) world. Yet, it has not cornered the market in dance music, since apart from its own music production, it is also dependent on imports from both the USA as well as from mainly Italy, Germany, Belgium and the Netherlands.

English mutations

By the end of 1988 London radio pirates Kiss FM and LWR closed

---

182 {p. 86}
183 {p. 89}
184 See the end of Chapter 2.
185 See the start of the popularity of house music consumption in the Netherlands.
186 See Appendix C, where even when population size is taken into account, British publications outnumber those from the other two researched locations.

down in order 'to try and get licences'[187] [Cheeseman, 1993b]. A 'new breed of pirate radio'[188] gained prominence [Cheeseman, 1993b]. These stations, which were even more anarchic than their predecessors, represented a new generation of DJs. Similar radio stations appeared in British cities like Manchester, where its legal local stations also featured house and dance music shows, such as Stu Allen's House Hour on Key 103 which increasingly broadcast 'harder' European sounds. Another prominent show in Manchester was 808 State on Sunset 102, by the DJs from the band State 808, who played a mixture of techno and rave hardcore sounds between 1989 and 1993. Phil Cheeseman remembered about the London radio pirates that:

> ... in 1989 they were playing the whole spectrum of music that you would hear at raves, which did include a lot of garage, Chicago stuff and the current New York free style house, as well as the harder stuff. You had the Balearic thing at the time as well. It was still like a real mixture, like all the first house clubs were[189] [Cheeseman, 1993b].

The term garage was used in England to indicate the soul vocalised sound from New York and New Jersey in contrast to the sometimes more energetic or sometimes more sex-orientated deep house sound from Chicago. However, in the USA everyone preferred the less restrictive tag of club music. At English house music events an example of a popular garage anthem is *Reaching* by Phase II (Republic Records, 1988). At the big open air raves of 1989, productions like Manchester State 808's *Pacific* (Eastern Bloc, 1989) and the New York Cliville and Cole production of *Seduction* by Seduction (Break Out, 1989) were memorable. The track list is seemingly endless.[190] However, one club record that had a profound effect on future productions and which ended up at Number two in the British charts was the blatantly sexual *French Kiss* by Chicago DJ and producer Lil Louis (FFRR, 1989). This track slowed down

---

187 {interview}

188 {interview}

189 {interview}

190 A compilation with Manchester club classics from 1988 and 1989 is *Classic House* (MC Mastercuts, 1994). An example of popular British productions (released by Mute Records' dance subsidiary Rhythm King) from around that time is *Beat This: Rhythm King* (Stylus Music, 1989).

completely in the middle and then picked up speed again while a female vocalist made orgasmic moans. Also, the Italian outfit Black Box left its mark both on the English house music party scene as well as on the British charts, where it reached Number One, with *Ride on Time* (Disco Magic & De/Construction, 1989).[191]

Cheeseman continued on the subject of pirate radio DJs:

> But some DJs, they got basically just harder and harder. I think you could trace it back to probably 1990; they stopped playing vocals. (...) that's where the hardcore scene really started ... you know, it gradually got faster ... and then of course all that Belgian stuff coming in. That scene all over the Belgian stuff. At the same time, people were beginning to make faster and faster records[192] [Cheeseman, 1993b].

'That Belgian stuff' was mainly from the R&S label, such as *The Complete Dominator* by Human Resource (R&S, 1991). Although it seemed a relatively fast record in 1991 at 128 BPM, the *Original Mix* sounds slow in comparison to current European material in 1994; on the other hand, at 138 BPM its *Mental Speed Mix* by Ceejay Bolland showed the way to new developments in the hardcore scene. Despite the repeated announcements by Manchester radio DJ Stu Allen that 'we know you like it hard'[193] [Allen, 1991], Dutch producer and journalist Ardy Beesemer explained to me that for the British market it is always wise to make a 'softer' mix than for North Europeans like the Dutch and the Belgians [Beesemer, 1992]. An English type of dance music was developing which was called rave music. Specific African-Caribbean influences have been added to English productions when MCs[194] started to appear on tracks, such as MC Kinky, who is featured on *everything starts with an e* by e-zee possee (More Protein, 1989). These MCs started out on party and club nights and were soon inseparable from many underground dance events, from DJ Sasha's Italian piano track set at Delight in Shelley's

---

191 See Chapter 6 for a discussion of *Ride On Time* with regards to its construction.

192 {interview}

193 {various radio observations}

194 An MC is a Master of Ceremonies, who talks the crowd into a particular frame of mind. See also Chapter 5.

Lazerdome in Stoke-on-Trent in 1990, to the jungle[195] sets in London in 1994. In 1991, there appeared a North English version of techno inspired rave music which was soon dubbed bleep music. One of the first examples can be found with LFO's *LFO* (Warp, 1991). More examples of this type of dance music can be found on the compilation *Bleeps International*, (Fast Forward Records, 1991), as well as on rave compilations like *Strictly Underground II* (Strictly Underground, 1994). As with the dance producers from the Benelux, the hip hop backgrounds of its producers could be heard in the use of break beat samples and speeded up hip hop drum loops, which often sounded like they were played at 45 rpm instead of 33 rpm. This trend started in 1990 and a multitude of examples can be found in dance productions from 1991, as can be heard on the English popular rave track *Shut Up and Dance* by The Green Man (Shut Up and Dance Records, 1992), which shows a particular common structure for hardcore rave tracks with seemingly unrelated parts, in the same way as a DJ, especially a hip hop DJ, would construct a mix between records.[196] For more examples of this type of dance music, compilations like *Illegal Rave III* (Strictly Underground, 1994) are useful; the latter contains the memorable track *Head In The Clouds* by Manix. *Charly* by The Prodigy (XL-Recordings, 1991) was one of the first tracks to make this type of music hugely popular; although initially intended as a joke for a specialist rave audience, this record charted [Phillips, 1992], showing the popularity of raves and rave music amongst a teenage singles buying crowd.[197]

Not all English dance music productions have taken this direction. A compilation like *Warehouse Raves* (Rumour Records, 1994) shows a cross section of mainly English classic tracks with a great variety of influences. An example of more obscure British contemporary house music is the compilation *None Of These Are Love Songs* (Caustic Vision, 1994), a title which ironically makes comment on the fact that most house related music deals with love and desire.[198] Even though ecstasy induced empathic love was for a while the main inspiration to the choice of music in 1988 and 1989, this title illustrates a

[195] Jungle is a particular type of hybrid between hardcore rave music and ragga. It has dub base lines at a slow pace while its drum samples and drum programming are twice the speed of the bass line. It has been around since at least 1992, but has gained a positive profile in London based music and club press in 1994.

[196] See Chapter 4; in the Netherlands a similar development occurred.

[197] See also Chapter 7 in the section on dance drugs, where this record is discussed in some more detail.

[198] See Chapters 6 and 7.

diversification within the dance music and house music market and therefore also a diversification of the definition of 'love'. Dance music has been produced to fit many different taste groups, such as progressive house (South England based danceable house music), handbag (populist vocal based garage and disco), European inspired trance, tribal trance (exotic world music samples put to dance beats)[199] or rave related jungle which has dub reggae and ragga influences.

The best and shortest way to sum up the six years which have followed the house music explosion of 1988 in England is to end this chapter with the sleeve note from 1994 club compilation *The Drum Album* (Drum Records, 1994). Even though this record is a promotional device for a brand of cider, the text shows an intimate knowledge of the early rave and house music scene and a working knowledge of what happened after 1989. In this context it articulates some of the attitudes, names some of the legendary nights and reveals something about the DJ centred record (show) business. However, the text warns that it must be 'read in an eyebrow raised, naive yet somewhat sardonic manner ("those were the days my friend, we thought they'd never end")':

Over the last few years we've all been out there having it right off! Tear arsing up and down the country on a pilgrimage of pleasure. From the murky warehouse days of Blackburn '89 mate and M25 orbital lunacy to the ooh so memorable closing nights of Shoom and Spectrum. Legendary nights at Venus, Atlantis, Shelley and Quadrant Park to name a few who are no more. (thank God in some cases). Been there, done it, bought the brain damage, you score the know[200] and even if you didn't, it don't really matter, 'cos time marches on and Clublandia PLC[201] has infiltrated every part of this fair isle. The hedonistic hallelujah chorus has affected a whole generation. The acid house baby boomers have now taken up residence either in mental asylums, prison or the far flung, lost in the plot, beaches of Goa. Other

---

[199] See the end of Chapter 7.

[200] A pun on 'hardcore, you know the score' {an often repeated phrase in the early 90s in the English music press}, in other words, you find out what it is all about.

[201] One has to interpret this as an ironic statement, since not all clubs and parties are owned through a system of stocks and shares. As explained above, free festivals and sound systems are still happening in 1994, such as *Rave In The Cave* in Lancashire or Manchester Hulme's inner city open air *Demolition Sound System* [Marshall, 1994], as well as a host of other parties in London and around Britain.

more fortunate souls grew up, got a proper job and joined Mr & Mrs Adulthood, the rest ended up DJing or promoting or both ... 6 years on and we have DJs as globe trotting superhero magazine cover stars, promoters as rock star hotel wrecking gossip column fodder, and a new sub genre of dance music invented every other week, from 'Handbag' to Tibetan Euro Progressive Folk Trance. The musical diversity seems never ending with clubs to cater for every pigeon hole available[202] [Gill and Lethbridge, 1994].

Conclusion

Initially, house music was played in London and places like Manchester, Nottingham and Sheffield. It seems that this music caught on in the North with a non-'gay' audience as a 'natural' progression to other American club music it was already dancing to, like disco and the vocal tracks with an electro type of backing which were also popular in New York's Paradise Garage.[203] At the same time in London, 'straight' club land was more involved with hip hop and rare groove. Although in places like Manchester house music was played on the radio, it was the pirate radio stations of London which had made this music available to a wider audience.

In England house music became part of a national phenomenon in the form of a complete entertainment package called acid house party or rave, which was exported to Europe, the USA and Japan. One cannot help but suspect that a particular colonialist discourse, which has been informed by a British imperialist past, has inspired the cultural exploitation of 'marginalised' (ex-colonised) (African)-Americans in order to produce an export product. However, rather than it being a type of 'sinister' and conscious plan, this process happened along an enthusiastic network of clubs, DJs, record labels and information media, which was not controlled by anyone in particular, even though some catalysing figures can be singled out, such as radio DJ Jazzy M, who lovingly played Chicago house music imports on London pirate radio LWR to a wide audience on the same day as it came off the plane, London DJ and A&R man Pete Tong who licensed and exploited dance records for FFRR/London Records from Chicago and New York, or London DJ and party promoter Norman

---

202 {sleeve note}
203 Also known as 'garage', in addition, see Chapter 5 for a description of Northern Soul.

Jay who exported the first English styled house music parties to Amsterdam in the Netherlands since the Dutch authorities were not as draconian about late night dancing as the British.[204] Hereby one can also conclude that, from an aesthetic as opposed to a economic point of view, house music is part of an international exchange of musical ideas. To return to Will Straw's definition of musical scenes,[205] most modern music aesthetics are not rooted in any isolated community [Straw, 1991]. For house music this international process has been so successful, that Simon Reynolds has stated that: 'It's difficult to imagine a genre more place-less...' [Reynolds, 1990b].[206]

However, as has been shown above, local characteristics can be found across the production of this genre. What follows are several Dutch interpretations of the term 'house music'.

---

204 For Norman Jay and the English influence on Amsterdam club culture, see Chapter 4.
205 See Chapter 2.
206 {p. 174}

4   Cyber clogs

Ondertussen is Nederland helemaal & totaal plat voor 'House'. De gezonde Hollandse polderjongens & meisjes gaan massaal voor een vrijetijdsbesteding die inmiddels al (of eigenlijk: wederom) tot vragen in de kamer heeft geleidt [Bos, 1992].

(Eng. trans.)[207] In the meantime, the Netherlands have completely fallen for 'House'. The healthy Dutch polder boys and girls have chosen en mass for a leisure pursuit which meanwhile has already (or in fact: again) led to questions in parliament.

Introduction

Since the term 'house' was imported, it took several years before a 'second generation' of house consumers gave it its own meaning in the Netherlands. Although house music had been known to dance music import enthusiasts since at least 1985 [van Vliet, 1992], popularity and mainstream attention of house music started with the arrival of English rave parties in the summer of 1988. Since then, the development of house music and its party scene began to follow its own local path, whereby in 1992 gabberhouse, known in the Enlish speaking world as gabba, became the most identifiable Dutch house music sound on the 'global' market.

---

[207] (Eng. trans.) means 'English translation'.

The early Dutch house music scene

As early as 1987, the first London styled acid house parties were organised in Amsterdam by a trendsetting organisation called Department Store, which were very exclusive. Music from Chicago was provided via friends in the London underground circuit. The people who attended (not more than about five hundred) were from the fashion world, as well as media people, art students and unemployed people (who liked to dress in outrageous, often expensive, outfits); a significant proportion of this crowd were reported to be homosexual [Adelaars, 1991]. The Amsterdam avant-garde 'in crowd' had found a new pastime which was suitably imported; in other words, it was based on an elitist 'know-how' which separated them from 'the masses'. Around the same time, night club Roxy opened in Amsterdam, where in 1987 and 88 DJs Eddy De Clercq and Joost van Bellen made a brave attempt at playing house music to what was, at the time, an unwilling public:

> Van Bellen, ook als DJ actief, herinnert zich dat om drie uur 'snachts nog maar dertig man over waren gebleven. En hoe glazen bier in zijn richting werden gesmeten omdat de acid-dreun totaal niet aansloeg bij het publiek[208] [de Vries, 1991].

> (Eng. trans.) Van Bellen, also active as DJ, remembers that only about 30 people were left at around 3 am. And how beer glasses were thrown in his direction because the monotonous acid beat was unwelcome with the audience.

To have only 30 people in this large club at 3 am was quite a disaster since in Amsterdam clubs were usually open until 5 or 6 am at the weekends and Roxy was situated within a large converted theatre with an extra floor on the balcony. However, by the end of 1988 the Bam Bam nights on Wednesdays with Joost van Bellen became a stronghold for the avant-garde of the house scene [Engelshoven and van Luijn, 1989].

In 1988 the London dance club and party scene made more noticeable waves in Amsterdam. In May that year *The Face* magazine reported a boat party on the canals organised by the Wag Club from Soho in the tradition of the Thames boat party trips.

---

208 {newspaper}

London radio station Kiss FM's Norman Jay played, amongst other music, acid house to an audience which included 120 London club tourists. Apparently the Dutch 'watched in bemusement' as 'the core clientele of the Wag Club seemed intent on trying to re-enact the complete works of Hunter S. Thompson in four days'[209] [Garratt, 1988]. The weekend described ended with an English styled rave party at the Amsterdam Roxy Club. Garratt made an attempt to explain what drives the British to travel so far for a party as follows:

> ... the urge to travel is a strange quality common to British clubbers. Nowhere else in the world will otherwise perfectly sane people hitch, hire coaches, or drive hundreds of miles just to attend an all-dayer that invariably features at least one DJ they can see at a local venue each week. Perhaps because of our archaic licensing laws, nowhere else does dancing in a warehouse at 5 am or at an all-dayer on Sunday feel so good. And nowhere else are clubbers willing to travel so far for their pleasure[210] [Garratt, 1988].

During the 80s it seemed that enterprising young British people came over to Amsterdam in a steady flow, where in the later part of that decade they left their mark on Dutch culture in the form of shops, club nights and rave parties. First of all the British were attracted to the 'easier' attitude in Amsterdam, compared to that in Britain, to restrictions on varieties of sex behaviour, the use of drugs and also of licensing laws. Secondly, Amsterdam provided economic opportunities in the form of gaps in the market [de Vries, 1991]. For example, Howard Shanon started an Amsterdam based entertainments magazine called *City Life*. Since 1988, several English rave party organisations, such as Sunrise, had organised parties in Amsterdam. Even Manchester night club the Haçienda, an early stronghold of house music,[211] celebrated its seventh birthday at Roxy in 1989.

After their first boat party, English DJs Graham B and Paul Jay formed the Soho Connection in Amsterdam. In addition to this Paul Jay edited and wrote for *Wild*, a club culture fanzine, and ran a shop specialising in party clothes. Graham B and Paul Jay were motivated

---

209 {p. 40}
210 {p. 40}
211 See Chapter 3.

to make their move to Amsterdam because the London scene seemed too competitive:

> There are, claims Graham, plenty of clubs in Amsterdam, but no real club culture, though they're working on it: building up mailing lists, introducing jazz dance with visits from UK dance troupe IDJ, starting their own show on the pirate station Radio 100, and trying to introduce the idea of following DJs and crews rather than just visiting clubs[212] [Garratt, 1988].

The parties organised by this team left a significant impression on Amsterdam club culture; four years later the Dutch press still acknowledged the major influence of Graham B and Paul Jay [de Vries, 1992]. In September 1988, Gert van Veen wrote a seminal two page article in the Dutch daily newspaper *De Volkskrant* on rave parties [van Veen, 1988] in anticipation of the first huge acid house party in the Netherlands, the London-comes-to-Amsterdam trance party, which was organised by the Soho Connection on Saturday, 3 September 1988. This event was organised in collaboration with Radio 100, in an old warehouse on the Levantkade (loods 22) and was attended by around 2000 people [Verhave and ter Weijden, 1991]. One of the main DJs was Londoner Danny Rampling. London boys and girls were reported by ethnographer Adelaars to be dancing on boxes which were placed around the large space in the light of two stroboscope lights, surrounded by orange-red smoke. Social backgrounds varied, but what people had in common was that they all wanted to dance into the morning hours [Adelaars, 1991].

Although some articles on acid house had appeared the month before, it was this event which triggered the enthusiasm of the press and of club audiences. In the same month, the Dutch national music paper *Oor* published its first big article on house music, which gave an overview of the history of disco and house music as well as a review of the consumption of house music in Amsterdam, Gent and London [Franssen, 1988a]. In the same issue an article appeared on the history of techno [Franssen, 1988b]. It was not unusual for the middle class section of Dutch youth to follow English trends; for instance in the 1970s, punk was introduced in that way. In the Netherlands there was relatively easy access to the English music press; English club magazines such as *The Face*, *i-D* and *Mixmag* as

---

212 {p. 40}

well as more rock orientated music weeklies such as the *NME* and *Sounds* were available in most larger urban centres during the 80s and 90s. The initial trickle of imported house records increased to a flow and record shop Boudisque was one of the first companies to start licensing house music for the local market [Verhave and ter Weijden, 1991]. In 1988 acid house broke into the Dutch charts with *We call it Acieed* by D-Mob (FFRR, 1988) and *Can You Party* by Royal House (Torso, 1988) [Verhave and ter Weijden, 1991]. By September that year English dance records such as Cold Cut *Doctoring the House* (Westside, 1989), The Beatmasters with the Cookie Crew *Rok da House* (Torso, 1988) and S-Express *Theme from S-Express* Torso/Rhythm King, 1988) had entered the Dutch national Top 40 [van Veen, 1988]. English acid house outfit Humanoid entered the charts in spring 1989 with *Stakker Humanoid* (Westside, 1989).

Apart from fashionable Amsterdam, there were other relatively isolated pockets within the Western metropolitan area of the Netherlands which had taken an interest in house music. For instance, at night in Maassluis, near Rotterdam, DJs Felix Huyser and Peter Rijswijk played acid house on their pirate radio station called Night Life, around August of 1988. They also attempted to bring acid house to the Rotterdam clubs, but met with some resistance:

> Een tijdje geleden organiseerden ze een Acid House-party in een Rotterdamse discotheek. Het disco publiek kwam binnen, keek vijf minuten rond en vertrok geshockeerd[213] [Dibbets, 1988].

> (Eng. trans.) A while back they organised an Acid House party in a club in Rotterdam. Its usual disco clientele came in, looked around and left in shock.

Instead of the mostly working class crowds who visited traditional dance clubs ('discos') it was the more bohemian 'alternative crowd', who used to be involved with punk rock, hip hop, electro and avant-garde electronic pop, who were attracted to acid house events.

At the same time in the neighbouring country Belgium, acid house had been taken on by several clubs in Antwerp and Gent. Dance club the Boccacio in Destelbergen near Gent, hosted specialist nights on Sundays until 2 pm the next day, with DJ Olivier Pieters. Apparently

---

213 {newspaper}

there was a decadent atmosphere, while it catered for all layers of the population. The audience was described as looking like 'Tin Tin on Acid'; short trousers, high socks, heavy black shoes and a hair cut with a little front lock [Dibbets, 1988], or otherwise clad in black or in extravagant disco outfits [Franssen, 1988a]. Here acid and latin house were played alongside European electro-punk and New Wave such as Fad Gadget and Kraftwerk as well as a Belgian dance music called new beat [Franssen, 1988a], which used similar technologies as house music for a much slower, lyrically obscene form of electro-disco. New beat had started in the mid-80s when Belgian DJs played records at 33 rpm instead of at 45 rpm, which is the speed at which they were supposed to be played.[214] Thereby the speed slider of the record deck was put to the maximum setting of 8+; hence the popular term for new beat was '33 8+'. By playing 45s that way a much deeper bass sound was created than intended by the producers and cutting engineers while the slower tempo allowed for a 'sleazier feel'. New beat was related to a European tradition of electronic dance music called electronic body music which will be described later in this chapter in the section on the development of different styles of dance music in the Netherlands.

Parties and surveillance

By the end of 1988 acid house was described in the Netherlands as a new 'subculture'[215] [Quint, 1988]. News of police raids on parties in Britain made it attractive to young people to engage themselves in the music, clothes and parties inspired by the raves across the North Sea. Dutch authorities initially showed some sympathy to the panic behaviour of their British counterparts. On 22 November 1988, the drug ecstasy[216] was placed on list 1 of the opium law (hard drugs) [Adelaars, 1991]. In December of that year, even clothing store chain C&A temporarily removed T-Shirts with the smiley logo on it because of its (unsavoury) connotations with these parties.

In January 1989 seemingly contradictory news items appeared.

---

[214] During the 80s, most European pressings of 12" dance singles used to be 45 rpm. In contrast, American 12" singles were cut at 33 rpm, which allowed for a deeper bass frequency.

[215] However, the notion of a 'subculture' has been doubted in the context of music consumption [Redhead, 1990] and of house music consumption [Rietveld, 1993].

[216] An entactogenic drug which was adopted by the acid house scene and which gained widespread popularity in proportion to the popularity of the music and its social events.

Although one newspaper stated that the Netherlands were behind in the acid house craze compared to other countries such as Belgium or England [Editorial: Pauze, 1989], in music paper *Oor* it was claimed that house music was flooding the Dutch discotheques, youth clubs and even radio and that it was spreading 'like a virus':

De hysterie die de dansrage veroorzaakt herinnert aan de discofever die John Travolta en Olivia Newton-John in 1977 teweeg brachten[217] [Engelshoven and van Luijn, 1989].

(Eng. trans.) The hysteria which the dance craze causes reminds one of the disco fever brought about by John Travolta and Olivia Newton-John.

Apart from the publicity which acid house parties received, there was also an economic factor which caused the preference of dance nights and parties over live music [Engelshoven and van Luijn, 1989]. Youth clubs and also some of the inner city live venues receive a subsidy from the government. This was a system which stemmed from the early 70s, when the drug underground and the generation gap problems which had started in the 60s were contained through the provision of subsidised spaces under supervision of trained social youth workers. By the late 80s these subsidies were reduced. Since it is much cheaper to entertain a crowd with one or two DJs rather than with one or two bands, it was a logical step to allow dance nights to take over from live entertainment.

From the beginning of 1989, an increasing amount of house parties were organised at a variety of locations, mostly near Amsterdam. Due to their popularity, one needed to have a flyer or invitation to gain entry, which could only be obtained at another house party the week before. Adelaars reported that the music was generally loud, the lights flashed in a blinding white and the noisy colourful crowd was surrounded by a lot of theatrical smoke [Adelaars, 1991]. The queues before the entrance of the parties became longer, since the sensational stories of the parties attracted more and more curious people. Some dance clubs became too full to provide decent dance space for people. The door staff became more choosy; people had to invent new props and outfits to be allowed entry:

---

217 {p. 18}

Scheidsrechtersfluitjes, scheepstoeters, een bril met ingebouwde schijnwerpertjes die zo mooi door de rookwolken priemden, shirts met een capouchonnetje, ruime eigengemaakte petten, Afghaanse mutsjes, fluoriscerende make-up, strakke wielrennersbroeken, doorzichtige kleren, blote buiken, geen kleren. (...) Alles was mogelijk, zolang het maar niet alledaags was[218] [Adelaars, 1991].

(Eng. trans.) Referee whistles, ship hooters, a pair of glasses with built-in spot lights which beam so beautifully through the smoke, hooded shirts, Afghan hats, fluorescent make-up, tight fitting cycling pants, transparent clothes, bare bellies, no clothes. (...) Everything was possible, as long as it wasn't everyday normality.

The schism between the 'original' party elite and what this group identify as the 'second generation' became apparent in July 1989:

Langzaamaan begint immers het Top Veertig-publiek op feesten af te komen: jongens met matjes in hun nek en meisjes met te veel soleil in hun coupe. Mensen die het verschil tussen New Beat en Deep House niet eens kennen en, erger, als een robot staan te dansen.[219]

(Eng. trans.) Slowly but surely the Top 40 public starts to attend the parties: boys with hair which is short on top and long in the neck and girls with too much soleil in their coupe. People who do not know the difference between New Beat and Deep House and, worse, who dance like a robot [Campert, 1989].

In the same year, complaints started to be voiced about violence and too much drugs use at urban house gatherings which was in contrast to the original feeling of togetherness [Kleijwegt, 1990]. Football fans and (mainly male) urban youth had discovered the pleasures of the drug ecstasy and of losing oneself in trance dance. However, their preference for the cheaper and harsher combination of amphetamines and alcohol caused feelings of aggression. In Amsterdam, the name 'gabbers' was used for young men who hung out with their 'mates' in groups in places like the Leidse Plein. In July 1989 they caused problems in the Amsterdam night club Mazzo,

---

[218] {pp. 47-48}
[219] {newspaper}

which needed to be emptied with the help of a lot of police. It was the notion of the gabber as party-goer which slowly but surely became a dominant factor in the production of a specific Dutch house music style. Journalist Ardy Beesemer gave some descriptions of gabber parties:

Een grote hoeveelheid (havenfeesten in Amsterdam). Bijna allemaal fout. Al die gabbers zwaar onder de dope. Een zompige atmosfeer. Veel hash en bier. En opgefokt; niks te maken met goede smaak in wat voor vorm dan ook.[220]

Ik denk dat het laatste (feest in Scheveningen) op de pier was. In de sportshallen worden grote feesten gegeven; 6000 tot 7000 goozers blazen het dak ervan af. Die atmosfeer; ik durfde de zaal niet in. Ik was blij dat ver weg op het podium stond te draaien. Ik dacht: hou 'ns op! In de kleedkamer stond ik na te rillen; dat tuig daarzo. Alhoewel, het is opvallend dat er eigenlijk weinig moeilijkheden op die gelegenheden zijn. Elke keer denk ik: naaa dit gaat helemaal fout[221] [Beesemer, 1992].

(Eng. trans.) An enormous amount (of harbour parties in Amsterdam). Nearly all sad. All those 'gabbers' under the heavy influence of drugs. A muddy atmosphere. Lots of dope and beer. And hyper; nothing to do with good taste in any way.

I think the last (party in Scheveningen) was on the pier. In the sport halls they give huge parties; 6000 to 7000 blokes blow the roof off. That ambience; I didn't dare to enter the room. I was glad I was DJ-ing far away on the stage. I thought, leave it out! In the dressing room I was shaking; that scum in there. Although the striking thing is that there is actually little trouble at those events. Every time I think, naaah this is going completely wrong.

By the end of 1989, the police stepped up their alertness to drug use and arrested three dealers and four users at the subsidised club the Melkweg in Amsterdam. However, according to weekly news magazine *Vrij Nederland*, they only found about ten pills, some cocaine and some heroine [Kleijwegt, 1990]. Police representative

---

220 {interview}
221 {interview}

77

Cees Rameau stated in context of this incident:

We hebben in de Melkweg een signaal willen geven. Dat kan overal weer gebeuren zo lang er openlijk gebruikt en verkocht wordt. Aan de andere kant: waar geen probleem is, moeten we dat ook niet oproepen. Dat geldt in het algemeen voor nieuwe middelen. Ik wordt hier op de afdeling voorlichting af en toe gek van de journalisten die vragen wat we tegen crack doen. Dat spul is niet of nauwelijks te krijgen, dus daar doen we niets aan. Wat we willen vermijden is dit: de patient is niet ziek, maar krijgt toch een asperientje[222] [Adelaars, 1991].

(Eng. trans.) We wanted to give a signal in the Melkweg. As long as there is overt use and dealing, this can happen again anywhere. On the other hand: we should not ask for problems if they aren't there. This applies generally for all new controlled substances. Sometimes here at the department of information journalists drive me mad with questions about what we are doing against crack. Because it is hardly possible to obtain that substance, we don't do anything about it. What we want to avoid is this: the patient is not ill, but receives an aspirin nevertheless.

As a result of police action three New Year's Eve parties were cancelled. In February 1990, questions were asked in the parliament on the connection between house and the drug ecstasy. Gert Koffeman, member of the Christian coalition party CDA and ex-chairman of the Christian police society ACP asked Minister of Justice Hirsch Ballin whether any action had been undertaken by the authorities. The questions arose due to the huge publicity given to the SOS House Party organised by Psycho Connection near Amsterdam. In the end this particular party was forced to be cancelled. The Amsterdam council put pressure on the owner of the boat on which the party was supposed to be held; he would have lost his mooring licence if the party would have gone ahead. In the first months of 1990 some parties were disallowed but others could go ahead. On Queens Day, 30 April, thousands of people danced in places like the fronts of Mazzo and Roxy under the slogan 'fight for your right to party'[223] [Adelaars, 1991]. However, the police did not continue with

---

222 (p. 50)
223 (p. 51)

the same level of action as they did in Britain; therefore the house music scene did not vanish 'underground'. As the house music scene escalated the drug ecstasy became widely popular. For instance, during the celebrations of football team Ajax winning the Dutch football cup, its supporters chanted:

Hash, coke en pillen, dat is wat we willen[224] [Adelaars, 1991].

(Eng. trans.) Hash, coke and pills,[225] that is what we want.

As the awareness of house parties increased in the Dutch popular imagination, house parties ceased to be the exclusive entertainment for the Amsterdam elite in either Roxy or Mazzo. Neither was it simply an urban form of entertainment for the (gabber) city youth of Rotterdam in clubs like Night Town or Feyenoord FC supporter stronghold Parkzicht. In spring 1990 the parties spread out from the western urban areas into the provinces [Abrahams, 1990]. By the summer of 1990, huge parties became the norm; however, these were organised more often for profit rather than for the fun of it. Although most party people had stopped wearing T-shirts with imprints such as a smiley or 'I love XTC',[226] there were still a lot of people wearing surf and skateboard clothes such as shorts, trainers, hip pouches and bandannas [Abrahams, 1990].[227] In addition, people wore sensual rips and holes in their clothing, like a vague echo of the razor slashed jeans which the Chicago house crowd used to wear in the mid-80s [DJ Pierre, 1992]. Like in Britain, party people became prepared to travel all over the country for dance parties. They even went over to London to keep up with the newest developments [Adelaars, 1991; Bakker, 1992]. Party organisations such as Black Love Cabaret, MTC, Soho-connection (with its travel agency for British ravers called Exodus) became established names [Kleijwegt, 1990]. Ardy Beesemer described some of the 'better' parties:

De Gaultier parties hebben een redelijk goede naam. Onlangs gaven ze een enorm feest op een kasteel. Het schijnt dat dat ook zompig was. Zo ordinair, die geblondeerde kapsels. Dit laatste feest was in de buurt van Breda. Maar meestal geven ze goede

---

[224] {p. 51}
[225] The form in which the drug ecstasy is sold is either that of capsule or of pill.
[226] 'XTC' is the Dutch popular abbreviation to indicate the drug ecstasy. See Chapter 6.
[227] Compare dress styles of British ravers in 1988 and 1989 [Rietveld, 1993].

feesten, vooral in de buurt van Amsterdam. Hun naam komt van de mode show op het eerste feest. Het is een deftige naam. De goozer die er achter zit is een patatkraamman uit Madurodam; niet een man met smaak; een grote dikke vent[228] [Beesemer, 1992].

(Eng. trans.) The Gaultier parties have a reasonably good name. Recently they gave a huge party in a castle. Apparently that was muddy as well. So common, those bleached hairdos. This last party was near Breda. But usually they give good parties, especially near Amsterdam. Their name is derived from the fashion show at the first party. It's a posh name. The guy who is behind it is a fish and chips man from Madurodam; not a man of taste; a big fat bloke.

House was becoming the dominant form of entertainment for Dutch youth in general. Even though, like in Britain, the death of the concept of a single youth culture was announced by Dutch sociologists, house seemed to have reunited various factions [van Woensel Kooy, 1989]. Apart from the terms house music and house party, a new verb entered the Dutch language, 'housen', which was an equivalent to the British word 'to rave'. It either meant to go to a house party[229] or to go to a club to dance non-stop to electronic dance music for hours on end.

In 1992, the house scene encountered new difficulties with the Dutch authorities. Questions were asked in parliament when the society for the hotel and catering trade (Horeca) complained that the organisers of house parties did not have any regard for the rules by which this trade was supposed to abide and cited a list of main offences which included lack of licences, tax evasion, fire hazard and free drug trade. However, by banning the parties, the scene would become criminalised which means less control for the authorities. The main problem for the catering trade was the loss of potential income and yet, the same organisations showed a reluctance to be associated with unruly hedonist events [Escher and Vermeulen, 1992; Schilders, 1992]. Party organiser DJ Per estimated that in March 1992, 30 to 40 parties were held per weekend, whereby in the weekend in the beginning of March out of 48 parties only 3 were illegal [de Jong,

---

228 {interview}
229 A house party is a rave, sometimes in a warehouse or on a boat or otherwise perhaps in a farm house, beach tent, urban squat or castle.

1992]. His argument was that if the necessary licences were refused, or when certain clubs would not allow a house party on their premises, then people would have to organise their own entertainment. Traditional dance clubs did not supply what was demanded. It was therefore up to the catering industry to shape up its act if it wanted to earn money from house culture [Schilders, 1992]. This public argument did give the house scene more adverse publicity, which meant that certain parties were cancelled again, especially in the area of Amsterdam and the surrounding areas.

One way of getting around the trouble of getting permission for the necessary licenses was by calling a dance event something other than a house party. These words, house party, therefore gradually disappeared from the party vocabulary since mid-1991. There were different other tactics to get around the problem. For instance, the band Quazar, with pop journalist Gert van Veen, organised a tour of parties along the traditional rock circuit. Since 1991 they have played their gigs with two men taking care of the technology accompanied by two female dancers, of which one also sang. At the end of their performance, the place was changed into a party with a DJ, smoke machines and special light effects [van Holst Pellekaan, 1991]. Ardy Beesemer, who was DJ at these events, described them as follows:

Van Friesland tot Limburg waren ze aan het klompendansen, werkelijk overal. Hoe extremer en raarder, hoe harder, hoe meer ze er van hielden. Het waren veel jeugdverenigingen en jeugdhonks in de kleinere plaatsen[230] [Beesemer, 1992].

(Eng. trans.) From Friesland to Limburg they were doing the clog dance, really everywhere; absolutely unbelievable. The more extreme and weird, the harder, the more they liked it. There were a lot of youth societies and youth clubs in the smaller places.

Another reason to refrain from using the name house party was an attempt to keep the parties reserved for an underground elite. For instance DJ Marcel Bakker stated:

Ik wil mijn feesten eigenlijk niet een House party noemen; ik noem het gewoon een dance party. Anders krijg je het verkeerde publiek die gewoon meeloopt, zo van: nu is het populair en gaan we

---
[230] {interview}

lekker housen, want we hebben alle top 40 platen die House zijn. Alsof dat zo zou zijn, maar dat is natuurlijk niet het geval[231] [Bakker, 1992].

(Eng. trans.) I don't really want to call my parties a house party; I just call it a dance party. Otherwise you get the wrong audience which is there to jump on the bandwagon, like: now it's popular and we'll go and have a good rave, because we got all the top 40 records which are House. As though they would be, but that is of course not the case.

In Rotterdam, the authorities were more lenient towards house parties than elsewhere. As a result, by 1992, raves of around 5000 people were not unusual and the biggest event of that year, Eurorave, which was held on the beach near the gigantic petrochemical industrial estate of the Europoort, pulled 20,000 gabberhouse and techno fans. According to English reports, the main dance style was like that of the old punk slam-dance [Laarman, 1991]. Alternatively, 'gabbers' from Rotterdam danced like they were riding a horse, a movement which was reported to be used on the football terraces the year before, when Feyenoord scored [Hulsman, 1991].

Elsewhere in the country huge events were staged, attracting up to 8000 people. On the other hand there were also smaller illegal clubs in squats which were organised without a profit motive. An example of this was Bash-O in The Hague, which was a techno club in the cellar of a squat which was open for the entire night, well into the morning [Schilders, 1992]. So 'house' had become a generic term for a particular type of dance entertainment, which, like rock before, could be produced and consumed in both mainstream and underground contexts [Verhave and ter Weijden, 1991].

Dutch house music

Initially, in 1988, 'acid' had been the popular tag for anything that was related to house music, which in the Netherlands is an umbrella term for acid house[232], deep house,[233] garage,[234] new beat, electronic

---

231 {interview}
232 See Chapters 3 and 6.
233 See Chapter 2.
234 See Chapter 2.

body music,[235] world beat and other dance music which uses similar technologies [Engelshoven and van Luijn, 1989]. In this context, the term 'house music' indicated more than the very specific definition with which it had started in Chicago.[236] The insistent four quarter beat, manic rhythms, a stress on synthesised sound textures and a disappearance of melody lines and traditional song structures was emphasised by the choice of music by Dutch DJs. Thereby a definition of techno (a term initiated by Detroit producers Derek May, Juan Atkins and Kevin Saunderson) would probably be more appropriate when speaking of a Dutch house aesthetic:

> If there is one central idea in techno, it is of the harmony between man and machine. As Juan Atkins puts it: 'You gotta look at it like, techno is technological. It's an attitude to making music that is futuristic: something that hasn't been done before'. This idea is commonplace through much of avant-garde 20th-century art ...[237] [Savage, 1996].

Together with Detroit techno, Belgian electronic body music such as the punk-vocalised robo-disco of Front 242 [Reynolds, 1990a] was of major influence on several versions of Dutch house music which appeared in the early 90s. Electronic body music[238] had part of its roots in the electronic music tradition of Europe, especialy that of Germany, from the perfectionist composer and teacher Stockhausen, the ambient music experimentalist Klaus Schulze [Mutsaers, 1994] and trance music makers Kraftwerk, to the early 80s electro-punk scene the Neue Deutsche Welle with groups like DAF and Einsturzende Neubauten. In the 90s the Frankfurt based DJ and producer Sven Vath has continued the German trance music tradition which had started in the 70s, mixing it with elements of house music. Of European record labels which have developed the notion of trance techno during the early 90s the Belgian R&S Records have lead the way, with tracks like *Mama* by Neuro (R&S, 1993), as well as the English label Warp.[239] The European tradition of electronic dance music, which also included English groups from the early 80s, like

---

[235] Electronic body music is a tradition of European electronic dance music with a punk aesthetic.
[236] See Chapter 2.
[237] {p. 19}
[238] See for example the compilation *Electronic Body Music* (Play It Again Sam Records, 1988).
[239] See Chapter 3.

83

Cabaret Voltaire, Depeche Mode and New Order, were in their turn of major influence on the early, rather isolated, creators of Detroit techno in the mid-80s [Savage, 1993b].[240] On the influence of electronic body music Alain Verhave said:

Ik draai voor Radio 100, een plaatselijke piraat in Amsterdam. Alle belangrijke DJs spelen daarop, dus veel mensen luisteren, ik geloof ongeveer 75.000 die ernaar luisteren. (...) Alle DJs op ons station maakte de switch in 88 van electronic body music. Het was opeens: hee, house![241] [Verhave, 1992].

(Eng. trans.) I DJ for Radio 100, a local pirate in Amsterdam. All the main DJs play on it, so a lot of people listen, I believe there are around 75,000 that listen to it. (...) All the DJs on our station made the switch from electronic body music in 88. It was suddenly: hey, house!

In line with the way of thinking of the zippy[242] and the punk/new wave avant-garde, some journalists employed by the quality press regarded house music as the only form of art which was still possible at the end of the 80s [Engelshoven and van Luijn, 1989]. Such a description may be understood as belonging to a discourse of European bohemia and fits neatly within the cultural boundaries of a European middle class *avant-garde* art sensibility. Since the days of Dada in the early 20th century, artists attempted to break down the hierarchical gallery system by propagating art by and for the people [Richter, 1965]. Combined with the machine aesthetic which developed during the early 20th century[243] [Huyssen, 1988a; Museum Of Modern Art, 1934] this created a sentiment for technological art combined with audience participation amongst a section of the European art community [Richter, 1965; Plant, 1993]. In the early 80s, before the words 'techno' house were coined, one English electronic dance music group, in sympathy with the ideas of dada, called itself Cabaret Voltaire after the dada theatre of Zurich during the First

---

240 Also see Chapter 6.
241 {interview}
242 Zen Inspired Professional Pagan.
243 See, for example, the Italian futurists [Apollonio, 1973; Tisdall and Bozzolla, 1977]; the German Neue Sachlichkeit [Lethen, 1970]; German cinema such as Fritz Lang's 1927 film Metropolis [Huyssen, 1988b]; European modernist architecture like that of Le Corbusier [le Corbusier, 1927]; or French fine artists like Leger [de Franca, 1983].

World War. Taking this perhaps modernist sensibility into consideration it may not be surprising that to some people techno house music was a form of avant-garde art.[244]

Although at the New Music Seminar of 1989 in New York the Dutch were mostly represented by rock bands, with perhaps the exception of rock-rap outfit Urban Dance Squad,[245] dance music was becoming the dominant form of pop in the Netherlands [van Veen, 1989b]. At the Dutch DJ and Dance Convention in October, it was agreed that 1989 had been the most successful year in the history of dance, with more dance hits in the hit lists than ever [van Veen, 1989c]. People who used to create hip hop started to record house music [van Vliet, 1992]. This is most likely the reason why traces of hip hop can be heard in many of the faster hardcore tracks which have utilised sampled and speeded up rhythm loops from hip hop records, whereby the song structures include the breaking up of grooves by moving from one particular part to another seemingly unrelated part in the style of hip hop DJ-mixing.[246] Examples can be found in *Feyenoord Reactivate* by Rotterdam Termination Source (Rotterdam Records, 1992), Cubic 22's *Night In Motion* (Big Time International, 1991) or *The Noise* by Holy Noise (Hithouse Records, 1991).

In 1990, D-Shake released *YAAAAH!*, which could be called a blueprint for what would be named gabberhouse. It sold 200,000 copies world-wide. The maker explained that it was not particularly intended for a 'gabber' audience, but rather that it was more an exercise to find a very hard 'drive', a trance-beat which would be harder than anything previously released:

> Monotone beat, dwingende baslijn — dat was de essentie van YAAAAH! — subtiele accentverschuivingen, waardoor een soort oergevoel opgeroepen wordt — dat is het gabbergevoel, het Cro Magnon-gevoel. (...) Het is een volstrekt pretentieloze genotscultuur. Niet meer dan dat. De muziek bevat geen enkel statement[247] [de Jongh, 1991].

---

[244] The concept of techno house was popularised; for example, in the name for the Belgian outfit Technotronic who released the poppy house track *Pump It Up* (ARS Records, 1989) and Dutch duo 2 Unlimited who chanted the already popular word 'techno' as in the techno house style produced pop song *No Limits* (Bite, 1993).

[245] A forerunner of bands like Rage Against the Machine and Senser which were doing well in Britain and The Netherlands in 1994.

[246] A similar structure can be found in the more mellow British hardcore rave tracks; Chapter 4.

[247] {interview}

(Eng. trans.) Monotonous beat, forceful bass line — that was the essence of YAAAAH! — subtle shifts of accent, because of which a kind of primeval feeling is created — that is the feeling of gabber, that Cro Magnon feeling. (...) It is a hedonist culture completely without any pretence. Nothing else but just that. The music contains no statement whatsoever.

The term 'gabberhouse' was first coined by Roxy DJ KC The Funcaholic, who also worked for record shop Blackbeat. Then D-Shake made it a public word by explaining it on television [Beesemer, 1991a]. Gabberhouse could be compared to hardcore punk: easy to make at home, purely technological, rough and very energetic because of its high tempo. Developments in technology took away restriction of speed, for a drum box could be set to play much faster than any drummer. Marcel Bakker, who in 1992 played garage and disco at the Amsterdam club The It, remarked on the tempo of Dutch gabberhouse:

Het is juist het punt dat het makkelijker is om energieke muziek te maken met een sneller tempo, omdat het tempo energie in zichzelf heeft. Het is een stuk moeilijker om langzamere muziek te maken die net zo hard en dansbaar is. Het is mogenlijk, maar je hebt veel meer een gevoel voor muziek nodig[248] [Bakker, 1992].

(Eng. trans.) The point is, that it is easier to create an energetic music with a fast tempo, since tempo has energy in itself. It is much more difficult to make a kind of slower music which is just as hard and dancable. It is possible, but then you need a greater sense of music.

The new technologies also made the idea of verses and chorus lines near to obsolete, since no band or singer had to remember a song structure. The combination of cheap synthesizers and sequencers had left the field wide open for experimentation by working class layers of the population who ironically were not interested in *avant-garde* ideas. One should take into consideration that the notion of *avant-garde* art is closely connected to values based on class and affluence [Bourdieu, 1984]. Steeped in a tradition of rock, it was not surprising that the majority of Dutch producers and consumers preferred a rock

---
248 {interview}

type of sensibility:

Derek May zei over dat onderwerp: 'het is rock muziek die op een snelle dans beat is geplaatst'. Het grotere publiek houdt van die herkenbare liedjes, terwijl echte techno een stuk moeilijker is; je moet open staan tot die muziek omerecht van uit je bol te gaan[249] [Bakker, 1992].

(Eng. trans.) Derek May[250] has said on the subject: 'it is rock music placed on a fast dance beat'. The larger public likes those simple recognisable tunes, while real techno is much more difficult; you have to be open to the music to be able to get off your head on it.

To Rotterdam label owner Van Vliet, taking the position of someone who preferred soul and disco, gabber was a sign of 'impoverished'[251] music:

We zijn het allemaal wel een beetje moe van die stampende boel, weet je wel? Sommige van die platen zijn o.k., maar ik wil wat *muziek*. Ik ben altijd een disco freak geweest en ik heb altijd van muziek gehouden. Op een bepaalt moment dacht ik niet dat dat nog muziek was; gewoon een enkel drum lijntje trekken met wat herrie er bovenop, het geluid van een *cirkelzaag* ofzo. Misschien is het leuk om in een staat van ectasy te komen op een XTC pil, maar het blijft op een bepaalt niveau, een plafondniveau, die gabberhouse. Je kan niet omhoog of omlaag. Dus het niveau van spanning gaat gewoon weg. De mensen doen gewoon een beetje gek, scheren hun hoofd, gedragen zich aggressief. Wel, dat is wat ik ervan denk ...[252] [Van Vliet, 1992].

(Eng. trans.) We're all a bit tired of that stamping stuff, you know? Some of those records are all right, but I want some *music*. I've always been a disco freak and I've always loved music. At some point I just thought that it (gabberhouse) was not music any more; just creating a bare drum track with some noise on top of it, the

---

249 {interview}
250 One of the originators of Detroit (in other words African-American) techno, which was closely related to Chicago house music. See Chapter 2.
251 As in musically uneducated: young and brass and stupid and kicking the shins of musically sensitive and 'wiser' creatures.
252 {interview}

sound of a *circle saw* or something like that. It may be fun to get to a state of ecstasy on an E, but it stays on a certain level, a ceiling level, with gabberhouse; you can't go up or down. So the level of tension just disappears. People go a bit crazy, shave their heads, behave aggressively. Well, that's what I think of it ...

However, instead of pleasure, what one gets is a trance inducing type of music, comparable with Gilbert Rouget's descriptions of certain African trance ceremonies [Rouget, 1985]. Biomusicologist Nils Wallin describes music which contributes to a trance state in participants of trance ceremonies as being, amongst other things, 'violent enough to evoke the necessary excitement', and 'flat (not too varied in dynamics but kept at a high intensity level) ...'[253] [Wallin, 1991]. I would therefore argue that the producers of gabberhouse have taken the use of music to enable a state of trance, an ancient method of reaching a communal dream state, to its technologically possible extremes[254] within a secular and urban cultural context.

In Europe, the religious aspects and even those indicators of an Afro-American 'gay' identity which were part of the Chicago house sound were subdued and mostly went unnoticed. Ideas of longing or of spiritual healing can hardly be found in the European versions of house. Roxy DJ Eddy de Clercq said:

Acid (...) is niet zozeer muziek als wel een nieuwe jeugd cultuur. Het is een gevoel. Dat komt door het repeterende. En Acid is slang, underground, anoniem, met een druggy atmosfeer. Het is puur escapisme, het heeft geen boodschap en geen troost[255] [Goedkoop, 1989].

(Eng. trans.) Acid (...) is not just music but a new youth culture. It is a feeling. That is because of its repetitive quality. And Acid is slang, underground, anonymous, with a druggy atmosphere. It is pure escapism, it has no message and gives no comfort.

Journalist Ardy Beesemer has said something similar:

... (house) muziek (...) heeft geen ruimte voor romantiek[256]

253 {p. 285}
254 For more on trance, see the last part of Chapter 7.
255 {interview}
256 {interview}

[Beesemer, 1992].

(Eng. trans.) ... (house) music (...) leaves no space for romance.

Perhaps one could speculate that in the Netherlands there was no need for a sense of hope as can be found in the African-American soul and gospel sensibility which speaks of 'better days'. From an economic and social point of view most Dutch people do not suffer a lack. Therefore pure hedonism could be afforded without a particularly positive or 'upperworld' message.[257] In addition, specifically the vocals of gabberhouse articulated 'satanic' imagery which is comparable with heavy metal and death metal. This has lead to accusations, for example, by the Dutch evangelical movement, that a house party and its sound track were the works of the devil[258] [Mulder, 1993; de Jong, 1993].

As house music became a more common cultural phenomenon a reaction by the dance club elite of Amsterdam was inevitable. In an attempt to rid themselves of acid house in spring 1989, an embrace of African-American deep house was spearheaded at night club Roxy with, for instance, PAs[259] by Chicago dance acts Ten City and Kym Mazelle. However, the majority of the Dutch party and club audiences had just started to like the concept of trance dancing to synthesizer loops [Barelds, 1994]; they considered deep house as lacking in wild energy. Some journalists and people from the house scene, such as Quazar musician Gert van Veen, asked themselves whether deep house was 'just old disco' or a progression [van Veen, 1989a]. The idea of progression is one which can also be found in the old modernist avant-garde discourse. However, in accepting that there are different styles for different local populations, the idea of progress disappears. Perhaps it would be more useful to define changes in music as mutations instead of 'perversions' of the 'authentic' or the 'original' [Benjamin, 1973; Baudrillard, 1983], which

---

[257] 'Upperworld' is a term used within the context of Shamanism to indicate the higher realms of spiritual consciousness in contrast to 'underworld' (the site of experience which is also called hell) and 'middle world' (the site of experience which is a routinely everyday experience) [Taylor, 1985].

[258] One has to bear in mind that satanic/devil is a definition of that which is considered to be harmful to a certain discourse on which a society has based its values (such as a non-hedonist work-ethic). On the other hand, a spiritual experience of a 'higher' level usually involves the bonding of a community and its values, which hold a similar function as the super-ego in Freud's body of thought [Marcuse, 1987].

[259] A PA is a Public Appearance.

is an essentialist notion. In the Netherlands, however, a conviction existed amongst the middle class press that house/acid/techno was 'global' and that it 'progressed'.

Journalist and house producer Ardy Beesemer suggested that gabberhouse was directed towards the genitalia [Beesemer, 1991c] rather than towards a polymorphously perverse sensibility which could be found at English raves [Rietveld, 1993].[260] In both Dutch and Belgian versions of house music the lower frequency range receives a higher stress than the mid-range, where traditionally the melody line or voice would appear; low bass sounds, on the other hand, affect the lower regions of the body. A head banging, or, at the faster speeds which appeared in 1992, a pogoing movement was facilitated by the non-syncopated four quarter rhythms. In addition, gabberhouse often displayed an ironic sense of humour. Marcel Bakker, who spoke from the position of the elite Amsterdam club-incrowd, criticised the methods and sentiments of gabberhouse as follows:

Alweer, dat is gabber, echte gimmick muziek. Je krijgt van die dingen zoals 'your son is dead' of 'you're not on the guest list'. Het geval met gabber is die somberheid; alles wat maar akelig en eng is vinden ze fantastisch. Vaak zijn de mensen die er op dansen aggresief. Ze gebruiken speed. Ze weten niets van muziek af, maar ze houden van dat aggressieve gevoel van bedreiging in die muziek. Ze houden van zinnetjes zoals 'your son is dead' or 'James Brown is dead'; het moet altijd zo eng en somber zijn[261] [Bakker, 1992].

(Eng. trans.) Again, that is gabber, real gimmick music. You get things like 'your son is dead'[262] or 'you're not on the guest list'. The thing with gabber is its gloominess; anything morbid or a bit horrific they think is fantastic. Often the people who dance to that are very aggressive. They use speed (amphetamine). They know nothing about music, but they love the aggressive feel of threat in that music. They love sentences like 'your son is dead' or 'James Brown is dead'; it always has to have something morbid or gloomy.

---

[260] In terms of sexuality and other attitudes, one can see similarities between gabber house and rock or heavy metal. For a discussion of differences in those terms between rock and dance music such as disco, see Dyer [Dyer, 1992].

[261] (interview)

[262] *Mr. Kirk's Nightmare* by 4 House (Reinforced, 1991).

Perhaps Bakker missed some of the sense of irony which was present in many Gabber tracks. Many producers, under aliases, attempted to make the hardest, yet wacky and 'druggy', noise at ever increasing speeds, whereby the potential of current music technology was taken to the limit. To their initial surprise, it became a commercial success. For instance, the underground Dutch house track *Anasthesia* by T99 (Who's That Beat Records, 1991), using hard hitting orchestra samples from Carl Orff's German 1937 opera *Carmina Burana*, became a Top Ten hit in the Netherlands. In October 1991 LA Style had a Number One hit with *James Brown Is Dead* (Bounce, 1991), which despite its crude harshness was written and produced by the classically trained pianist Denzing from Rotterdam [de Wolf, 1991].

Parallel with the developments in the party scene, Amsterdam and its bohemian incrowd had definitely lost its exclusive grip on the creation of the Dutch house music aesthetic. For example, from 1990, a lot of gabberhouse was produced in industrial Rotterdam. With its working class tradition of being no-nonsense and 'straight forward', the hardcore attitude as opposed to soulful gentleness suited its population better, even though its more elitist club crowds had a preference for funk and jazz. The sounds which could be heard all over the city were mostly of the building trade, since the heart of Rotterdam had been bombed during the Second World War. For instance, the noises of pile-drivers and circle saws could still be heard during the 90s. Added to that were the sounds produced by tugs, boats and cranes on the busy river Maas. This idea was confirmed in the English press, where the subtitle of an article on this subject reads: 'Rotterdam is a working class town. We are hardcore.'263 In the article it was claimed that:

> The most extreme track in history (!) comes from a project called Euromasters and is called *Alles Naar De Kl**te*, which basically translates as 'Everything Is B*ll*cks'. This track is a mixture of super fast brutal beats, some speed metal riffs and very strange Dutch samples insulting the Amsterdam DJ Dimitri264 [Laarman, 1993].

Gabber sometimes displayed an agressive defence of local identities.

---

263 {p. 13}
264 {p. 13}

In the names of the projects, a loyalty towards Rotterdam and a hatred for Amsterdam was expressed, for instance *Rotterdam Ech Wel* ('Rotterdam is real') and *Amsterdam Waar Lech Dat Dan* ('Amsterdam, where is that?') by Euromasters (Rotterdam Records, 1992), with a comic style sleeve on which the Rotterdam Euromast (a 150 metre high panorama tower left over from the world exhibition) urinates on Amsterdam, which falls apart under the force of its stream. This underlined the football connection, whereby traditionally Rotterdam Feyenoord fans and Amsterdam Ajax fans hate each other. At some Rotterdam gabber parties an over-excited crowd shouted the slogan 'Joden, Joden'[265] ('Jews, Jews') which is a symbolic address to Ajax [de Wolf, 1992]. However, the slogan was adopted by other people as well [Editorial: NRC-Handelsblad, 1993], showing a rather anti-Semitic undercurrent in Dutch culture of the early 90s. In protest, when this slogan was heard, some DJs would turn the sound off; alternatively there were also some DJ who refused to return to a venue where this slogan had been used during their visit as a guest DJ [Editorial: NRC-Handelsblad, 1993]. From observation it seems that mostly heterosexual young men consumed gabberhouse, who showed a certain level of misogyny on top of their intolerance to other towns and to ethnic minorities. For instance, one record shop owner recalled two girls entering his shop for some gabberhouse; he remembered it because it was such a rare occasion [Hulsman, 1991]. The title of popular track *No Women Allowed* by Sperminator (Rotterdam Records, 1992) stressed this point.[266]

In 1992, the extremely fast and hard hitting dance beats of gabber were favoured by the rave scene of the USA. For instance, in Chicago, *Poing* (with, on the flip side, *Feyenoord Reactivate*) by Rotterdam Termination Source (Midtown Records, 1992) was selling better than its home made product. By March 1992 it had sold over 70,000 copies world-wide [de Jong, 1992]. In New York it became part of the sound track for its suburban youth, with clubs the Limelight and the Tunnel in the forefront. For me it was a bizarre experience as a native from Rotterdam to have travelled to Chicago after having lived in England for years and ending up in the Limelight in New York to hear *Feyenoord Reactivate* for the first time, since it

---

[265] {newspaper}

[266] As an example of how cultural contexts are important to the interpretation of the meaning of a text, in March 1995 I have witnessed a female DJ at London 'mixed gay' fetish club Fist, who used this particular track as part of her DJ set. Its ironic use in Britain has been confirmed by Kelly Rust in her BA dissertation on women in the British gabba scene [Rust, 1996].

incorporates the melody of the team song for the Rotterdam football team Feyenoord to which I was able to sing along in Dutch. On the world-wide popularity of gabberhouse Marcel Bakker remarked in 1992:

> Gabber is nu over de hele wereld populair, van Oostenrijk tot Australie. Mijn neefje in Australie is een DJ en heeft een labeltje. Wat daar populair is is het zelfde als hier, zoals dat gabberachtige harde werk en dan een piano-break met wat soulstemmen en dan gaat'ie verder (...) het zal rock en roll overnemen; het verspreidt over de hele wereld[267] [Bakker, 1992].

> (Eng. trans.) Now gabber is popular all over the world, from Austria to Australia. My nephew in Australia is a DJ and has a small label. What is popular there is the same as here, like that gabber-like hardcore sound and then a piano break with soul voices and then it goes on again (...) it will take over rock and roll; it's spreading all over the world.

In the process of trying to outdo each other in being harder, faster and more outrageous the Dutch have defined their own aesthetic. In this sense, one may claim that house in their own definition is as Dutch as tulips.[268] In 1991 Alain Verhave claimed that gabberhouse was:

> ... iets wat zich heel duidelijk afscheidt van de vorige generaties en de jeugd heel duidelijk het gevoel geeft: dit is van ons[269] [Beesemer, 1991c].

> (Eng. trans.) ... something which separates itself very clearly from the past generations and which gives young people very clearly the feeling: this is ours.

According to Ardy Beesemer, in 1991 there were around four hundred people involved in the Dutch production of house music. This means that everyone knew each other, leading to both

---

267 {interview}
268 Originally imported from the Orient (East Mediterranean) the Dutch cultivated the original species of tulips into a distinctive flower shape which, for many years now, can be called specifically Dutch.
269 {p. 66}

incestuous co-operations as well as bitter rivalries. It also meant that several producers wrote different types of house music under various guises[270] [Beesemer, 1992]. Not all Dutch house music was constructed like a sledge hammer under the influence of amphetamines and beer. Other forms, first in the shadow of gabberhouse, gained recognition after the initial peak in international popularity of gabberhouse in 1992.[271] For instance, in 1990, Rik Zwaan and Rob Pieck formed Black Tulip as a vehicle for the voice of African-American singer Wendell A. Morrison from New Jersey and caused a stir in New York with their white labels[272] of *Jam On It* (Tink!, 1990) and *A Song Of Love* (Tink!, 1990). The same production team was involved in a variety of projects which were all rooted in garage and disco culture[273] [Pieck and Zwaan, 1992]. Disco and 'happy house' DJ Marcel Bakker was co-writer of the 1991 hip house flavoured *Beat of Zen* by Sonic Surfers (Fifth World, 1991), which was played across the international dance club network. Happy house was a tag which I heard often in the context of a type of dance music which had a positive message in contrast to the 'death metal-mentality' of gabberhouse. By 1993, Amsterdam based labels like Work and Fresh Fruit released happy house tracks which applied samples from mostly African-American garage tracks to new backing tracks. These ran at higher speeds than the original bpm-s of the tracks from where the samples had been derived. However, in comparison to Dutch standards where in 1994 gabberhouse was as fast as 180 bpm, these tracks of at around 135 to 140 bpm were relatively slow. In some ways this new mutation could be regarded as an accelerated form of garage music, such as Beat Freak's *Loop Trick* (Work, 1993). However, the speed of tracks forced a simplification of the Latin-American syncopations which were so characteristic for American dance records. An example was *Do You Feel What I'm Feeling?* by Luvspunge (Spiritual Records, 1993), where a funk-based guitar riff was the main syncopation of the track, since at 140 bpm a bass, which needs space and time to develop its relatively large sound wave, cannot do more than enact a simple repetitive pattern. An

270 See Chapter 6.
271 A particular indication of the maturing of the Dutch house scene is that since 1992 several house music orientated zines have been published; see Appendix C. Until 1991 the only publication which catered specifically for the house party scene was the British produced and Amsterdam based *Wild*.
272 White labels are vinyl test pressings which can also be used as promotional material or for a small press run of a track. See Chapter 6.
273 See Chapter 5.

example of Dutch fast but friendly tracks was the 'warm' techno[274] developed by DJ Dimitri and his partner Eric Nouhman [Beesemer, 1991b], such as *Palmyra* (Outland Records, 1993). Incidentally, a local characteristic has been added to the house aesthetic with, for example, the track *Cnossus*, which can be found on the flip side of the latter record, where the groove and sound textures remind me of a Dutch street organ.

Some gabber stylistics of the Rotterdam house productions had an effect on the more sophisticated productions of Erik van Vliet's Rotterdam based Stealth Records, which released a positive and yet unmistakable Dutch techno sound with bass drums and snare in the foreground of the soundscape of the mix. Their compilations *Techno Grooves*, especially Mach 5 (Stealth, 1992) were a good example of their A&R style, which at times allowed for some fast moving vocalised garage tracks as well, such as BP Johnson, *I Believe In The Power* (Stealth, 1992). Music journalist Alfred Bos set up his own label in 1992, to produce tracks which seemed fitting to the cyber age zippy; his product was a mixture of trance, rave and ambient house, such as Cyberia's *Albatross* (Hypercycle, 1992). Friendly techno inspired tracks which showed no trace of a gabberhouse stylistic could be found on Saskia Sledger's Eindhoven-based Djax label, which released a lot of material from Chicago and Detroit and similar sounding tracks by British, Dutch and Belgian artists [Steele, 1994]. A good example was the haunting contemporary acid house trance track *Circus Bells* by Robert Armani (Djax-Up-Beats, 1993). Trance techno house matured in an exciting direction, which had a recognisable North West European texture and structure, like Jark Prango's *Complete Control* (Fresh Fruit, 1993) which built layer after layer of sound to a catargic crescendo or Paragliders's *Paraglide; Blue Sky Mix* (Superstition Records, 1993) which gave the listener a sensation of flying at breakneck speed at more than 140 bpm. Trance is a particular language of electronic dance music making which takes to a logical conclusion the notion of letting 'the self' go and 'dissolve' in a sensory overload of repetitive sounds [DJ White Delight, 1994]. Hereby song structures are determined by its effectiveness to take the dancer 'out of this world'.[275] Since trance is not dependent on words and works purely functional on a physiological level for a dance

---

274 See Chapter 6.
275 See Chapter 7 on the dissolution of the self.

crowd on the road to escape, the electronic dancing 'tribes'[276] will most likely continue to produce music in this direction, in sensual and aggressive variations, both in the USA as well as in Europe.[277]

Conclusion

Although house music was known to Dutch disco DJs during the mid- to late 80s, it did not gain wide popularity until the format of acid house parties together with over-excited British press stories entered the Dutch popular imagination in the autumn of 1988. The first English styled parties were held in Amsterdam and later spread all over the country. The verb 'housen' became a commonplace word to describe the entire experience of going to such an event.

As the house party scene developed, the Dutch started to produce their own house music. Dutch productions gained their own identity in the process. Since 1991 a mixture of African-American acid house and techno, Belgian hard house, German trance, English rave as well as African-American garage and deep house hybridised into several Dutch house music styles. On the 'harder' and faster end of the range of styles there appeared 'death metal[278] house music', gabberhouse, which with a speed of 160 to over 200 bpm stretched the possibilities of electronically produced rhythm tracks to their limits. Trance and ambient productions with a distinctive European 'feel' were produced by self declared 'zippies'. The Dutch also produced happy house, a club music which was a mixture of disco and garage, and which has a pace of around 135 bpm. Like rock music, house music has become a type of international musical language, which nevertheless shows signs of local accents and 'dialects'. In this sense, during the early 90s, the Dutch created their own styles of house music which showed their connections to different 'global villages' but which also demonstrated a recognisable variety of Dutch sensibilities.

---

[276] Tribal life styles have been celebrated amongst the zippies, nomadic 'travellers' and 'crusties' of Britain, as well as amongst the house party people [Wave, 1994].

[277] Check out Goa trance, for example, which has gained popularity in London and elsewhere since 1994.

[278] This is a type of hardpaced trash rock music which uses 'underworld' imagery.

Part III
Jack into electromagic

5 Disco's revenge

One does not proceed by specific differences from a genus to its species, nor by deduction from a stable essence to the properties deriving from it, but from a problem to the accidents that condition and resolve it[279] [Deleuze and Guattari, 1986].

... the past is precisely what we are made of[280] [Eagleton, 1990].

... the breaks of the records from the 70s became the medium for the records in (...) the late 80s[281] [Tong, 1990].

House (...) it's not actually disco's revival, it's disco's revenge[282] [Knuckles, 1990].

Introduction

As the last three chapters have made clear, house music has been a forever growing and changing cultural event; hopefully an attempt to define a static essence of the genus of house music has thereby been prevented. However, in each of the researched localities evidence has been pointing to disco music, specifically New York disco from the 70s, as an important influence on the formation of the production and consumption of house music. Thereby it has become clear that house music is a dance club music which started out as a kind of DIY disco

---

279 {p. 19}
280 {p. 378}
281 {transcript}
282 {transcript}

music which was designed by, and for use by, DJs. It is therefore of importance to briefly address a history of dancing to recorded music, focusing mainly on New York disco music and its specific style of DJing.[283]

Disco music was specifically designed for an escapist 'otherworldly' dance event which relied entirely on recorded music [Joe, 1980]. It enabled the DJ to create a total soundscape which went beyond the use of its separate building components of single recorded songs. In the resulting audio environment people could, in principle, dance without a break. To sustain attention and to move the dancers in an emotional sense, some DJs have developed an amazing skill of building a pace and choosing the 'right' lyrics at the 'right' time, whilst mixing two to three musical pieces at the same time. The DJ is perhaps not only a kind of curator,[284] but at best could fulfil the function of a Shaman.[285] In the latter sense, the DJ is the Master of Ceremonies, the high priest(ess) of physical vibrations, the manipulator of moods. In other words, as a mediator of recorded dance music, the DJ is central to the creation and communication of this type of music. This chapter will discuss the development of disco DJs and their working environment, as well as the format of the 12" dance single (which used to be called a disco single), before moving on to their contemporary mutation, the house DJ. There will also be a very brief comparison with types of cult dance hall entertainment other than house music which use recorded music rather than live musicians, such as the Northern Soul tradition in the North of England and the sound systems which stem from the Caribbean islands.

---

[283] For a brief discussion of 70s disco DJs as heroes, see Appendix D. For a short description of the author's experience as a house DJ, see Appendix E.

[284] See Chapter 6.

[285] This notion has been mentioned frequently in the Dutch press when describing Acid House parties and its DJs. Also in England this idea has been mentioned. For example, in Autumn 1993 a club called Megatripolis was started in London club Heaven, which claims to spread the message of 'Shamanarchy' through the path of 'Techno Tribalism'; this idea falls in place with the hippie ideology of the late 1960s as well as with the philosophy of the British free festival circuit of contemporary nomadic tribes of people who have disaffected from the 'blueprint' way of life and who call themselves 'travellers' [Earle et al., 1994; Lowe and Shaw, 1993].

Discotheque

The word 'discotheque' stems from France, where the club La Discotheque was established before the Second World War, which provided a social drinking environment while one listened to (imported) jazz recordings. During the Second World War dancing to jazz recordings became a form of defiance against the German occupation:

> Although the German forces occupying France had outlawed dancing to America-type music as imperialistic and decadent, they could not kill it. It simply moved underground and survived alongside, and with the help of, the French Resistance. History has it that when the logistics of war made it impractical for fun-loving French nationals to continue dancing to the live sounds of the big bands of the period, inventive diehards rigged up loudspeakers and other paraphernalia of the emerging phonograph industry and played whatever recordings of their favorite bands they could lay their hands on[286] [Joe, 1980].

Not only in France, but also in other occupied territories in Europe, such as the Netherlands, an illicit party network flowered which used recorded American music.[287] This is an interesting point in the context of the sometimes outlawed dance parties in Britain in the late 80s and the 90s.[288] In the first couple of years after the war clubs like Chez Castel, with its mirrored walls and 'charismatic host', and Whiskey au Go-Go officially opened their doors to the public[289] [Joe, 1980].

In the USA, the jukebox gained popularity during the impoverished 1930s [Harker, 1993]. Neighbourhood juke joints were for a mostly African-American audience, whereby the word 'to juke' is of West African origin and has sexual connotations, indicating unruly behaviour and an expressive individualistic type of dancing [Joe, 1980]. During the 50s rock and roll made African-American music, and thereby the jukebox and its related dance style, acceptable to a European-American mass audience. Then the twist craze, an

---

286 {p. 13}
287 My father, who was affiliated to the Dutch resistance during the Second World War, remained loyal to American jazz and swing all his life.
288 See Chapter 4.
289 Whiskey au Go-Go became yet another generic term for a type of discotheque, which was used well into the 60s by many clubs.

uninhibited form of dancing related to juking, was started by Hank Ballard and the Midnighters, followed by Chubby Checker whose recordings made it widely popular. People stopped dancing according to formalised dance steps and instead became creative by moving the body in syncopation to the beat.

In Manhattan's Times Square area, The Peppermint Lounge opened its doors and brought the twist to New York's fun loving elite. The Peppermint Lounge was a live venue. However, it influenced the dancing styles which would become popular at discotheques. One of its more prominent dancers, Terry Noel, became one of the first celebrated DJs at Arthur's Discotheque. Although the concept of employing a DJ was imported from France, Terry's choice of records was inspired by what he liked to dance and twist to, such as soul, rock and ballads [Joe, 1980]. However, in sharp contrast to juke joints, during the 60s most discotheques were places for the upper classes to socialise. At these types of places the music had ultimately a secondary function. In New York the first disco of this kind was probably Le Club which opened in 1960 [Harvey, 1983]. The more dance orientated, but exclusive Arthur's followed in 1965 and in 1977, after a period in which the dance club had not been fashionable, the indoor dream world for the rich, famous and bored New York social elite, Studio 54 opened its doors, which to the mainstream disco fan:

> ... commands as much international reverence as that of the Vatican. It is the headquarters of the World Discotheque Movement[290] [Blackford, 1979].

When one hears and reads about places like these [Blackford, 1979; Joe, 1980], one may be forgiven for thinking that engaging oneself with disco music was an activity which only involved a social group with a particular conservative sensibility. The music that was played in the discotheques of the late 70s was a sanitised form of what during the 70s had become a sound track for and by young homosexual men as well as for African-American and Latin youth.

The mainstream disco consumer indulged in a Disneyland version of a psychedelic experience. The roots of the creation of a dream space through the use of lights and props most likely stemmed back to events which took place in the 60s in California, in the counter-cultural world of hippies. For example, San Francisco's rock dance

---

[290] {p. 10}

hall Avalon Ballroom experimented with the particular psychedelic lighting rigs which some rock groups had started to use:

> The incredibly sensual combination of earthy, pulsating rock music and ever-changing patterns of surrealistic lights freaked the minds of the already freaked-out hep cats of Haight-Ashbury — birthplace of this country's (the USA — sic) subculture of music, drugs and sex/love[291] [Joe, 1980].

Ken Kesey's mobile *Electric Kool-Aid Acid Tests* were also part of the Haight-Ashbury hippie scene, whereby LSD and MDMA[292] induced events included slide projections, smoke effects and strobe lights as visual companions to rock jams [Wolfe, 1989]. Strobe lights, the main popular light source for English acid house parties in 1988, have a particular disorientating and fragmenting effect:

> Stroboscopes are used sparingly in most discos. Partly because they send people potty in no time at all, and partly because they turn rhythmical dancing into a nightmare. Your ears try to persuade you of one tempo while your eyes are picking up an entirely different beat. Your feet get caught in the crossfire and you wind up like a victim of cerebral palsy, jack-knifing maniacally across the floor in an uncontrollable mazurka[293] [Blackford, 1979].

This is exactly what the dancers at late 80s acid house parties were doing, as well as playing with their hands and fingers in order to create light patterns for their own eyes. However, in mainstream English discos of the 70s, which Blackford describes, this possibility of intense experience with a chance to discover that one may be prone to epileptic fits was not favoured. Therefore, the glamorous mirror ball was the ultimate symbol of 70s disco. This was a ball covered with little fragments of a reflecting material suspended in the middle of a dance space. Any light focused on this implement is fragmented into many directions; as it slowly rotates, it seems as though the entire dance space floats around the dancers in a gentle dream-like manner. In the 90s this is still a favourite tool in most dance clubs.

---

291 {p. 19}
292 LSD and MDMA are both psycho active drugs which are discussed in Chapter 7.
293 {p. 44}

In 1970 the dance club Sanctuary opened in New York City, which in retrospect almost seems like a blueprint for any of the underground house parties held 14 to 24 years later, even though its main sound track was based on rock recordings. The use of the space was seminal, as well as the DJ technique of Grosso, who originally had started out as a substitute for Terry Noel at Arthur's:

> ... Sanctuary was located in a former church in Manhattan's Hell's Kitchen neighbourhood, evolving into a wild scene of druggy abandon. The DJ, Francis Grosso, was the first DJ-as-auteur/artist/idol. To quote Albert Goldman in his 1978 book *Disco*: 'He invented the technique of 'slip-cueing': holding the disc with his thumb whilst the turntable whirled beneath, insulated by a felt pad. He'd locate with an earphone the best spot to make the splice then release the next side precisely on the beat (...) His *tour de force* was playing two records simultaneously at a stretch. He would super the drum break of *I'm a man* over the orgasmic moans of Led Zeplin's *Whole Lotta Love* to make a powerfully erotic mix (...) that anticipated the formula of bass drum beats and love cries (...) now one of the clichés of the disco mix'[294] [Harvey, 1983].

Although the sound textures have changed and the speed of the music has increased considerably, in house music the clichés of 'bass drum beats and love cries' can still be found ad infinitum.

Even though in the late 70s, at the height of its 'mainstream' popularity, disco seemed like a 'bland' pop event, in its role of being seminal to house music and its related forms, it has never been that far removed from the way it is currently thought of; a hedonistic, drug induced, libidinally charged soundtrack for a purely escapist event, which has taken on board elements from African-American dance culture as well as from European surrealist and psychedelic notions of resistance and community. Add to this a 'gay' hedonistic attitude which emerged when the first mainstream disco scene decayed in the early 70s. Although 'the beautiful people', the rich socialite elite, had temporarily grown bored with the concept, the need for escapism from social conditions was strong with 'gay' people as well as with African-American and Latino social and

---

[294] (pp.26-27)

cultural groups[295] '... the same cross-section of tenacious minorities that had aided the concept's birth in the late 1950s and early 1960s'[296] [Joe, 1980].

It was in 'the underground clubs which catered to blacks, latins and gays',[297] like Salvation in 1969, that a breeding ground was provided for the new dance music which was later to be called disco [Harvey, 1983]. The resulting (weekend) escapist cult which danced to recorded music with pulsating rhythms and a soul sensibility in an environment engulfed in psychedelic lighting was what later still resulted in certain forms of house music.

Disco music

In the early days of underground African-American disco, the records which were used would be less 'DJ friendly'. The rhythms and speed varied per record, which meant that it was an effort to blend one record into the next. At first the soulful songs from Motown records were used as well as soul music obscurities and later on the contoured Gospel vocalised Philly sound became popular. By playing the songs in a certain order, a method of story telling was developed by the New York club DJ. For instance, Larry Levan, DJ at the legendary and seminal club Paradise Garage[298] would create sets of five or six records, then leave a gap and start as he put it, 'a new paragraph'[299] with a fresh introduction, such as an acapella or a special sound effect [Harvey, 1983]. To overcome the problem of variety in speed between tracks, special effects such as an echo unit could be utilised to make the change from one record to another easier. Some DJs added a third turntable to their equipment so that quick switches could be made between records, especially if small sound bites[300] were being used, or in case two records were being played simultaneously while the next song needed to be cued.[301] With the advent of first the disco single and later the drum box, it became increasingly easier to make

---

295 These categories are (of course) not mutually exclusive.
296 {p. 21}
297 {p. 26}
298 See Chapter 2.
299 {p. 28}
300 Parts of a track or of a song such as a sax riff or a vocal chorus, or perhaps just an orchestra stab.
301 Put a record ready for action at exactly the right speed, on the beat at the right place.

one record flow into the next in a near seamless fashion.

The first commercially available disco 12" single was *10 Percent* by Double Exposure (Salsoul, 1976). The original album track had been three minutes long and was changed by DJ and remixer Walter Gibbons into a 'musical landscape in excess of nine minutes' which 'defined the possibilities for a DJ/club influenced and oriented music'[302] [Harvey, 1983]. The 12" format for one track allowed the grooves to be wider apart than on a 7" or on an album where it would have to share space with other tracks. This meant that there was more space for the dynamics of the sound, especially the bass, which needs a wide groove in vinyl when it is 'high up'[303] in the mix. Gibbons repeated the orchestrated introduction of *10 Percent* twice and followed this up by the insertion of a break which strips the track to its drums with an added electronic keyboard riff.[304] The vocals do not appear until well over one minute into the track. Also later in the track the 'intro' is repeated several times, while the song finishes with a rhythm track, which would make it easier to mix the record with the next one without a break for club and party dancers. In this type of structure, rather than being placed at the centre of attention, the vocal part gets an equal status to the groove and to the overall sound textures. Over the next eight to twelve years the trend of stretching songs with added groove tracks would slowly mutate into the first instrumental DJ tracks.[305] The most reputable labels[306] in the field of disco music production were Salsoul,[307] as well as West End, who had dance hits like Taana Gardner's *Heartbeat* (West End, 1980) and Loose Jointz *All Over My Face* (West End, 1980);[308] and Prelude, who released dancefloor classics like D Train's *Keep On* (Prelude, around 1981) and Sharon Red's *Beat The Street* (Prelude, 1982).[309] In addition, labels like Casablanca, who released Giorgio Moroder and Donna Summer's tracks such as *Love To Love You Baby*

---

302 {p. 28}
303 Meaning: of a high volume in relation to the other instruments a track comprises.
304 Incidentally, this sparse break is still to be found, as a sample, on numerous contemporary house and garage tracks, although perhaps surprisingly this break does not appear on the 1992 remix by house reconstruction and remix giants Masters At Work (Double J Records, 1992).
305 See Chapter 2.
306 See also the supplement to the magazine *DJ* on disco music [Lee, 1993].
307 See the compilation pack *Salsoul Classics* (Indigo Musik, 1988).
308 See compilation series *The West End Story* (West End, 1994).
309 Prelude has released its own compilations as well.

(Casablanca, 1975),[310] put out a considerable amount of quality dance products. As has been mentioned in Chapter 2, during the 1980s in the dance scenes of the USA, the remakes of disco classics became a common practice and, in the late 1980s, samples from existing disco records[311] were placed on sparse rhythm and bass tracks. Any of Todd Terry's DJ tracks, which are built mostly from samples, are excellent examples of the latter, such as his remix of Shawn Christopher's *Don't Lose the Magic* (Arista, 1992), his production of *Somba*, House of Gypsies (Freeze Records, 1992) and his prolific compilations, such as *Sound Design* (TNT, 1992). An example of a recent reconstruction of an old disco classic is the Masters At Work remix of *Ten Percent* (Double J Records, 1992).

Even though the disco single became quickly popular with a wider audience, during the 1970s it was designed specifically for use by DJs. As independent elements of DJ craft, the disco and especially the instrumental or dub house[312] single, may sound odd, repetitive and even boring when listened to out of its dancefloor context; it is only when played to and interacted with a dancing crowd, that house music, as a medium, is complete.[313] In addition, a dance record is also pretty meaningless when it is separated from other dance records. One should look at dance singles as words which are looking for a sentence; they need to be combined to create a soundscape. As disco singles became available, the technique of the disco DJ could be developed into a sophisticated form of 'sonic overlaying of elements' [Harvey, 1983]. The result on the turntables was a complex simultaneous montage or collage of found materials (to put it in European art historian terms) or a creative and impulsive re-use of the cultural output of one's 'ancestors' like one does in jazz (to put it in the terms of African-American cultural studies)[Harvey, 1983; Toop, 1984; Berry, 1992].

For a comparison with the above description of the first DJ techniques, here is a version of the working method of a Dutch house DJ, Eddy de Clercq of the Amsterdam Roxy club, who in his case tried to create a dreamy trance atmosphere rather than an erotic one:

---

310 On request of Casablanca boss Bogart, the extended mix lasted seventeen minutes [Dannen, 1990].

311 Either 'classics' such as those from labels like Salsoul and Prelude, or from contemporary dance hits.

312 See Chapter 6 for the concept of dub and the instrumental.

313 See Chapters 6 and 7.

Af en toe werk ik ook wel met drie pick-ups. Twee om de ritmes te mixen en een derde om daar weer melodie en geluiden overheen te zetten. Vaak mix ik er dan sitarmuziek doorheen. Als je dat doet bij nummers van Fingers Inc., dan lijkt het bij wijze van spreken een plaat. Of soms laat ik Indiase ragas een half uur meelopen, dat geeft een heel aparte sfeer. (...) Dat vindt ik zo mooi aan acid: alles is mogenlijk. Het hangt helemaal af van je eigen stemming en van de reactie van het publiek. (...) De mooiste mixen gebeuren altijd spontaan[314] [van Veen, 1988].

(Eng. trans.) So now and then I actually work with three record decks. Two for mixing the rhythms and a third to layer melody and noises. Often I mix in sitar music. If you do that with a tune by for instance Fingers Inc., so that in a way it seems as though it is a record in itself. Or sometimes I play Indian ragas for like half an hour along with something else because that gives such a special atmosphere. (...) That is what I like about acid (house): everything is possible. It all depends on your own mood and on the reaction of the audience. (...) The most beautiful things always happen spontaneously.

This flowing kind of mixing was also specific for disco and later for house; the pace would increase almost unnoticed until the audience would be in an elated state of frenzy. However, there are other kinds of DJ styles. For example at sound systems of African-Caribbean origin,[315] which in the late 1960s may have had one turntable (rather than two), a singer or a speaker[316] will perform over a dance record which is often left sparse in its vocals for that purpose [Back, 1988]. If the record is especially liked, the DJ can, for instance, play the introduction twice by manually reversing it at a fast pace and then releasing it again. At other times the needle can be taken up while the MC entertains the crowd with a rousing talk, after which a favourite bit is played again. This technique, which can send the crowd wild

---

314 {newspaper}
315 Historically, these sound systems started out playing calypso. In Jamaica this was replaced by reggae and in the 80s by ragga.
316 The speaker used to be called a 'toaster', but since the 80s MC is more common. Although one may presume that like a 'toaster' giving a toast, the MC is a Master of Ceremonies. In London 1988, however, for some people it was an abbreviation of 'Mic Chanter' [Back, 1988]. The use of the term depends on the style of music being played and on the historical moment and geographical space where the sound system performs. The use of the word 'toaster' is more often heard in the context of 70s reggae and especially a dub reggae.

with desire for that particular tune, can be found in various versions at current soul, ragga, hip hop and dance hall sound systems. The New York hip hop DJ style with its rapper MCs,[317] who often make (critical) comment on their social environment, has been partly based on that kind of sound system style which was imported during the 70s to neighbourhoods like Brooklyn, Queens and the Bronx in New York, adding to it a specific African-American jazz sensibility [Toop, 1984]. There, the DJ would cut fast between different often rare records, displaying agility and an improvised playfulness in combining elements from the past with radically new music, such as in the early 80s with electro, in an almost bebop kind of way. This method was, and still is, quite different from the practice of the British and Dutch mobile disco DJ[318] who plays a variety of songs and dancetracks in the style of a radio DJ. In contrast to the latter the spoken part in between records is more cabaret style, perhaps addressing individual persons in the crowd or making the occasional joke. The (American) disco DJ, in contrast, became the subtle mood manipulator, the specialist of the 'slow mix'. According to British writer Andy Blackford, in the 70s this smooth DJ style was called 'to segue (pronounced segway)'[319] [Blackford, 1979].

Away from the early influence of hip hop, the style of smooth slow mixing could develop especially well in Chicago, resulting in a plethora of DJ orientated jacking house music tracks [Berry, 1992]. However, although the disco element is like a root grammar for the structure of house music and its related styles, elements of hip hop and rap can be found in contemporary house tracks. In Chicago, Fast Eddie and Tyree added a rap style to house, calling it hip house. A lot of American garage tracks such as Degrees Of Motion's *Shine On* (Esquire Records, 1992) insert a male rap part into what is otherwise a melodic (female) vocal track; this type of structure can also be found in pop versions of dance tracks. In England both elements of hip hop and disco DJ styles can be found in its dance tracks. Although the DJ often mixes the separate tracks into one soundscape, there is often an MC who whips up the crowd. Both rave and jungle tracks have a

---

317 Or fast, rhythmical and often poetic speakers.
318 Since the 60s the mobile disco DJ has travelled with a small sound system and lighting rig to play at club venues, pubs, parties and weddings. Since the late 70s clubs have acquired their own custom built sound systems and therefore do not need to rely on the mobile anymore. In the 90s this type of DJ is a versatile cheap form of entertainment who will play whatever pleases the crowd, which is usually a mixture of current chart pop and 'golden oldies'.
319 {p. 36}

rhythm track based on speeded up versions of hip hop drum tracks (breakbeats) and have instrumental parts which chop and change between what seem to be traces from several tracks.[320] Thereby hip hop has become like a type of accent or inflection which has been added to house music.[321] Other influences, such as European trance, which is related to a European form of disco music, will be discussed in the next chapter with a focus on the development of production technologies.

Disco and house DJs

In order to carve out a place in a rather overcrowded market, particular records need to be found which other DJs have yet to acquire, such as rare older records which are either re-appreciated or nostalgically remembered as well as new records which are to be 'broken'.[322] For the latter category of records, DJs in the USA can become members of a record pool, where for a fee, all the new important dance records and 'not for sale' DJ-mixes are sent by mail. In 1975, Steve D'Aquisto, Vince Aletti and David Marcuso set up the first record pool; now there are several to choose from. In Britain one joins the mailing lists of promotional agencies, who want to see their records in chart returns for dance hit lists, as well as a report on how well the record does on the dance floor. If the audience likes a record but does not go out to buy it, then at least people will come back to the DJ who plays it. Some DJs obscure the labels of their records to prevent people from buying 'their' records, which are after all the tools of their craft.[323] As Dutch DJ Marcel Bakker puts it, he hates to see people 'picking the currants' he has 'found in the porridge'. He especially enjoys it if he can make a record a hit which has only a low press run, for instance an import from a small label of which only a few copies are available in the import shop. For him, as it is for other

---

[320] At the time of re-editing this text in October 1995, several styles within the genre of Jungle have moved away from the chop and change rave style towards a more sophisticated musical style in terms of sound textures and a complex use of syncopation; see for example Goldie's album *Timeless* (FFRR, 1995).

[321] This is a viewpoint affected by the fact that this thesis focuses on house music, whereby related musical forms are almost inevitably positioned as its derivatives. If seen from, for instance, the point of view of a British teenage raver in 1994, both hip hop and ragga as well as house and techno would rate as main sources of inspiration.

[322] To break into the market; a new record has to be 'sold' to the crowd.

[323] See Chapter 6.

110

professional DJs, being a DJ involves more than spending one hour a week in the local hip record shop and then playing the newly recommended records on just one night a week [Bakker, 1992].

Although some DJs 'with a national reputation'[324] can earn between £2000 and £10,000 a night [Greenhalgh, 1994], most DJs are not paid in relation to the time and money they spend on the research for and the construction of their sets. Ideally £500 a week is needed to cover costs[325] and to make an average living of around £1000 a month net, instead of the £25 to £75 a night which most received (research data 1992-95). Rather than a focus on money, it is their enthusiasm and love for music which DJs like to share that motivates them in the first instance. To be a good DJ is not so much a job, but more an 'addiction' which occupies most if not all of his or her waking time.[326] DJ Norman Jay confirms this by saying that it needs hundred percent commitment which takes over your life; he adds that 'the only good DJs are the ones for whom it is their lives'.[327] [van Veen, 1992]. Sometimes just to look at a DJ one may be forgiven to think one sees an 'addict'. 'Pale' and red eyed from working late nights, sometimes having to play at more than one club on a night, carrying heavy boxes of vinyl from squat to castle and whatever club in between, DJs are vulnerable to exhaustion and the chemical 'remedies' which pull them through on a short term basis.[328] To return to the old examples, Larry Levan stopped being a DJ for five years due to the stress that went with being a successful DJ [Bakker, 1992]. On the other hand, Frankie Knuckles, who had started out with Larry Levan at New York's health and entertainment club for male homosexuals The

---

[324] {p. 15} This does not mean they are good DJs, but rather that their name has appeared often on flyers, in club/party night adverts and in magazine articles.
[325] In 1994 imports are between £6.99 and £7.99 per copy, whilst British releases are £3.99 per copy. To be innovative and ahead of the competition, a certain amount of imports are needed, even though the audience does enjoy an old tune or two (the so called 'classics'). To be an able professional, at least £70 is spent on vinyl each week. Added to this is the cost of transport; not all venues are within easy reach of public transport and boxes of records are very heavy to lug around, therefore a car or taxi is needed. Some DJs employ a driver, since they themselves are often too exhausted to be able to drive safely.
[326] Although specialist press for DJs used to be exclusively addressed to males (for instance with 'send in a picture of your sexy girl friend' for girlfriend-of-the-month competition in *Mixmag* 1983), since the late 80s there has been an increase in female DJs, first in the 'gay' scene, but also in other dance scenes. In the early 90s it has become fashionable in the dance club scene to employ a female DJ. Hopefully, soon female DJs will be a normal, rather than a fetishised, trend.
[327] {newspaper}
[328] The favourite stereotype is that of the 'moody DJ', who is always in a grumpy, arrogant mood, of which a comic story can be found in club fanzine *The Illustrated Chortler's Companion*.

Continental Baths in the early 70s [Smith, 1992], is still going strong in 1994 since he takes care of his health [Martin, 1992].

One may claim that at its best (and there are not many of those around) the DJ is not only a researcher and a curator, as well as a technician, but also an author/artist.[329] Certainly a DJ can become as much a pop star as any other musical entertainer. There is a difference between the enthusiast who plays records and the professional DJ. Although a DJ is a mediator between the recording artist and audience, the DJ is also a communicator by means of using records in a particular manner. By feeling their mood, finding out what makes them tick and by combining this information with the choice of records available that night, a relationship is set up. If the DJ is successful in catching the feel of the night and by knowing how to manipulate this to the advantage of the available material, it may well be that a following is created. The more the audience is taken away from its daily realities and sense of rationality, the more susceptible it becomes to the influence of the DJ. In anthropological terms, the professional house DJ can be seen as a kind of Shaman, who helps people to bring them out of themselves.[330] By letting the crowd dance non-stop and whipping them up with an incessant beat, it can get into a state of mind which is comparable to a kind of communal trance. As one African-American Chicago house music dancer said, 'I dance until the walls around me fall away'[331] [Elliott, 1992].

In creating a dream world of emotions through the use of stories, keywords and sounds, the sharing of that dream 'glues' a community together. Many house records beckon to 'release yourself' or to 'let yourself go' and in doing so the daily world with its problems seems to disappear. The crowd allows itself to be emotionally manipulated by the DJ, and if perhaps all the circumstances are right, after about six or seven hours s/he can make the crowd hold hands and jump for joy or weep and sit down on the floor, as has been witnessed for instance at the *Sound Factory* in New York where Junior Vasquez

---

329 See Chapter 6.
330 See Chapter 7.
331 {interview}

presided during the early 90s.[332] This does not mean that the lyrics will be of a totally escapist nature. Assertions against bad boyfriends are made, as for instance in *Trouble* by Kim Beacham (East 111, 1992) or *Shoulda Known Better* by Candy J (Vinyl Solution, 1993). Race relationships are mentioned for example in *Follow Me* by Aly-us (Strictly Rhythm, 1992) or in a more allusive manner in Joe Smooth's *Promised Land* (DJ International, 1988). So long as the sensibilities are shared by the crowd, it will make them melt into a single unit. Both disco and house usually use lyrics with ambivalent meanings or otherwise just a couple of repeated words or grunts which are not specific, but which carry perennial emotions such as hope, love, sex, anger and community in a rather generalised manner; this music is therefore able to hail a huge, otherwise culturally differentiated, audience. Perhaps this could be part of the explanation of its waves of huge popularity as well as the ability to draw and completely engage crowds which may have a frenzied core of up to two thousand people, as was witnessed at a Sunrise event in 1989 [McLarnan, 1990].[333] In this way the DJ, by playing the mood of the crowd in the right manner, can to some people approach the meaning of a demi god, or of a secular type of priest at least.

This feeling will be enhanced by the use of drugs by the crowd, which makes the crowd more open minded, susceptible or vulnerable (depending on which angle one takes) to the emotional manipulations of the DJ.[334] In Britain, where in 1994 most nightclubs open their doors between 9 pm and 10 pm and still close at 2 am, there are in effect only three to five hours for the crowd to work itself into a moment of loss and abandon; in this context drugs are helpful to reach a state of mind which would otherwise take nearly twice as

---

[332] The frenzy with which the audience gives itself up can be witnessed at many good raves and clubs. In the English clubs the audience manages to 'get wild' within an hour or two. Memorable nights I have witnessed are Nude Night in the Haçienda, 88-89; Flesh at the Haçienda, 92-93; Trade at Paradise Factory, 93, all in Manchester; the Funhouse, the Roxy, the Loft and Paradise Garage, 83 in New York; a very special club in its Shamanic function was Delight with DJ Sasha at Shelley's Lazerdome, 90-91 in Stoke-on-Trent as well as the Whirley Gig in London, 93. Megatripolis in Heaven, London, 93 tries ever so hard with its policy of shamanarchy, but I have not seen its audience carried away just yet, probably due to the intellectual aspects of the club, which don't quite allow for a complete rejection of rational behaviour.

[333] As has been explained in Chapters 2, 3 and 4, other factors which are social rather than structural (such as a British public moral panic) can also be attributed to the ability of house music to draw huge crowds.

[334] See Chapter 7.

113

long.[335] Manchester club conceptualist Paul Cons has described in a rather cynical manner the effect of drugs in the context of the status of the DJ since the rave days of 1988 in England:

> Ecstasy warms people to whoever is DJing, it could be a white rabbit. People stomping their feet, clapping their hands and cheering at the end of a night is far more related to the drugs they're on rather than (to) the DJ[336] [Greenhalgh, 1994].

A receptive crowd, either because of recreational dance drugs or because of the reputation of the club night and of the advertised DJ, is much easier for the DJ to work with. Yet, blunders can be made when the DJ does not know a crowd, or when a crowd is not receptive to a particular set. Therefore, some resident DJs, who are very successful in a particular club, such as Junior Vasquez, often refuse to do guest spots elsewhere, especially when they also rely on the sound and mixing equipment of their regular club. Even so, a professional house DJ should be able to take on this challenge and eventually carry the dancers to where s/he wants them to be, without having to rely on a drugged crowd or a fashionable reputation, or without having to resort to a kind of populism for which some mobile DJs are renowned.[337] At such occasions the art of mood manipulation is put to the test. Some DJs play a prepared set regardless of what the previous DJ has been playing; it may not link up at all, but simply announces that a different person is now in charge. This may work when a reputation has been built in advance. Yet, a more careful approach wins more fans in the end. For instance, one could start with a popular track which crosses over between the last record of the resident DJ and the direction the guest DJ wants to take. This could then be followed by a similar production of a more obscure track in order to find out how far the crowd can be taken on that path. This way the DJ can zigzag through a variety of styles and moods until a compromise is reached with the crowd. The most frustrating thing that can happen to the guest DJ is if the organiser

---

[335] The fact that the entactogenic MDMA, or E, lasts for around four hours makes it ideal within the context of current British club licensing laws; in contrast, cheaper and more traditional party drugs such as the hallucinogenic LSD or the stimulant amphetamine, or speed, take at least eight hours to wear down.

[336] {p. 16}

[337] Here I take a risk at being more subjective than an ethnographic account would justify; however, my opinion is based on both experience and observation and is meant as a recommendation on the basis of this.

panics prematurely while the guest DJ is analysing the situation and brings back the resident before the point of compromise has been reached. However, once this moment of balance occurs, the DJ can then lead the crowd to new and different highs, which, in my opinion, is a skilful art within the field of communication that deserves to be applauded.

After disco in the USA

The peak of disco came in 1977 with the film and record *Saturday Night Fever* (Sony and RSO Records resp., 1977). Every group and artist, even classical orchestras put a bit of the four quarter beat (bass drum-hand clap) disco flavour to their music in order to secure a hit. African-American artists were forced by their record companies to produce disco music, rather than funk or rhythm 'n' blues [Joe, 1980]. The market was flooded with 'second rate'[338] dance music by artists and producers whose heart was not in it. In addition, disco in the influential style of the club Studio 54 was more about trash than substance. By the end of the 70s mainstream disco had attracted a lot of ridicule, not least from the corner of raw rock 'revivalism' called punk rock.[339] The slogan 'Disco Sucks', found on T-shirts and bumper stickers showed a general backlash [Hughes, 1994]. In the early 80s the death of disco was declared by a group of middle-of-the-road rock radio stations. Frankie Knuckles remembers:

Well see in 19 er, was it 1981? (...) there were a couple of radio disc jockeys in Chicago, Steve Doe who was on one of the major radio stations in Chicago who proclaimed that disco was dead and what they did was in Kominsky Park which is a White Sox ball park they took like every disco record they could find in Chicago and they blew them up in the middle of the stadium and from that, from that day on disco was dead all over the country you know and, it's like the whole dance music scene as far as any type of

---

[338] With 'second rate' I mean that the music was not made with the same sensibilities and without a finer understanding of the aesthetic forms from which disco had developed, such as funk, soul and gospel.
[339] Even though the history of punk is related, in a rather complex manner, to disco and dance culture, not least through its connections with gay and lesbian culture [Savage, 1991], one could, in analogy to presenting house music as disco's revenge, suggest with Joe that punk was rock's revenge [Joe, 1980].

music that related to disco or sounded like it, you know, went completely underground, (...) came completely from underground and most of the major companies wouldn't go anywhere near it at that particular time, you know, so it forced it underground[340] [Knuckles, 1990].

In New York, as in Chicago, dance music remained an intensely engaging activity for the groups of people who had danced to disco music before it gained its popularity in the late 70s. These were mainly African-American and Latino homosexual men as well as a more general crowd of Latino[341] and African-American youngsters. 'Gay' clubs Paradise Garage and the Warehouse have been discussed earlier.[342] The Roxy and the Funhouse are examples of the latter from around 1983, when dance music started its third wave of popularity. Instead of the old-styled disco it was mostly electro that was being played at these clubs, such as Whodini's *Magic Wand*, *Hip Hop, Be Bop (Don't Stop)* by Man Parrish and *The Smurf* by Tyrone Brunson (MC, 1994).[343] Electro was the first purely electronically produced dance music, which incorporated certain hip hop influences. In 1983 I witnessed the Roxy on a Saturday night. A temporary floor had been laid over what was otherwise a skating ring. The DJ was in the middle on a platform at that time, using a Roland TB303 Bass Line and drum machine to enhance his set. The crowd created a visual display with break dancing or by creating acrobatic human pyramids. There, John 'Jellybean' Benitez played:

... records every Saturday from around midnight till 8 am — for an audience of between 1000 and 3000 kids —, making it 'the seedbed for electro-bob'. (...) On my visit it reminded me of a meeting between hardcore punk and disco[344] [Harvey, 1983].

The club with its incredible sound system was a testing ground for

---

340 {transcript}
341 This includes female Latin-American (Latina) youth. I have chosen the term Latino, since that is the name which Americans of Latin-American descent such as Puerto Ricans have chosen for themselves.
342 See Chapter 2.
343 As witnessed in the Funhouse and on New York's dance orientated radio stations Kiss FM and WBLS in New York, June-October 1983.
344 {p. 31}

producers such as Arthur Baker,[345] who would go down there with an acetate[346] of a new mix; if a tune worked there, it would work anywhere [Garfield, 1983/84]. In 1983 I observed Jellybean's DJ work in the Funhouse. It had a boxing ring in the middle of its space which served as a platform for dancers, who often brought in a change of clothes in order to keep the perspiration at bay. The energy of the dancers was as frantic as one would have seen in England in 1988 during the acid house craze. This was not only inspired by the music, but also by a combination of the crowd, the club, the drugs (such as amphetamines and ecstasy)[347] and the skill of the DJ. Translated to, for example, an English or Dutch context, electro did not invite the same frenzy, even though break-dancing became a very popular pastime for many young people in the 80s and, for example, some enthusiastic formation dances to its derivatives were witnessed in Manchester's Haçienda club in the mid-80s.

Before house in England

At the time when the Funhouse was at the peak of its popularity, DJ Mike Pickering observed that the atmosphere of this club was actually very similar to the Northern Soul weekend events which took place in Northern England during the 70s [Pickering, 1983]. At Northern Soul events Tamla-Motown and other (rare) soul records as well as Philly records were being played [Pickering, 1983], which was the same music that inspired the early disco styles. Like underground disco, the Northern Soul events involved late long hours of dancing [Rushton, 1982] which required several changes of clothes [Blackford, 1979]. Since the dancers were devoted to dancing at an unstoppable pace, some even brought talcum powder with them to avoid the floor getting slippery from the condensed sweat which started to drip from the ceiling. Northern Soul dancers were fuelled by the use of amphetamines, such as Dexedrine tablets called 'Dexies'. In the 70s its crowd was young and mostly Northern working class and as such they could perhaps empathise with the sentiments of escape from a sense of oppression and the need for an

---

[345] Arthur Baker, who was central to the development of electro, had been the keyboard player for the classic disco orchestra Vince Montana's Salsoul Orchestra in the late 70s [Jules, 1989].

[346] A vinyl cut made by engraving the groove with a needle at the cutting room. It is a rather expensive one-off; records are otherwise pressed at a pressing plant.

[347] Dance drugs are discussed in Chapter 7.

117

exclusive community which was also of importance to the African-American, Latino and dominantly 'gay' dancing crowds in the USA. The difference was, that in New York and Chicago the music was tailor made for its crowd, whilst in the Northern Soul scene people were dancing to records made by strangers from a different scene on the other side of the Atlantic. The Northern Soul scene may have generated boundless energy to dance, but it did not produce its own records.[348] Rather than developing and changing the sound to its own needs and embracing the soul of the process of music making which keeps dance music alive, it formalised soul and still to this day often celebrates the old soul 'classics' and rare grooves in a static traditionalist 'trainspotting' manner. In their own slogan, they 'keep the faith'[349] to 'true' soul [Garratt, 1989]. As Andy Blackford puts it:

> The rules were few when it came to Northern Soul music. The artist had to be American and black. And he had to have the authentic, easy on-beat rhythm with just a hint of syncopation which was the good old Tamla hallmark[350] [Blackford, 1979].

Several of the original Northern Soul DJs did get into dance music production work during the 70s and the 80s. One of them was Ian Levine, who became the originator of HiNRG productions while he was a DJ at London 'gay' club Heaven. Examples of his production work are the classics *So Many Men So Little Time* with Miquel Brown (Record Shack, 1983) and *High Energy* with Evelyn Thomas (Nightmare Records, 1984), which tied in with the 'gay' disco scene of Heaven as well as with the European-American New York 'gay' clubs [Levine, 1990]. Another Northern Soul veteran is Pete Waterman of production team Stock, Aiken and Waterman[351] which has been responsible for the production of dance-pop acts like Bananarama with *Love In The First Degree* (London Records, 1987) and Kylie Minogue who had hits like *I Should Be So Lucky* (PWL, 1988). As described in Chapters 2 and 3, as early as 1985 he imported house tracks, rhythm sections of which inspired the backing of his pop dance

---

[348] Yet, without the kind of mysticism which goes together with the notion of 'rare grooves' there would not have been an underground dance scene in Britain which existed independent of the fashion of Disco or of other trends.
[349] {slogan heard often in the context of Northern Soul}
[350] {p. 65}
[351] See Chapter 3.

hits [Waterman, 1992]. At the same time he has been responsible for importing and giving a British release to several European dance acts. Some Northern Soul fans applied the love they had acquired for dance music to contemporary dance forms and became successful house DJs, such as Mike Pickering, who in the 90s titled the album by his pop dance group M-People *Northern Soul* (DeConstruction, 1992). In the 80s other acts had already appeared which were inspired by the Northern Soul scene, such as Dexy's Midnight Runners' first album *Search For The Young Soul Rebels* (EMI, 1980). The influence of the scene could also be traced to many British pop groups who used female 'black' singers with American accents to recreate a kind of 'authentic' soul sensibility. However, this new music would not be played at Northern Soul events.

Conclusion

The focus of this chapter has been on the role of the DJ in house music, which has been placed within a historical context. A house (music) DJ has a specific manner of linking records together, called 'the slow mix', which follows a method developed by New York disco DJs. As records are sequenced in various combinations, individual tracks will take on a slightly different meaning each time they are played, due to a change in intertextuality, which also incorporates a variety of social and cultural contexts. DJs who travel around can find that what works with one crowd does not work at all with another. The DJ has to work at making people like a new sound. The crowd needs to be warmed to a particular choice of records, which is often easier if the DJ has a good reputation. This is not only built on the hard work a professional DJ undoubtedly puts into his or her act; it also depends on the quality of equipment, the use of space a dance club provides and, arguably, the type of dance drugs, if any, the majority of the crowd is 'on'. A discussion of DJs has not been possible without mentioning crowds or clubs. Dance spaces, dance drugs and the relationship between the crowd and the DJ will be discussed in the chapter on consumption of house.

First, however, will follow a chapter which describes the production technologies which are involved in the creation of those records which are the DJ's tool kit. Hereby some of the particular political, legal and economic frameworks in which these technologies and their products have acquired their meaning will be addressed. Also the cultural position of the DJ as well as of the audience as producers of a house music event will be clarified. As has been shown in the previous three chapters, in contrast to, for example, the puritanical attitude of English Northern Soul fans, when house music was imported to Europe, house fans contributed their own localised versions. Perhaps this was due to the DIY aspects of house music productions, which did not necessarily require expensive lush orchestrations or skilled gospel trained groups of African-American singers. The next chapter will show that house music can be produced on relatively cheap and consumer friendly electronic equipment which is sometimes second-hand. Like disco, house music has been produced by and for both an American and European home market, which may be due to the fact that house music is part of a dialogue between African-American soul and disco on the one hand and North European electronic body music and its variants on the other, with a generous helping of Italian disco thrown in along the way. Since creative DJs like to give their crowd something a bit special, exports and imports cross the Atlantic in both directions, cross-fertilising dance music and inspiring endless mutations. Finally, it seems to me that house music is made for the dance floor by DJs who know their own crowd best, or otherwise by producers who are in touch with their market(s).

6 Digital desire

The rock star, up on stage, bathed in light, inaccessible, is an outdated image from a defunct society. In a world where information plus technology equals power, those who control the editing rooms run the show. DJs are editors of the street[352] [Gallagher, 1994].

The signature is superseded by the trademark[353] [Reynolds, 1990b].

... computer writing institutes a factory of postmodern subjectivity, a machine for constituting non-identical subjects, an inscription of another of Western culture into its most cherished manifested. One may call it a monstrosity[354] [Poster, 1990].

Introduction

Although the practice of the club DJ has shaped the style of house music, this has occurred within the limitations and new possibilities which electronic recording studio technologies can offer. In this chapter there will be a description of some of the developments in music technologies with relevance to house music. A discussion will then follow on the identities and discourses which surround the use of these kind of technologies. Of importance is the notion of authorship, which ties in with concepts such as origin and creation of the text and

---

352 {p. 87}
353 {p. 175}
354 {p. 126}

its meaning. Moving from the creative process and issues of copyright to matters of representation, the discussion includes a consideration of the kinds of desire, and their resulting pleasures and bliss, which are generated through the textual structuring by reproductive electronic technologies which are employed in house music.

Music technologies

The development of electronic musical instruments has been of major importance while from the late 80s onwards, computer technology has made a major impact. Samplers and computerised sequencers are standard equipment in any studio which produces dance music. Both have different functions in the process of digital recording. A sampler is a digital recording device with which one can manipulate the sound textures that have been recorded with it.[355] The sequencer is able to record, memorise and replay a sequence of notes in the way that a word processor works with a written text.[356] When programmed it can trigger sound generating modules such as synthesizers,[357] drum machines[358] and samplers, in a similar manner as a word processing application which triggers a printer. The sequenced sound pattern is communicated via a cable network currently called MIDI, or Musical Instrument Digital Interface.[359] In 1994, personal computers such as Atari and Apple are both popular hardware to use with sequencing software such as Steinberg's Cubase.[360] Through the use of an

---

[355] The sound texture and pitch of the recorded sound bites can be changed. It is also possible to reverse the recorded soundbite. A sampler like the Akai S1000 has a 'time stretch' device with which one can manipulate the length of the recorded sound as well.

[356] As is the case with the writing procedure on a word processor, the programmer does not need to be fluent in performance skills, since mistakes can be corrected, sequences can be restructured and rhythms can be 'quantised'. However, this does not mean that the programmer does not know anything about music, or indeed is unmusical, as some would put forward in the discussion of digital music technology. This is to confuse the notion of technical musical skill with the notion of musical knowledge. As will be explained later in this chapter, electronic technology invites a different type of performance skill.

[357] A synthesizer is an electronic sound generating device, which can be triggered by devices such as a special keyboard or by a programmed sequencer.

[358] A drum machine is a sequencer with pre-programmed drum sounds.

[359] In 1982 the first MIDI sequencer became available [Harker, 1993].

[360] Atari initially is more widely used in the home market of music production, since it had a built in MIDI interface and had gained popularity due to the wide range of computer games which were available for this personal computer.

SMPTE[361] code, the sequencer can be synchronised with a multi-track tape recorder, so that non-digital music recording as well as sequenced overdubs[362] are possible [Braut, 1994].

The synthesizer started its life in 1929 when an instrument appeared that had four oscillators,[363] which were controlled by paper rolls. In the same year the Hammond organ was first produced, which in terms of the way that it works may also be seen as a precursor of the synthesizer. Through the ecclesiastical connotations of the organ the Hammond was first seen in churches and due to its relatively low cost gained popularity in the gospel churches of the USA and Jamaica [Durant, 1984], whereby it influenced the musical styles of African cultural descent, such as soul and R&B. Another electronic sound generator at the beginning of the history of the synthesizer is the Theremin. This device electronically produces a single sinus wave which can be controlled by the distance between an extending pole and the hand of the musician. The resulting sound is comparable with that of an electronic fretless stringed instrument with a single string, whereby the 'width' or 'vowel' sound can be varied by changing the shape of the hand. It took until 1954 before a computerised synthesising instrument was developed, which was the RCA Mark II Columbia-Princeton synthesizer [Harker, 1993]. However, this instrument, which could be controlled with a type of keyboard like the Hammond organ, filled up several rooms [Krause, 1983]. Finally, in 1964, 'the first practical synthesizer'[364] was put on the market by Moog:

> Donald Buchla and Robert Moog produced the modular synthesizer with integrated circuitry (so) that electronic music leapt beyond the bounds of academia into the mainstream of modern music[365] [Krause, 1983].

The sound-waves which oscillators of the Moog produced, could be manipulated by filters. Other companies followed on a small scale,

---

361 SMPTE is 'the standard originally developed by the Society of Motion Picture and Television Engineers', pronounced SIMP-ty {p.105} [Braut, 1994].
362 To overdub is to record a new track along an existing recording, so that it becomes part of that recording.
363 Oscillators are devices which generate sound waves. The British techno/rave outfit LFO named themselves after the Low Frequency Oscillator, which could be found on analogue synthesizers of the late 70s and early 80s.
364 {p. 127}
365 {p. 127}

but the technology was often only used as an effect like The Beach Boys did with the Theremin on *Good Vibrations* (Capitol, 1966). In the early 70s electronic music technologies became part of the popular idiom. On the mainland of Europe a combination of the availability of capital combined with an avant garde sensibility facilitated the existence of projects like Tangerine Dream and White Noise which appeared on radio programmes like the Dutch *Superclean Dream-machine* in the mid-70s. Kraftwerk were one of the more prominent danceable electronic music outfits, whose recordings *Autobahn* (Phillips, 1974) and *Trans Europe Express*366 (EMI, 1977) heralded the beginning of electronic trance dance music, which is:

(a)s Kraftwerk's Ralf Hutter described it to (David Toop) in 1987: Letting yourself go. Sit on the rails and ch-ch-ch-ch-ch. Just keep going. Fade in and fade out rather than trying to be dramatic or trying to implant into the music a logical order which I think is ridiculous. In our society everything is in motion. Music is a flowing artform367 [Toop, 1992a].

The Italian Giorgio Moroder produced electronic studio based dance music with a similar cyclical groove, but added a 'sexy' 'black' female voice to his music, like the 17 minute *Love To Love You Baby* (Casablanca, 1975) featuring disco Diva Donna Summer in a project [Dannen, 1991], which may be described as the throbbing predecessor of electronic pop dance outfits [Toop, 1992a]. The Euro-disco format often consists of one or two male electronic composers, preferably fronted by a 'black' female singer. David Toop comments on European disco music in the 70s:

Although the African component, the cyclic trance rhythm, was central to disco, the African-American gospel element was optional. Europeans, often African or Afro-Caribbean Europeans, found themselves welcome at the party. Their talent for the endless loop and the chant, along with an un-American angle on sexuality, overrode previous difficulties with language and expression. This was the new, ecstatic language of continuous motion368 [Toop, 1992a].

---

366 The title track was later sampled for Afrika Bambaataa's *Planet Rock* (Polydor, 1982).
367 {p. 21}
368 {p. 21}

In the late 1970s in New York, radical electronic outfits such as Suicide and impLOG created cyclical trance mayhem combining the nihilistic and DIY ethic of punk with driving dance rhythms produced on cheap drum machines. Similar outfits such as The Normal and the dry witted Fad Gadget could be found in England. These groups were part of a 'movement' which at some point was identified as the industrial scene, which according to Jon Savage groups together electronic music makers such as Brian Eno, Cabaret Voltaire and The Residents [Savage, 1983]. In Germany the Neue Deutsche Welle produced an even harder edged electronic yet highly sexed groove sound with bands such as the Conny Plank[369] produced DAF and Liasons Dangereuses. In the mid-1980s, the Slovenic band Laibach were ahead of European tekno and gabber house with their sonic experiments in the use of orchestra, film score and opera samples, celebrating an aggressive 'masculine' military sensibility.[370] In the arena of African-American dance, synthesising technologies were also incorporated. For instance in the 70s the African-American band Parliament used the new technologies in a dance music which articulated an African-American science fiction type of imagination,[371] known as P-Funk [Killbourn, 1986]. This kind of fantasy was a source of inspiration for a form of house music produced in Detroit called techno, which for its stylistic influences looked to European technocrats such as Kraftwerk[372] [Franssen, 1988b] and the more poppy Gary Numan, as can be heard in the early work of Juan Atkin's Cybotron [Savage, 1993]. Since 1985, Detroit techno producers also listened to their Chicago counterparts in dance party music, as can be heard for example on *No UFO's* by Juan Atkins' Model 500 (Metroplex, 1985) [Cheeseman, 1993a]. For a European audience, more well known examples of original Detroit techno are Derek May's Rhythim Is Rhythim projects, like *Kaos* or *Strings of Life*, as well as Model 500 *Off To Battle* (Jack Trax, 1987).

---

369 Conny Plank was also responsible for production work on many of Germany's electronic acts, including Kraftwerk's albums (up till *Autobahn*) [Bussy, 1993].

370 Techno radical Moby fits within this European and mostly European-American cultural history, which despite similarities in the use of production and consumption technologies seems at times far removed from the Frankie Knuckles school of African-American house music. Yet, both histories have met and crossed over on several dance floors and studios, creating several hybrid forms current in the dance music of the early 90s.

371 For an interesting discussion on the subject of African-American science fiction, see Mark Dery's interviews with Samuel R. Delany, Greg Tate and Tricia Rose [Dery, 1993b].

372 Especially Kraftwerk's single *Home Computer*, which can be found on the album *Computer_ World* (EMI, 1981) has been sampled by a lot of electro-dance acts [Bussy, 1993].

In New York the dance scene moved into its hip hop inspired electro dance phase during the early 80s,[373] while DJs in Chicago began to produce their own instrumental jack tracks for their 'houses'.[374]

In the early 80s American companies Moog, Oberheim and Sequential Circuits independently developed the polyphonic[375] synthesizer. These Silicon Valley based companies were very small and not able to market their products on a large scale, so their use remained restricted to users who were already successful in their musical careers to some extent. For example, the English band New Order have always reinvested their profit into new technologies, thereby keeping ahead of the developments which put them in a vanguard position of electronic pop music production, with for instance the innovative best selling 12" dance single *Blue Monday* (Factory, 1983).

Japanese micro chip technology changed this hierarchical situation. In the case of house music it was, for instance, the availability of cheap Roland technology which created its specific sound, such as the drum-machine series TR808,[376] TR727 and TR909 as well as the TB303 Bass Line which was able to produce sounds and sequences for bass patterns and the now classic analogue keyboards such as the monophonic 101 and polyphonic Juno 106, Juno 6 and Jupiter 6 [Robinson, 1993]. Earlier instruments such as the monophonic Sequential Circuits Pro One and also the Mini Moog were, and still are, of importance as well as the Oberheim DMX series. The Roland drum machines and the TB303 Bass Line were especially popular with urban African-American DJs in the early 1980s. They used it in order to add an extra beat or bass sound to the records of their set. Because all the early Chicago house tracks have been created using some of this equipment, these instruments are still in demand with house musicians, even though the manufacturers have long since deleted the production line of these instruments. It should be noted that none of these instruments are samplers or indeed digital. Their analogue simplicity was partly responsible for the minimalist but 'warm' sound of early house music, which mainly consisted of tracks which were

---

373 See Chapter 5.

374 See Chapter 2; a house is a club or dancing 'posse' (a socially bonded group of people); to 'jack' is to dance in a certain jerking sexually suggestive and possessed manner.

375 Polyphonic as opposed to monophonic means that more than one key can be made to trigger a sound at the same time, so that chords can be played as well as two hands can be used to play simultaneously.

376 The British electronic dance project State 808 (and the related dance music radio programme 808 State on Manchester radio station Sunset 102) derived its name from this machine.

created to be played simultaneously with existing records. A specific Dutch version of house has been influenced by Detroit techno as well as by TB303 driven Chicago acid house,[377] exemplifying an ongoing trans-Atlantic musical exchange. Techno was influenced by European electronic outfits, it is produced by African-Americans in a city which, amongst other things, was famous for its soul tradition. For instance Detroit record company (or label) Motown Records established itself there as one of the most famous soul producing labels from 1959 onward [Mitchell, 1990]. Together with soul labels like Stax they influenced different dance scenes such as New York disco and Chicago house, providing an important part of the dance track of English Northern Soul nights and weekenders. Amsterdam techno DJ Dimitri refers to Detroit techno as 'soul' techno, not only for its soul and gospel context of cultural production, but also because of the use of 'warmer', often analogue, sounds. This is in contrast to the 'harsh' digital sounds and choice of samples, such as the sampled orchestra stabs and opera chords, of Dutch gabber house [Beesemer, 1991b]. In relative terms, a similar hard 'coldness' can be found in some of the sound spectrum of Belgian techno as well as English 'hardcore' rave music.[378]

As electronic music technology gradually became more sophisticated as well as cheaper, the pop sensibility of this technology increased with English outfits such as The Human League and Depeche Mode in the late 70s and the early 1980s. Although synthesizers originally produced distinct electronic sounds which suited the futuristic fantasies of the avant garde, they became popular when they were able to 'simulate the sounds of conventional instruments'[379] [Goodwin, 1990]. In 1964 it became possible to reproduce conventional sounds with the Mellotron [Harker, 1964], an instrument with a keyboard which triggers magnetic tape loops with pre-recorded sounds like choirs and string quartets as well as special

---

[377] For example the Dutch label Djax-Up-Beat, which also releases the 'un-Dutch' recordings of various Chicago and Detroit artists.

[378] Although techno from both continents is concerned with an almost psychedelic and shaman-ritualistic use of music technology for a dance audience, the African-American form of techno has an emphasis on sexualised body movements and themes, while its European and European-American counterpart seems more concerned with angry power. Compare for example the compilation *XL-Recordings; The Second Chapter, Hardcore European Dance Music* (XL-Recordings, 1991) with the compilation *The Deepest Shades of Techno* (Reflect, 1994). The fact that one compilation is from 1991 and the other from 1994 does not affect the argument; of importance is the socio-geographical and cultural historical difference which creates a different accent and meaning.

[379] {p. 261}

effects such as a thunder storm. In the 70s it was used by progressive rock groups [Goodwin, 1990]. In a sense this was a precursor of the keyboard with 'realistic' sounds. Since the late 80s it has been possible to buy keyboards with pre-recorded sampled sounds which have been manipulated and synthesised. Since 1986 they have been financially within reach of most people, since a squeaky but useful Casio sampling keyboard could be bought for around £80 [Goodwin, 1990], while in 1994 a high quality mid-range priced Korg M1 can be bought at £1200 new and £700 secondhand. The Korg M1 has been so well programmed that anyone who plays it can sound like they have spent time in an expensive recording studio or at least like they own the top of the range in sampling equipment, which would cost at least a few thousand pounds. Most television advertising sound tracks are constructed using these mid-range types of keyboards, which produce sounds which seem to be more 'perfect' than real acoustic and 'conventional' sounds. Therefore, Jean Baudrillard's concept of the hyperreal [Baudrillard, 1983] could be applied to this type of simulated soundscape[380] which has been created in the tradition of naturalism [Goodwin, 1990]. However, sometimes in underground dance music these instruments can be heard with a different usage, when the textures of sounds rather than the suggestion of an authentic player is foregrounded. For instance despite the fact that its sounds are digitally recorded and synthesized, the organ sound of the Korg M1 workstation is a popular replacement of the analogue synthesised bass in American underground club music. Examples can be found on product from labels like New York's Strictly Rhythm and Nervous Records from about 1991. As second-hand instruments, 'dumped' by the advertising and major pop industry, keyboards like, writing in 1994, the M1 have only just started their lives on the underground scene, despite the boredom voiced by certain producers of the 'over use' of their pre-programmed sounds. Taking into account what has happened to electronic equipment in the 80s in the dance music scene, it is most likely that their sounds will become 'classics' like those of the Roland equipment range.

To avoid repetitiveness in sound textures, however, one could buy new sound chips and cards or otherwise synthesise new sounds, depending on what type of synthesising module is used. Most of the older synthesizers had no pre-programmed or sampled sounds but

---

[380] Simulations and the political implications of this concept will be discussed near the end of this chapter.

128

for a lot of people this made the synthesizer 'inaccessible'. In 1994 there were roughly two types of synthesizers; the programmable synthesising module and the populist pre-programmed sound module which often contains sampled sounds. Korg for example brought out a 'sister' digital keyboard to the M1 called the Wavestation which allows for the synthesising of a huge variety of sounds, including the 'classic analogue' sounds of synthesizers from the 80s.[381]

Another possibility is to sample one's own sound textures. Although its price put it out of reach for most people when it appeared on the market in 1979, the Fairlight Computer Musical Instrument was the first commercially available sampling device, followed by the cheaper Emulator, Synclavier, Ensoniq Mirage and Akai.[382] The sampler allows one to enlarge the sound palette to a seemingly infinite range of possibilities. Single drum sounds, small segments of instrumental sounds such as a guitar or a stringed instrument or perhaps the sound of a pen hitting a bottle can be manipulated and used as source material for new textures.

To producers and remixers the sampler is also a useful tool which enables the reconstruction of a song. Parts of a song which are repeated in its structure, such as the chorus, only have to be recorded once. Often the most successful parts of the recording are sampled and inserted where they are needed as well. Remixers use a similar method to create a new track, using only a few key elements of the original recordings.[383] Sometimes only a few words from the original vocals are used as a rhythmical device for what is otherwise an instrumental dub. This technique follows from the working method of the DJ, who sometimes uses the sampler as an extension of DJ equipment.[384] A contemporary example is Junior Vasquez, who presides over The Sound Factory in New York, who uses his equipment in an imaginative and sophisticated manner:

... Junior's working the decks, a sampler, EQ-ing out the mid-

---

381 The American Sequential Circuits programming team now works for Korg; this may explain why the sounds from the analogue range of synthesizers from Sequential Circuits have a dominant presence on the Wavestation.
382 In the early 80s it was also possible to buy a sampling box which contained one chip which could record one sound; this device was especially popular with drummers of smaller bands.
383 Often, only the vocal lines are re-used on top of a completely new backing track.
384 Mixers are available with which one can sample one part of a record while one is playing a set.

range[385] and has even found a sly way to play records backwards. Check a Junior set and you'll find Mariah Carey's *Dreamlover* running backwards on one deck, forwards on another and the main vocal lick looped on his sampler[386] [Marcus, 1994].

Existing songs and tracks can be cut up and parts such as hook lines can be recorded on the sampler, after which the samples could be triggered in a new order by the sequencer. In this manner, a new version can be obtained with the addition of a 'fresh' drum-machine track and a certain number of synthesizers. When this type of 'remix' has not been commissioned by the original songwriting perfomer or by other representatives which own part of the copyright of a song or its recording, its commercial release may be stigmatised as an act of theft and the product will be regarded as a bootleg. A discussion of copyright in this respect will follow later.

Without a DJ tradition of using recorded music as elements of a soundscape for a dance, equipment such as samplers would not have gained the importance as they have now within dance club music. In 1877, Thomas Alva Edison invented the phonograph or 'voice-writer' [Chanan, 1995], which was 'the forerunner of today's record player',[387] while Edison's colleague Emil Berliner created the first 'disk-type record'[388] [Joe, 1980]. Gramophone records have been commercially available in the USA since 1894. During the first half of the twentieth century, especially after 1936, the use of jukeboxes[389] [Harker, 1993] in public spaces in the USA enabled (dance) music which was from another area or which was lavishly orchestrated to be accessible to a wider audience; live performances are relatively expensive and logistically cumbersome in comparison. Although even before 1940 in France records were played in clubs by a DJ, in the USA it took until the late 1950s before the DJ took over from the jukebox[390] [Joe, 1980]. A major progression has been the specific use of two record players in the 60s[391] to enable the DJ to cue up the next record.

---

[385] The mid-range in the audible sound spectrum often represents vocals. To EQ out this range means that with the use of a graphic equaliser that part of the sound spectrum is made inaudible. In effect, the vocals have been 'removed' from the sound palette of the record.

[386] {p. 32}

[387] {p. 16}

[388] {p. 16}

[389] Jukeboxes are automated record players which can be programmed and which are often coin operated.

[390] See Chapter 5.

[391] See Chapter 5.

With the addition of felt mats on top of the turntables one could cue the record without having to jam the mechanical parts of the record player. Using two record players in combination with a DJ mixer and a pair of head phones,[392] the DJ is able to blend one record into another at the correct speed, making the beats of the rhythms join up, or inserting parts of one record on top of another one. It has therefore become possible for the mixing of records to become a sophisticated skill, to the extent that DJ Spooky claims: 'Gimme two records and I'll make you a universe'[393] [Gallagher, 1994].

In the 70s specialist turntables called decks came on the market. Since the late 70s the Japanese have produced Technics SL1200 and SL1210 [Larwood, 1994], which have become the most popular amongst professionals [Farrin, 1994]. Decks are different from domestic turntables in that they allow the DJ to be in control of the change in speeds between records. Technics has a patent on its magnetic drive device, which is useful for several reasons; the turntable can accelerate from being stationary to its desired speed within a small fraction of time and while the motor still runs, one is able to stop the record by hand or to move forward or backward without causing friction to its mechanical parts. DJs were enabled to begin competing with each other with sometimes acrobatic skills, especially in the hip hop scene. Although I haven't seen a person spinning on his or her head on top of a record deck yet, rumours are that some have mastered this over-exerting skill.

In the case of house music and related musical forms the slow mix is usually favoured over the cut and mix styles of hip hop and some dance hall reggae.[394] Since songs and tracks are made to overlap, a sense of harmony may be achieved if the melody scales of the different songs fit. Although there are arguments on the subject amongst DJs,[395] this is not of primary importance to a groove based dance music like house. In house music one may find DJ mixes and even records produced by professional DJs which have a vocal which seems 'out of tune' with the bass line. A tendency to foreground

---

[392] Headphones are used so one hears what is going on in the mix before the audience hears it. For a more detailed description of DJ mixing, see Tony Langlois's article on English house music DJs [Langlois, 1992], which is correct except for the simplistic claim that house music 'is a genre of electronic popular music developed in Britain in the late 1980s' {p. 229}, thereby disregarding its legacy in American urban dance club and party music.

[393] {p. 86}

[394] See Chapter 5.

[395] See for instance electronic bulletin board *BPM List*, e-mail number bpm+@andrew.cmu.edu., between 15 and 19 November 1992.

rhythms and textures, rather than melodies, has been strengthened by this groove-centred DJ method throughout the 1980s.

Manipulation of recorded sounds in the studio became a possibility after the Second World War when magnetic tape, invented in 1928 by Fritz Pleumer in Germany, was used for music recording.[396] In 1947 the magnetic tape recorder was used for the first time in a commercial context for the American Bing Crosby radio show, although it was 'then transferred to 16-inch disc for transmission'[397] [Harker, 1993]. In the same year Capitol started to use tape for their recordings and in 1950 tape recording replaced disc recording altogether both in the USA and the UK [Harker, 1993]. Experimental composers were keen to play around with the new technology, so for example in the early 1950s Schaffer and Henri created musique concrete by manipulating recorded sounds in the ORTF Studios in Paris, where sounds, such as voices, were cut, filtered and run at different speeds [Krause, 1983]. On the other side of the Atlantic, during the 1970s and 1980s in the USA, teenagers with DJ aspirations, but who could not afford records or record decks, would construct 'scratch' pause-button sound collages with the help of (preferably) two audio cassette decks, mainly using material recorded from radio shows, such as dance club music and hip hop [NMS, 1992b]. Closer to the locality from where I am writing, in London recording tape was used during the 1960s, to provide non-stop music at parties and clubs which was not possible when the DJ used only one deck. From there the idea sparked for Londoners that two record decks could be useful to provide the same effect, except that the choice of records could be adapted to the mood of the audience [Blackford, 1979].

In 1958, the first Shure Brothers 4-track tape recorders became available in the USA [Harker, 1993], which enabled different instruments to be recorded on separate tracks in a parallel fashion (as opposed to the serial collage methods described above). It was also possible to overdub parts of the recording. This led to the possibility of creating (instrumental) 'dub' tracks. By the late 1960s in Jamaica, due to a lack of finance for studio time or new tapes, different singers used the same instrumental track as backing for the recording of their own song; the individual vocal performances could vary dramatically.[398] This type of recording performance was based on the

---

[396] Paul Theberge dates magnetic recording back to 1898 [Theberge, 1993], although my original source was David Harker [1993].

[397] {p. 11}

[398] See, for example, various material released in the 70s by the Jamaican label Studio One.

practice of Jamaican sound system parties, where instrumental tracks were played by the DJ with either an MC or singer providing vocal entertainment to dedicated crowds of dancers [Hebdige, 1987]. With the use of multi-track recording techniques, these instrumental tracks developed into the sophisticated overlaying of sounds of dub which were created in the early 1970s with King Tubby in the vanguard [Toop, 1992b]. In New York the development of instrumental dance club tracks trailed behind the Jamaican dubs. Although Walter Gibbons produced the first soundscape in disco with Double Exposure's *Ten Percent* (Salsoul, 1976), adding extra parts wherein the track was stripped to its percussive groove,[399] it was not until the early 80s that the instrumental made its appearance as a dub mix in New York club music. DJ, producer and one time A&R[400] for disco label Prelude Francois Kervorkian remembered:

> Around 1980/82 we were aware of Mad Professor, King Tubby and Black Uhuru's *In Dub* album. It was the first time in New York we'd made that reggae connection and so we used it in an uptempo style[401] [Knott, 1994].

A host of separate developments in instrumental dance music creation such as German proto trance, Italian Euro-disco, English HiNRG, English electronic pop, Jamaican dub, Chicago DJ tracks and New York dance club instrumentals were beginning to cross over on the dance floors of New York, Chicago and Europe in the early 1980s. This network of connections became the beginning of dance music like, for example, house music as we know it today. This would not have been possible without the technologies as described above.

DIY market

Digital recording has enabled the increase of the possibility of cultural and generic cross-over as well as an increased speed in the time of reaction on different musical products. Initially this type of technology was developed by the end of the 70s in order to overcome the static noises and the distortions which troubled analogue

---

399 See Chapter 5.
400 A&R stands for Artist and Repertoire; this person researches and suggests new artists to a record company.
401 {p. 26}

recording methods. As has been the case with all other (re)productive musical technologies, although exclusive at first, sequencers, samplers and DAT machines can now be afforded by the person 'on the street' at a grassroots level. A composition could be created at home without being dependent on large investments by the major music industry and therefore without their interference [O'Shaughernessy, 1992]. In 1988, one Dutch 'technophilliac' exclaimed:

De sequencer heeft van de computer het meest creative opname-instrument gemaakt dat je je maar kunt bedenken. (...) Geen geld is nodig voor dure studio's, gebrekkig bandmateriaal, noem maar op. De sequencer blijkt net die creative oppepper te zijn die veel thuis-muzikanten dringend nodig hebben. (...) Een amateur componist, Home Compu's noem ik ze, de opvolgers van de Home Tapers, kan nu met de diskette met zijn muziek erop naar de studio. Stop de diskette daar in de Atari en hop, daar klinkt zijn compositie puur professioneel uit de studio-luidspreker. Als de muziek bevalt, zou de producer het bij wijze van spreken direct op CD kunnen kieperen. Mooier kan toch niet?[402] [Boer, 1988].

(Eng. trans.) The sequencer has made the computer one of the most creative recording instruments you could imagine. (...) No money is needed for expensive studios, dodgey tapes, you name it. The sequencer itself is just the kind of creative stimulant which many home musicians need.(...) Amateur-composers, I call them Home Compus as follow-up to the Home Tapers, are now able to bring their music on a floppy disk to a studio. Once there, bang the floppy into the Atari and bingo, there you have this composition which sounds all professional from the studio speakers. If the music is liked, the producer could in principle dump it straight onto CD. What could be better?

The home production of CDs straight from one's PC (personal computer) has become a possibility [Waugh, 1994]. A consequence of the possibility of independent home recording is that the production of recorded music has been democratised;[403] a less censored form of

---

[402] {newspaper}

[403] The notion of democratisation of the production of music in the context of contemporary music production technologies has been discussed extensively by popular music theorists such as Alan Durant and Andrew Goodwin [Durant, 1990; Goodwin, 1992].

music can appear on the market. The early house tracks from Chicago, with their sexually explicit lyrics and raw unpolished productions are an example of this, as are references to male 'gay' relationships in New York club music, the hard hitting Dutch gabber house or the manic British rave tracks which contain sly references to the (illegal) use of the dance drug ecstasy. Since it is now possible to release one's own record and distribute it either oneself or through an independent distributor [The Timelords, 1988; E-Block, 1994], a kind of grassroots folk sensibility has been returned to popular music.[404] Tracks are produced for a home market and have acquired local characteristics, such as the use of Dutch language on some Dutch techno tracks. On the other hand, in a global market characterised by rapid exchanges in communication, the use of similar technologies and spaces of consumption has made it possible for certain tracks to 'make a cross over' from one scene to another. Despite local differences, dance music which can be grouped together under the tag 'house' is part of an international cultural aesthetic which shares certain formal qualities. Its differences are like accents and colloquialisms which bring welcome fresh ideas and which allow dance music to mutate into new directions.

As with other DIY musical genres, the multitude of home produced underground one-off dance track projects has brought with it a relative anonymity of the producers as well as a relatively short life span for most tracks. The anonymity of the recording artists is enhanced by the fact that their work is represented by a DJ as part of a continuous sound track, rather than as a unique live performance or a representation of such.[405] Rather than the artist within circles of underground dance, to use Roland Barthes' terminology [Barthes, 1973], it is often the myth of a certain dance record company which sells records. Within consumer circles it is customary to speak of a

---

[404] For a more thorough discussion of this notion, see Chris Cutler's idea that a 'folk community' can be created due to particular uses of contemporary music technologies and Richard Middleton's prising apart of the concepts in this piece [Cutler, 1984; Middleton, 1990]. Also of interest in this context is Peter Manuel's study of the prolific use of audio cassettes in North India, which has contributed to a specific development of local forms of popular music [Manuel, 1993].

[405] Ironically, although in Europe house related dance music has become popular during the late 80s and early 90s, the British national television pop chart programme Top Of The Pops, which for a long time used the technique of miming, has (re)introduced the concept of live vocalists to their weekly BBC show. Some producer teams alleviate this problem by hiring a singer to sing their 'stolen' vocal samples live; others hide behind a choreographed dance outfit, as the Dutch outfit Doop did in early 1994. In European countries like the Netherlands there are not many computer music ensembles which have an identifiable vocalist.

135

'label','in order to indicate the company name as denotation of its connoted public image and reputation. Customers in dance specialist shops, both in Europe and the USA, often request product from a particular label and the specialist press write about these organisations as being genuine creative forces.[406] In one such article the attitude of the consumer is summed up as follows:

> A rather spankin' DJ in his own right, Sherman once confessed to me that he bought everything that came out on DJax Up Beats (sic.) whether he'd heard it or not. 'You just know that it's going to be fucking brilliant' he raved ...[407] [Steele, 1994].

This development shows the importance of A&R personnel, who have a similar function within a record company as the DJ in a club. These are the people who decide on the musical profile of the label. In the area of dance club music, the A&R job is often performed by DJs, since they know what makes the dance floor move and what works from the flow of imported records. Therefore the DJ is also central to the musical image of a dance label. For example, in the case of the Dutch label Djax-Up-Beats, it is DJ Saskia Sledgers who runs all aspects of her label [Steele, 1994], while the London based Junior Boy's Own is run by several people, including DJ and producer Terry Farley [Harris, 1994].

An economic consequence of home production is that amongst the independent producers artist development is carried out at one's own risk. This could mean that the enterprise requires more investment than can be gained [de Kort, 1987]. However, an independent producer who releases product on white label,[408] could make a small profit after selling as little as 500 units, which is probably the full potential of the market value of an underground dance record. In contrast, the major record companies see the career of a 'star' as a long term investment. These companies are structured on the basis of large investments and sophisticated marketing techniques. Eddie Gordon, formerly head of A&R at a division for major record

---

[406] For a historical example of dance label adulation, see: Elvis Mitchell, *The Motown Album; the sound of young America - three decades of magic!*, Sarah Lazin Books, 1990.

[407] [p. 39]

[408] A white label is a test pressing, which larger companies use as a marketing tool in order to test the market. A DIY independent producer can use this type of product as a one off release which is sold directly to specialist shops and DJs. It is called a 'white label' since a test pressing is manufactured by the pressing plant without a marker on the label to indicate the source of production.

company Polydor, said:

> Majors can take 10 weeks to get a record on the street — and if there's too much stuff coming out, they put it back. It's also a great deal more expensive for them to release a record than it is for an indie.[409] With company overheads it probably costs £10,000 to release a single[410] [A. Jones, 1992].

The resulting high cost of production means that they are not able to afford to release a track which would sell a few thousand units. A large company with its many departments like A&R and marketing works too slow and its large investments force it to be too conservative and static in its artistic policies to be able to keep up with the developments in the dance market [Norris, 1990].[411] However, the major recording companies are able to pick up the more successful independently produced tracks without having to take a great financial risk in advance. Sometimes an entire independent label is bought in order to get hold of the contract of a desirable artist or successful record. Therefore another way of representing the home grown dance music industry is by likening it to nursery whereby, as in a type of cottage-industry [Fish, 1992], the independent music producer has to make the first investments and take the first risks.[412] A compromise in this situation is made when a smaller label becomes a subsidiary of a major one or when a major like Sony starts its own dance department which has a relative

409 An 'indie' is an independent record label.

410 {p. 8}

411 Rather than investing in new talent, a new format was used to re-release back catalogues; vinyl is being replaced by CD. Dance music is dependent on vinyl because of its roots in the technique of the DJ, who still prefers to use vinyl as a mixing medium. The dynamics seem different; the 'rawness' of the bass, which affects the pelvic part of the dancing body is not distracted by a 'perfect' high range dynamic. Erik van Vliet from Rotterdam Stealth label gave me a CD called *Food for Woofers; Car Hifi Demo* (FFW, 1992) to prove differently, which does produce a decent sub-bass sound; however, it does not move the hips. Vinyl pressing plants are disappearing; for instance, in 1993 the last plant was closed in the Netherlands and, since there were no pressing plants in Portugal, Portuguese dance producers had to go to London to have their material pressed [Pereira, 1993]. Even though independent labels have started to release on CD and ambient and trance DJs have started to use CD mixers, the argument of CD versus vinyl sometimes seems to be synonymous with that of major record industry versus independent dance labels.

412 An English example is from Jazzy M, who, for an advance of £12,500, had the group Chime taken over from his Ozone label by Pete Tong's FFRR label, which is a subsidiary of London Records. This group then went on to become the highly successful Orbital [Jazzy M, 1993]. The Dutch Stealth label, who, having learned from its own similar experiences, now provides its artists with a two year deal [van Vliet, 1992].

independence in its policies and strategies. Subsidiaries are in touch with 'the dance floor', such as FFRR for London Records, which had DJ Pete Tong as A&R person when they released The House Sound series during the late-80s. Thereby the hierarchical structures within the major companies have been exchanged for network structures [Negus, 1992]. This kind of company structure could be described as a result of 'the cultural logic of late-capitalism'[413] [Jameson, 1984].

As the outlines of the hierarchy become blurred, notions such as 'mainstream' and 'underground' music production seem to have lost their relevance in the process. However, some small labels such as London based labels Junior Boy's Own and Strictly Underground, as well as Happy Records and Simply Soul from Detroit and New York's Strictly Rhythm proudly stay independent so they can release whatever they like. Although their output is directed at a small and specialised dance market, their investment per track is relatively low and the profit they make from small releases is their own. Different marketing strategies ensure that unusual dance music can find a voice. The Manhattan based company Strictly Rhythm for instance releases a huge variety of tracks in small quantities, on the understanding that only a few releases which will be successful enough in order to keep their enterprise and less commercially successful releases going [NMS, 1992a]. As mentioned above, the notion of success for a small independent is quite different than for a major record label; a similar amount of sales might mean a big flop and a great financial disaster for the latter, while for the former it might mean the success they had always hoped for. The method of promotion is different as well, in that dance records depend very much on the selling techniques of the shops which are specialised in dance club music [Davies, 1992]. In summary, 'the cultural logic of late-capitalism'[414] [Jameson, 1984] has not yet completely erased the notion of 'mainstream' and 'underground':

> It's pure market forces. (...) (Dance club) music is enormously popular on an underground level and people want to buy those records to play in clubs. If the majors aren't gonna do it then the independents are gonna do it. House is always independent; all the first house records were on independent labels. Club music was always independent. You know, Salsoul, Prelude and

---

[413] {p. 63}
[414] {p. 63}

Westend[415] were all independent labels. (...) Majors got involved when they thought it was worth investing in. They like to jump on the band-wagon once in a while; they hate to be left out, but they don't take risks; they only go for things when they're tried and tested[416] [Cheeseman, 1993b].

Since albums are a more worthwhile investment for products which need to be sold in high quantities, this low-risk policy has resulted in a flood of releases by the 'majors' of dance compilation records which are aimed at a home market, with tracks that are already popular.[417] One may conclude that when speaking of power relations within the record industry, a sense of 'dominant ideology' can still be identified despite the localisation of the global market and despite the development of the network model rather than the model of the hierarchical pyramid within major company structures.

Creative process

The expansion of studio practices and technologies does not exist in a vacuum. Simon Frith has suggested that the development of studio technologies and studio based music is a direct result of copyright law. Since 'copyright laws protect the composers rather than the performers'[418] [Frith, 1983], it is the composers who have had the investment capital to build and expand on the technological improvements of their studios [Blake, 1992]. This means that even early in its development there was a market for the then primitive and rather expensive electronic equipment. This market no doubt stimulated the development of recording technology as well as minimised the occupational possibilities of the traditional 'authentic' performer. In 1982 the British Musicians Union (or MU) proposed a ban on synthesizers and drum machines, because it feared that musicians in a traditional sense, such as string players and drummers, would become unemployed [Moy, 1991]. In 1988 a similar

---

415 These were the most influential disco labels for the current house and garage producers.
416 {interview}
417 Only the specialised dance labels release compilations which can be used on the dance floor; there are more tracks on one side of a home use compilation, so that the range of the dynamic of the sound is not as wide. For instance, the bass frequency takes a lot of physical space, while bass is necessary for a dance record to work in a club.
418 {p. 17}

statement was made on samplers, when the general secretary of the MU, John Morton, expressed a fear that the years of practice a traditional musician needs to perfect a sound could be stolen with such ease. However, at the same time he acknowledged that many of its members used the new technologies [Bradwell, 1988]. The occurrence of a new technology offers new creative possibilities. For instance, without the development of electronic and often digital technology, the growth of the stylistic aspects of house music would have been different. This then opens avenues to a new group of music makers. Beadle suggests that the technology of sampling:

> ... shifted the balance of power from singers, songwriters and instrumentalists to producers (...). Producers could emerge as artists in their own right[419] [Beadle, 1993].

These producers can also be described as contemporary songwriting musicians. Many names have been thought of to signify this new breed of musician who uses electronic music technologies. 'Home Compu' [Boer, 1988] connotes a DIY attitude. A relationship between musicality and the use of machines is suggested in the name 'Enginician' [Moy, 1991]. Kraftwerk call themselves 'Musik Arbeiter', or 'Music Labourers', who don't 'make music' but who practice 'sound chemistry' [Carvalho, 1992].[420] 'Technophilliac' is a term used by Claudia Springer to suggest an erotic relationship between computer technology in a wider sense and its (male) user [Springer, 1991]. This last theme will be discussed at the end of this chapter.

Within a cyberpunk context Bilwet suggests a more general name which indicates the inherent connection between the user and computer technology. 'Wetware'[421] as opposed to software (such as sequencing programmes or sound patches) or hardware (the computer) is the unpredictable organic ingredient which creates new patterns:

> Wetware is a body attached to machines (...) It need not result in slavish submission, for wetware has a secret weapon up its sleeve:

---

419 {p. 25}

420 This is a self definition which seems to have connections with German ideas on the machine as was defined during the epoch of the neue Sachlicheit in the 1920s and 1930s.

421 After Rudy Rucker's book *Wetware*, where 'wetware' is the genetic element, the DNA, which is part of the computer. With *Software*, this novel can be found in the collection *Live Robots* [Rucker, 1994].

its (all too) human traits. The nickname wetware is a homage to the do-it-yourselver who tries to make the best of things but always forgets to read the instructions. (...) Through ignorance, the urge to sabotage, and unbridled creativity, technology always goes haywire; from these accidents the most beautiful freaks forth, and after aesthetic treatment are effortlessly declared art. To wetware the user is not a remnant or something suppressed, but a born hobbyist who can hook together any old or new media into a personal reality, where an error message is at the beginning of a long series of resounding successes[422] [Bilwet, 1993].

Examples of these kinds of 'accidents' are numerous in the world of innovative dance music. I will discuss three of these, one which was registered in the process of 'participant observation' of my own music writing. When I was a musician in 1983, whilst creating a bass line for a track later called *Love Tempo* (Factory, 1983), I 'mistook' the sequence of notes, which were then played in a different pattern than intended with an added beat here and there. As a result, the bass line was made to swing in and around the metronome beat. After its recording, adding vocals and other instruments, it made people dance their hearts out in a constant re-interpretation of the syncopating rhythm in clubs like Paradise Garage in New York or the Music Box in Chicago.

In Chicago, 1984, Larry Heard created his classic Mr Fingers track *Mystery of Love* (Jack Trax, 1988) in a similar manner:

This is an endorsement for Roland I guess. I had the clock out, I think, from the Roland 707 [drum sequencer — sic] and hooked the wire into the arpeggiator clock in on the Juno 6 [a Roland synthesizer — sic], and it just happened. I just hit a chord with two hands on the keyboard and the Juno 6 arpeggiated it. I never could recreate that, it was just something that happened in the midst of me experimenting, and I got it on tape[423] [Trask, 1992].

Acid Tracks by Phuture (Trax, 1987) caused havoc in England in 1988. The name, rather than the music itself, was partly responsible for the mushrooming of a party scene outside of its regulated club environment. However, acid house parties, which later in the UK and

---

422 {p. 5}
423 {p. 50}

the USA mutated into 'raves' and in the Netherlands into 'house parties', did employ a dance soundtrack which used the beats and technologies of house music, whereby the European trance element of acid house fitted the occasion perfectly. Without *Acid Tracks*, perhaps the trajectory of house music outside of its African-American club environment may have been different.[424] Again this dance tune came into existence as part of an 'accident' or random event. When Spanky of Phuture bought his Roland TB303 Bass Line machine, it had no sequences programmed into its memory. Instead it produced scrambled sequences and played 'something crazy'[425] [Smith Jr., 1992]. Spanky explained what happened next:

> I had run across it and I called him (DJ Pierre) on the phone to come and listen to it, and he got to it and he started turning the knobs changing my frequency (settings of the EQ) of it, and that's what it started from.(...) But the funny thing when the batteries ran out the same exact acid was coming back in[426] [Smith Jr., 1992].

There DJ Pierre added:[427]

> Not *Acid Tracks* though. That has to be recreated every time. (...) It would be the same notes of being the same order it'd be there, but it just might be going to a different beat in some parts[428] [DJ Pierre, 1992].

These 'accidents' however need a social context to obtain a meaning. I was intrigued listening to similar sequences when I lost the batteries of my TB303 machine, however it did not seem 'appropriate' at the time in the particular musical and social context to use such 'effects'. *Acid Tracks* as a finished piece with drums, keyboards and voice added, was created in an environment that was ready for this type of 'crazed' random sequence. To use this sequence was certainly not a random act. It was the house sensibility of Chicago in a club like Ron

---

424 See Chapter 3.
425 {interview}
426 {interview}
427 Spanky (Earl Smith Jr.) and DJ Pierre, who are both from Chicago, were interviewed together at the offices of dance label Strictly Rhythm in New York City, where, in the summer of 1992, DJ Pierre worked as A&R person.
428 {interview}

Hardy's The Music Box, that gave it its initial meaning. 'Acid' connotes the fragmentation of experience and dislocation of meaning due to the unstructuring effects on thought patterns which the psycho-active drug LSD or 'Acid' can bring about. In the context of the creation of Acid Tracks it was a name to indicate a concept rather than the use of psycho-active drugs in itself.[429]

As the computer has no inherent function, it could be said that '... each user interface creates its own culture'[430] [T., 1993]. As has been shown with the way in which the tag 'house' has acquired different meanings[431] as well as with the example of the creation of Acid Tracks, it is the social context and its specific historical relations that shape the legitimate knowledge around the use of reproductive technologies. Whether it is the sampler, the DJ or perhaps the body of the dancer in the club that could be defined as an interface, each contribute to the creation of a culture which is specific. In a similar manner Ross Harley has argued that in the context of rock and pop many discussions in relation to digital technology are 'based on technological determinist lines',[432] although it is the political and cultural context in which technologies are used which gives them their function [Harley, 1993]. For instance, a DJ will give a sampler a different function than the kind of producer who attempts to create a naturalistic reproduction of a musical performance, in which case the use of technology is hidden. Another example is a contemporary almost electronic sounding ambient-techno type of dance trance music which can be generated with the use of didgeredoos and hand drums, rather than electronic instruments, as I witnessed in England at sunrise by the Stone Circle during the Glastonbury Festival of 1995.

In contrast, the way in which a piece of information technology, such as a computer, works, limits and opens new possibilities in the way we make sense of our culture; the medium is by no means neutral. The following discussion will focus on some of the general philosophical and political issues which are at stake as a result of the use of the reproductive technologies described above.

---

[429] However, it cannot be denied that recreational drugs are not important to the realm of house music. See Chapter 7.
[430] {p. 11}
[431] See Chapters 2, 3 and 4.
[432] {p. 211}

Authenticity, authorship and intertextuality

Musicologist John Shepherd has proposed that music can be analysed with the use of semiotics as a form of communication which for purposes of abbreviation can be designated as 'text' [Shepherd, 1991]. One could therefore regard a house music record as a text, which is created on a sequencing device in a process which these days, using software programmes like Cubase on an Atari or Apple computer, is equivalent to writing a text on a word processor. The sequenced results can be likened to a montage of other texts. This occurs because other texts within a particular aesthetic realm are a source of 'inspiration', inevitably leaving traces in the structures of the new text. Since a text is written in a particular tradition of communication, it follows that no text can be entirely original; a text always refers to other texts, otherwise it could not be understood. The use of the sampler has made this intertextuality more apparent, since a song can be created from the sequencing of snippets of sound as well as from recognisable fragments from other records. This practice has led to accusations of theft. In an assertion against this stigma, the following may state a position within the context of the discourse of house music and DJ culture:

> Stealing, as several people explain, is when someone else hears your idea and gets it out on disc locally before you do. It's nothing to do with borrowing or adapting riffs from old records. These are DJs, after all[433] [Garratt, 1986].

A self-conscious sense of intertextuality does not seem to be much of a problem to DJs, whose livelihood depends on the assembly of texts. It is the order in which they play their choice of records that makes or breaks their career. Their play list is their trademark. When a rather complex style of 'DJing' (British word) or 'spinning' (American equivalent) is employed, one is more likely to speak of a 'set'. The slow rolling groove of Frankie Knuckles, the techno sound 'washes of Derek May and the backward loops of Junior Vasquez are all very different and are recognisable in their remix work. Individual DJ styles can be distinguished from the choice of records, the way they are layered and the narrative order in which they are placed. Its complexity ranges from blending one record into another to creating

---

[433] (p. 23)

layers of tracks that employ vocals or a drum track from one record mixed with another. There are different degrees of creativity involved in this process, which can be polished to a high state of perfection when the competition is high between DJs. For instance, several Chicago DJs brought their own tracks to the clubs in order to enhance their performances.[434] These could range from basic bass and drum tracks to entire reconstructions of known songs, as Frankie Knuckles did. DJs spend a lot of time and money on research, in order to find records that no-one else has. In many different taste cultures that involve a DJ cult, whether it is Northern soul, hip hop or house, DJs often hide the identity of the records they use (for example by soaking off the label, sticking another 'wrong' label on top or by using a magic marker). Thereby DJs are protecting their right of authorship, which is what makes people pay to get to hear them. Authorship and thereby copyright ownership are connected to notions of property in the context of capitalism. Although a DJ set is not recognised by copyright law as being an original piece of work, the DJ knows only too well from practice that this is the case in terms of admiration from the punters, as well as in terms of income. Since the romantic notion of the unique expression of the individual artist is at the same time connected to the notion of competition, one could argue that capitalism and contemporary romanticism of the expressive 'genius' are intimately connected. Benjamin has argued that in the capitalist age of mechanical reproduction, the aura and authenticity of an original piece of art has disappeared; since '(t)he presence of the original is the prerequisite to the concept of authenticity', a reproduction cannot attain this quality [Benjamin, 1973]. However, these elements remain intact in the practice of the professional DJ who uses reproductions as building blocks for an authentic ritual soundscape. A similar issue is at stake for the producer and dance remixer, often a DJ, whose trademark is a specific choice of sound textures and a particular manner of (re)structuring a track. This secret knowledge will give the producer an aura of 'magic', which in turn will give him or her economic power.

It may be useful to see the modern DJ as a type of curator. In 1990 Brian Eno suggested:

If the author becomes someone who 'merely' assembles a network

---

434 See Chapter 2.

of texts, and then lets you, the reader, join them up (...) can he or she be said to be responsible for the shapes that emerge? Should we now then place curators in the same category as we place 'original artists'? (...) it is perhaps the curator, the connection maker, who is the new storyteller, the meta-author.
(...) We will stop dividing the world into 'authors' and 'readers', and start to recognize instead a continuum of involvement in the writing process[435] [Eno, 1990].

As consumers of records themselves, DJs tend to reinterpret them through a particular order of the records played, and by choosing only a specific part of a record as relevant, as well as sometimes simultaneously combining two or three tracks. This then produces an original text. Like a curator, the DJ takes the dancer along a gallery of sound experiences.[436]

The dancer then in turn re-interprets this text through movements of the body, perhaps alone or in dialogue with other dancers. The 'reader' therefore, whether in the role of dancer, DJ or user of sampling technology, contributes a mind set that is culturally specific and productive in itself. In *The Death of the Author*, Barthes in effect argues that the origin of meaning is with the reader:

Thus is revealed the total existence of writing: a text is made of multiple writings, drawn from many cultures and entering into mutual relations of dialogue, parody, contestation, but there is only one place where this multiplicity is focused and that place is the reader, not, as was hitherto said, the author. The reader is the space on which all the quotations that make up a writing are inscribed without any of them being lost; a text's unity lies not in its origin but in its destination[437] [Barthes, 1977].

It is perhaps confusing that Barthes still uses the conventional meaning of the 'origin' of the text, which begins elsewhere in an author. At the same time this 'author' is presumed to be at the end of its existence in a conceptual sense. However, the doubt of the position of authorship and the doubt of origin and therefore authenticity of a text is clear from the above. Perhaps a more

---

[435] {p. 14}
[436] CD-I interactive computer programming pushes the discussion on authorship yet further, since the programmer leaves it to the software user what creation will ultimately be produced.
[437] {p. 148}

146

workable definition of the author may come from Foucault:

> ... the author. Not, of course, in a sense of the speaking individual who pronounced or wrote a text, but in the sense of a principle of grouping of discourses, conceived as the unity and origin of their meanings, as the focus of their coherence[438] [Foucault, 1989].

This definition unties the romantic idea of an authentic truth that ultimately lies within the writer. It is the 'grouping of discourses'[439] and therefore the procedures which legitimate a text that are important to Foucault in the creation of meaning [Foucault, 1989].

In the discourse of house music it is the method of the DJ and the use of electronic technology such as sampling which create a text. Through the technique of fading and blending recordings, this text seemingly has no beginning or end. The texts used are themselves combinations of other texts. The order in which records are played makes comment on them. In a musical piece which uses recognisable samples a similar process occurs. This radical intertextuality creates a fabric of texts, each connected with another through cross referencing. The sensation which the shifting of meanings creates in this situation may be what Barthes describes as 'jouissance' or bliss:

> Text means tissue; but whereas hitherto we have always taken this tissue as a product, a ready-made veil, behind which lies (...) meaning (truth), we are now emphasizing, in the tissue, the generative idea that the text is made, is worked out in a perpetual interweaving; lost in this tissue — this texture — the subject unmakes himself, like a spider dissolving in the constructive secretions of its web[440] [Barthes, in: Wiseman, 1989].

Barthes uses this description in the context of literature of a modernist kind, the 'writerly text'. However, the notion of text as tissue in which 'the subject unmakes himself'[441] is one which can be applied to house music without much difficulty. As house music has a trance inducing beat, which seems to induce a sensual celebration of communitiy and which (in African-American gospel influenced productions) deals with a sense of religious bliss, its prominent

---

38 {p. 227}
39 {p. 227}
40 {p. 86}
41 See quote above.

intertextuality adds to the effect of ecstasy.[442] By never quite locking the meaning of the text into place, a desire to acquire a totality, an Imaginary, is created. Perhaps it is this desire which makes people dance all night and urges them to come back for more. However, the (intoxicated) dancer also may want to 'let go' of all desire to acquire a sense of totality. In that case the untying of the subject occurs in a state of complete jouissance, in a loss of its construction in language. This could result in a sense of vertigo, a type of freefall whereby one floats along with the currents of the sounds and rhythms and with the shifting meanings of soundbites. In these shifts of meanings, only surface values remain. Complete escape is thereby achieved; the dancer is lost in a type of ecstatic 'bubble' [Baudrillard, 1988a].[443] One could therefore argue that vocal tracks with recognisable song structures create a sense of pleasure, confirming the listener's sense of self by providing an imaginary 'mirror', while the further the tracks are removed from this familiar structure, the more likely it is that a sense of trance-like bliss can be achieved.

At the same time, it is the regular metronomic beat which frames this bliss. The often relentless four quarter beat is the only guide through a wash of sound textures and vocal urges to go for it and party and to need someone and to love someone and to feel it and to lose it completely. Although the beat is outside of the body, the development of soundsystems over the last twenty years now enables the sound volume to be that high in clubs, that its vibrations can be felt by, and its low bass frequencies enter, the body of the dancer. Thereby it begins to resemble the heart beat of the mother as the dancer is like a speechless infant in the moist and warm womb-like environment of the crowded dancefloor. The ecstatic bubble therefore takes on an emotional meaning which may explain why the house beat has become popular across cultural divides; up till the moment of writing, everyone has experienced the sensation of being inside the womb of one's mother, where one is surrounded by the sound of her heartbeat. When one performs physical exercise, the heart beat increases. Add to this effect a rhythm at a speed of 120 to 150 bpm (and perhaps higher if the dancer has an unusual amount of adrenaline in the bloodstream, or a substance with a similar effect, as

---

442 More on the definition(s) of the terms 'ecstasy' and 'trance' in the last part of Chapter 7.

443 'To each his own bubble; that is the law today' (p. 39) [Baudrillard, 1988a]. This statement refers to the fact that contemporary information technology allows a person to stay fixed in one place while communicating with the world. Escape from that world can also occur in one's own head, rather than in a physical place.

can be the case with the use of amphetamines such as the recreational drugs speed and ecstasy), then it may be possible that at times the dancer's heartbeat seems to 'synchronise' with the beat.[444] In that case separation between 'the self' and the outside world disappears; the dancer 'is' the music, like the infant imagines that it 'is' the mother. In this context, Richard Middleton's suggestion that music can be considered as a 'primary semiotic practice' supports my argument:

> The initial connotations of sound-structures (the origins of which may go back beyond the repetitive 'coos' of the mother even into the womb: the (equally repetitive) sound/feel of maternal breathing and heartbeat) are prior to any emergence of a subject, locating itself in opposition to any external reality (...) just as its quintessential structural tendency may be described as infinite repetition, or, in terms of psychological development, as the 'primal metaphor', in which everything is combined in a 'great similarity'[445] [Middleton, 1990].

House music serves the function of 'primal metaphor' in an excellent manner. As the dancer loses a sense of alienation, (s)he is 'reborn' in a world where only the music and its rhythm is the law. It is therefore in the actual process of the production and consumption of house music, at the moment of dancing to (i.e. physically engaging with) its sensual repetitive beat whilst being part of a warm[446] crowd, that its most effective meaning is created:

> ... it is a mistake 'to listen' to House because it is not set apart from its social and cultural context. (...) When House really jacks, it is about the most intense dance music around. Wallflowers beware: you have to move to understand the power of house[447] [Thomas, 1989].

In other words, in order to 'interface' with the bliss which house

---

444 However, at that speed a truly synchronised heart beat would not be comfortable or even possible. Even so, Russell Newcombe has pointed out that heart beats of 150 bpm have been found at raves [Newcombe, 1991].
445 {p.288}
446 Well, let's be honest about it: a hot and sweaty crowd with a generally friendly and unrestrained attitude. This discussion is expanded upon in Chapter 7, where I speculate on several metaphors which could be used to describe the relationship between DJ and audience.
447 {p. 33}

music can incite, one needs to participate. Its language and indeed its 'knowledge'[448] cannot be observed and remarked upon from any presumed outside 'neutral' point of view. Without being submerged in its physical presence, house music is quite meaningless; in other words, without physical and subjective interaction it does not produce a meaningful experience.

Copyright in the age of digital reproduction

The kind of definition of an origin of meaning and therefore of authorship as has been discussed above may indicate some of the problems concerning the definition of copyright. Cultural critics such as Barthes, Foucault and Benjamin as well as Baudrillard have an interest in the empowerment of the audience and ultimately the masses. House music is a good example of a kind of music which could achieve this. On the other hand, current copyright law is informed by an ideology which ultimately keeps hierarchical structures, which are based on ownership, intact. Institutions which traditionally capitalise on musical products such as record companies and publishing houses, have an interest in the current status of copyright law, which, in Britain, protects the rights of ownership of intellectual property by institutions and, since 1988, of individuals. In Britain the 'moral right' of the individual author has only just been recognised in the Copyright Designs and Patents Act of 1988 [Redhead, 1995]. However, the right of this type of author is a rather fragile one and seems to be defined in terms of capital power rather than in terms of 'origin' [Chesterman and Lipman, 1988] or of 'authenticity' [S. Jones, 1992]. Even so, with the widening and shifting of the definition of the author, one may doubt the practicality of the implementation of current copyright law. Either more needs to be included, which may ultimately stifle creativity, or otherwise concepts such as plagiarism need to be reconsidered.

In Britain, there are two types of copyright, the copyright of the sound recording, which is usually owned by the record company, and the copyright of the composition which is owned by the composer and writer but often shared with a publisher. Compositions are usually defined in terms of notation in the tradition of Western European

[448] This 'knowledge' includes constructions of identities, desire, aesthetic formalism as well as ethics in work practice and in human relationships and is experienced as a feeling, a sensibility rather than as a consciously articulated knowledge.

classical music, even though one does not need to register the copyright with notation sheet paper [Bagehot, 1989]. Musical forms which are based on a genre which stresses textures and rhythms, or what is called a 'groove' do not have the same level of copyright protection as those which are based on genres which stress lyrics and melody [The Timelords, 1988; Rose, 1994]. A lot of the DJ tracks produced under the umbrella name house music can be described as groove based. This means that the genre is financially vulnerable. Important parts of house music tracks are unprotected whilst being endangered by law suits concerning the use of samples. In addition, copyright law is biased towards those who can afford to file law suits rather than those who may need more protection. Ironically, as has been shown earlier in this chapter, copyright law has economically affected composers more favourably than performers and therefore recording studio technologies over performing technologies [Frith, 1983]. By not fully recognising the creative performing qualities of the use of affordable studio technologies such as samplers or the use of record decks, an entire section of artistic endeavour is ignored and perhaps even endangered. Perhaps if users of these technologies had a greater access to capital investment, entirely 'new' and 'original' tracks could be created, using 'real' instruments and 'real' performers. Yet, although DJ and club cultures may have their roots in an economic resourcefulness, they have resulted in the creation of culturally valid texts, within the context of a popular cultural tradition [Rose, 1994]. It seems clear that developments in digital technology, as well as in the production and consumption of music, are outdating copyright law at a fast pace [S. Jones, 1993].

Copyright law has no specific provisions to deal with the act of sampling. In Britain a precedent has not been set to date,[449] since most cases have been settled out of court. An American case concerning the use of sampling technologies in hip hop has set the mood for future proceedings. In 1991, a precedent was set on the use or rather the 'misuse' of samplers, when Gilbert O'Sullivan took Biz Markie to court in New York.[450] Biz Markie, a rap artist and therefore steeped in the DJ culture of hip hop, had 'lifted' eight bars

---

[449] The research for this section took place in spring and early summer of 1992. Since then (between 1992 and 1994) the British MCPS (mechanical copyright collectors) have taken the dance label Shut Up And Dance to court over sampling infringements and won the case. The label went bankrupt due to resulting costs, but still no precedent was set [Hyneman, 1995].

[450] Grand Upright Music v. Warner Bros Records (780 F. Supp. 182 (SDNY 1991)) [Schumacher, 1995].

of the introduction of the song *Alone Again (Naturally)*, by Gilbert O'Sullivan (MAM, 1972). Using this riff as the basis for his song, he also used some of the lyrics (a sample of three words) and adapted the title, calling it *Alone Again*. Biz Markie's argument was that he had meant it to be a 'parody'. In other words, this is a type of comment on another text, which is quite legitimate within the limits of current copyright law, both in the UK as well as in the USA. Nevertheless, the label of the artist, Cold Chillin', as a subsidiary of Warner Brothers, should have had the legal expertise to recognise the dangers should a substantial part of a song be used without copy clearance in advance. The case appeared when 250,000 copies of the album *I need a haircut*, which contained the song, were already available on the market. Since the song was not a 'straight' cover, Gilbert O'Sullivan did not give his consent. As a result, Judge Kevin Duffy, Federal Judge of the United States Court for the Southern district of New York who, it is alleged, has no experience in these kind of cases, ruled that the Biz Markie's album should be taken off the shelves by the following Monday, adding that 'thou shalt not steal'[451] [Ware, 1992]. The case ended in an out of court settlement, although a criminal prosecution was considered [NMS, 1992b; Schumacher, 1995].[452] In Britain the Copyright Designs and Patents Act of 1988 section 107, which is a section used to tackle piracy, could also be used to put sampling under criminal proceedings. Since 1956 in Britain the copyright owner has to give permission in advance for the use of a 'substantial part' of a work (which could be a sound recording). This is a rather vague term which seems open to definition [Bradwell, 1988]. However, James Ware, lawyer for Gilbert O'Sullivan, had no doubts regarding this issue when he argued in the British music trade magazine *Music Week*, that: 'If something is worth copying, it will, even if the extract is very short, be a substantial part of the original'[453] [Ware, 1992].

This American case has set the mood for a precedent on what is considered to be a 'substantial part'; the criminal offence of 'theft' is now defined as the use of a sample of a part of a song as the basis for a 'new' piece of work, whilst adapting the title and the lyrics for one's

---

451 {p. 4}

452 Thomas Schumacher's useful overview of the debate surrounding the cultural politics of sampling in the USA, especially in the context of rap and hip hop, was published after this thesis had been researched and written up [Schumacher, 1995]. It is recommended to the interested reader.

453 {p. 4}

own purposes. Although producers, such as the 'Enginicians' and the 'Musik Arbeiter', are more careful now in clearing the material they use, often the beginning and the underground artists, the 'Home Compu' and 'Wetware', have not got the capital or the knowledge to do so. In addition, there seems to be a certain unwillingness amongst house music producers to give in to the whims of the major record industry. In *DJ*, a British magazine 'for DJs and club people', the following quote has been highlighted by its editor:

> There's a really anti-sampling feeling going through the record industry and it's not the artists but the record companies and publishing houses. Even if the original artists says (sic) go ahead use my record, their record company can just turn around and say no or charge you ridiculous amounts of money for it. It's ridiculous because there's 10,000 reasons why you should be allowed to sample and only about two why you shouldn't[454] [Harris, 1993].

From an artistic point of view, Foucault's taunting question: 'What difference does it make who is speaking?'[455] [Foucault, 1984], makes sense when one accepts culture as a common good. However, within the context of a capitalist political economy of music, copyright of ideas is given a higher priority. Therefore, the difference in who is speaking is determined by who has the money, knowledge and willingness to assert the exploitation of a cultural product.

As concepts such as the author are redefined, so is the issue of authenticity. The authentic is tied to ideas of origin of a work of art as a fixed point, a 'presence in time and place' [Benjamin, 1973]. In Foucault's notion of the author, coherence is found within the realm of a discourse, its procedures legitimising only certain acts of 'truth' and therefore authenticity. However, in being aware of these procedures, one has to doubt forever an absolutely true reference point to which the notion of authenticity has been tied. As Foucault points out: 'The political question, to sum up, is not error, illusion, alienated consciousness or ideology; it is truth itself'[456] [Foucault, 1980].

Therefore, it would only be when an alternative discourse (which legitimates its own 'true' and 'normal' methods of production and

---

454 {p. 26}
455 {p. 120}
456 {p. 133}

consumption), such as that of DJ culture, becomes accepted in 'mainstream' culture that it becomes possible to argue for a different type of legislation.

Digital identity constructions

The notion of the author and specifically the identity of the author has been altered by the use of reproductive communication technologies as well as through a different method of consumption and way of 'reading' [Barthes, 1977; Foucault, 1989]. A space of anonymity has been created where one can play with the notion of identity. Computer musicians do not work in permanent easily identifiable bands, but rather in projects, whereby each project has a different combination of contributors, who often hide behind fictitious identities, such as the Dutch Speedy J. (Jochum) or Jean Baggerag[457] (Ardy Beesemer). The production of dance music in the studio is comparable to Mark Poster's notion of a 'game of masks' when he writes about the hidden identities of the users of computer communication [Poster, 1990]. The recorded voices and instrumental fragments from any culture, gender or race could be sampled and inserted into a new musical structure to become part of a forged identity. An English example is tribal house which is partly rooted in the cultural politics of a tradition of 'world music' which uses musical patterns and sounds from 'ethnic' recordings, such as African chants or the Australian Aboriginal didgeredoo. The 'other of Western culture'[458] [Poster, 1990] is thereby inscribed as a manifestation of a desire which wants to contain as well as control this 'other'. The owner of the technology of production is able to create identities and representations which approximate to the Lacanian notion of the Imaginary.[459] To an extent 'the other' actually becomes 'the self' when simulated by digital communication technologies [Baudrillard, 1988b]. Baudrillard suggests that the Imaginary ceases to exist when one simulates a reality, since at that moment the Symbolic overtakes

[457] This is a play on the Dutch term 'gabber' (see Chapter 4). 'Bagger' means mud or slush.
[458] {p. 128}
[459] According to subject theories based on the influential ideas of psychoanalyst Lacan, the imaginary comes into existence when a person imagines to have an immediate grasp of the real, even though it can only be known from the symbolic which represents and articulates it. A metaphor which is used to explain this process is the action of looking at a mirror, which then represents ('reflects') a sense of an imaginary self which seems to be an unfragmented unit in control of its actions and thoughts.

the Real altogether. In his own hyperbolical terminology he explains the effect of simulations as follows:

> The real is produced from miniaturised units, from matrices, memory banks and command models - and with these it can be reproduced an infinite number of times. It no longer has to be rational, since it is no longer measured against some ideal or negative instance. It is nothing more than operational. In fact, since it is no longer enveloped by an imaginary, it is no longer real at all. It is a hyperreal, the product of an irradiating synthesis of combinatory models in a hyperspace without atmosphere[460] [Baudrillard, 1983].

A record of a musical piece which has been constructed from layers of synthesised and decontextualised sounds could be seen as a type of simulacrum. This is defined by Fredric Jameson as an 'identical copy for which no original ever existed'[461] [Jameson, 1984]. An example of a simulated performance is the use of the sampled voice. Utilising a vocal from a different song in a remix or a new dance track, it seems as though someone has been singing to that particular track, while in fact the vocal line has been taken apart and restructured to fit a new piece of music. In European dance music there is a growing practice of the recycling of vocal lines of African-American divas in a manner which disregards the social and historical context of the original recording. Simulations therefore interfere with the notion of authentic identity.[462] For instance, in 1989, using the name Black Box for their project, the Italian producer team Goove Groove Melody based their piano driven track *Ride on Time* (Disco Magic & De/Construction, 1989) on some of Lolleatta Holloway's vocal lines from *Love Sensation* (Salsoul, 1980) [Cheeseman, 1993a]. Ms Holloway was distressed when she heard the result. *Ride on Time* reached number one in the British charts while she had never had that kind of success. To add insult to injury, her image was 'stolen' when the sampled vocals were 'performed' by another woman, Katherine Quinol, when Black Box appeared on television [Bradby, 1993]. After legal action was threatened Black Box offered her a financial reward in the form of an artist's contract. She initially

---

460 {p. 3}

461 {p. 66}

462 A process which is of interest in the context of a cultural critique as well as the copyright debate.

furiously refused this contract since her opinion on how her vocals were used had not been taken into consideration [ITC, 1992]. Her performance had been sampled and manipulated to fit someone else's imagination, which is painful when one identifies oneself with one's performances. In this sense it can be argued that the aura and authenticity of her performance had been violated as well as her sense of being as an 'unified subject'. In the British Copyright Designs and Patents Act, 1988, the concept of 'moral right' has been introduced in order to prevent this type of representational violence. However, this type of violence is subject to definition. A first act of 'violence' in this particular string of events was committed when a bootlegged record appeared on the Italian market, which contained several 'anonymous' acapellas, including Holloway's vocal lines for *Love Sensation*. Acapellas are much sought after tools for DJs, who use them in the mix with instrumental tracks. From there it is only a small step to create a new record from the available material. Because the acapellas had not been named, their original source had been effaced. It could therefore be argued that the use of vocals from the song *Love Sensation*, was an act in the 'hyper space' of cyber space which disregards the existence of any 'real' Lolleatta Holloway and her long lived experience which created the unique sound of her voice on the song. Traces of those vocals had become part of a simulation of a performance called *Ride on Time* for which an 'original' did not 'exist'.463 The notion of a 'moral right' is rendered meaningless in the face of the 'amorality' of a simulation.

According to cultural critic Fredric Jameson, contemporary cultural production is characterised by a sense of a-historical 'depthlessness' [Jameson, 1984]. Following this line of thought we therefore experience life as being in an eternal present. In contrast to the pessimism of Baudrillard and Jameson who see no way out of this seemingly meaningless and rather superficial cultural condition, Sol Yurick accepts the contemporary experience of everpresence as a creative event. He writes:

If the mythology of the past is *everpresent*, at least in the *memory* (distant signals presently felt, but not in any order) then it too is simultaneous even though the event is long gone. Seen in this way, event, and thus time, and thus life, become merely informational; that is to say an abstraction that can be handled in

---

463 In other words, an original was not recognised.

a non-real way with real effects. This is, after all, what dreams and surrealism are all about[464] [Yurick, 1985].

Dance clubs celebrate the everpresence, a *Living For The Moment* (Mercedes, Vinyl Solution, 1994), to a high degree. The creation of a new world of perception for even just one night has become part and parcel of its tradition. To Yurick the ability to affect our sense of reality is like an act of Voodoo magic; so long as the communicants believe in the reality of communication, it is real. This idea is not completely new but rather connects with a semiotic ontology which states that reality can only be understood and perceived though structures of articulation such as representations. Yurick wonders whether computer generated:

> ... systems manipulate the universe or a simulation of the universe? What certain intellectuals in modern society propose is electro-magic[465] [Yurick, 1985].

Baudrillard's notion of 'amorality' and Jameson's notion of 'depthlessness' as well as their conclusion that we now live in a time which heralds the end of history specifically affects those who have been at the top of the social hierarchy during the modernist era. On the other hand, culturally 'marginalised' social groups are (re)claiming the authority to write their own history and to embrace their own myths. In recycling and recontextualising texts from the past, a cultural history can be actively written and re-written. This activity is comparable with a tradition of oral story telling and can be found as part of a discourse of cultural resistance within the structure of African-American cultural politics which incorporates the moral obligation to honour one's cultural ancestors [Berry, 1992]. Before the arrival of the sampler or the record player, jazz musicians used parts of earlier songs and musical pieces in order to present a culturally coherent and historically informative performance [Toop, 1984]. In this manner a sense of cultural identity is produced which bonds an African-American community of consumers. A different sense of cultural authenticity, not in terms of isolated author or unique performance, but rather of a cultural tradition is hereby (re)stored in a cultural memory [Pratt, 1990]. Electronic reproductive technologies

---

464 {pp. 166 -167}; italics and brackets by Yurick.
465 {p. 24}

157

have made this process more efficient. To use samples of 'classic' disco records underlines a particular history of house music which focuses on an African-American and Latino cultural heritage within the 'gay' scene. Examples of a more confrontational use of these technologies in an African-American context can be found within the tradition of rap and hip hop [Rose, 1994]. Elsewhere, European and European-American industrial rock as well as techno celebrate a European cultural history with the use of samples of 'classical' music. As Andrew Goodwin puts it: '... the Age of Plunder is in fact one which recuperates its history, rather than denying it'[466] [Goodwin, 1990].

To write one's cultural history through the use of quotes is not necessarily an ethnocentric event; African-Americans have acknowledged a European influence, for instance, by sampling German band Kraftwerk [Dery, 1991], while the production of English tribal house such as *Earth Tribe* by Transglobal Underground (Nation Records, 1994) could be represented as a homage to non-European cultural 'ancestors'. Thus, developments in electronic reproductive technology are not the cause of an effacing or a (re)writing of history; rather it is the cultural context in which this technology is used which gives a (political) meaning to its ability to create cultural products which are more 'more real than the real'[467] [Baudrillard, 1987].

The manifestation of desire through the use of reproductive electronic technologies is therefore a political issue which revolves around the notion of power. In the context of gender studies and cyberculture Claudia Springer quotes D'Alessandro: '... for technophilliacs, technology provides an erotic thrill — control over massive power, which can itself be used to control others'[468] [K.C. D'Alessandro, in: Springer, 1991]. This desire for control could lead to 'techno erotics'. In view of a presumed patriarchal fear of female sexuality, one could consider the consequences of this concept in the context of digital recording technology. In European and Westernised cultures, gender roles are being eroded, especially now biological signifiers lose their importance with regard to gendered power relations when using computer technologies [Lury, 1993; Springer, 1991]. It could be argued that as computer technology and

---

[466] {p. 271}
[467] {p. 30}
[468] {p. 305}

reproductive technologies in effect decrease the importance of male domination, it is the technology itself which could be seen as threatening to the person who identifies with a traditional form of masculinity. 'The other', which threatens a loss of control over one's identity, could be contained through the use and mastering of that same technology, especially if its significance can be collapsed unto a construction of a sexuality [Huyssen, 1988b]. As has been described above, using Italians Black Box and Giorgio Moroder as examples, it is a common practice for European dance producers, who are mostly 'white', male and heterosexual, to employ especially 'black' female voices to articulate masculine desire. There are several reasons for this, one being that the African-American female vocalist has a prominent place in the history of soul music, which stems from its historical roots in the structure of gospel church ceremonies which feature a matriarchal front singer [Bradby, 1993; Pratt, 1990]. However, within the context of gender politics of patriarchy, the female diva is convenient because, like the early Hollywood female star, she symbolises the notion of a 'phallic woman', which presents no threat of castration to a traditional masculine identity[469] [Lury, 1993; Mulvey, 1989]. In addition, by sampling and disassembling the voice of the potentially threatening object, it can be controlled and represented in the place where the subject, the technophilliac, wants it to fit. Through the mastering of the threatening equipment, control is regained, over machine, woman and the non-'white' person all at once. This way the desire to alleviate the dread of lack of control and loss of an identity which is based on a definition of 'the other', is satisfied. The mystique with which music technology is sometimes presented by male technophilliacs to the female 'outsider' seems to be one of the barriers for women who want to have access to a similar control. In cyborg fiction, which produces the metaphors and 'terminal identity fictions'[470] [Bukatman, 1993] with which western patriarchal culture deals with electronic reproductive technologies, '(w)omen are typically associated with biological reproduction while men are involved in technological reproduction'[471] [Springer, 1991]. If

[469] Her seemingly central role and articulation of 'masculine' sexual desire mean that she does not remind the male of the fact that some people are not in the possession of a penis. In the context of a patriarchal society this lack could be a frightening thought to someone whose feelings of superiority are based on the fact of having such a genital organ. A reminder of a lack could create a fear of castration, whereby both lack and threat have been collapsed in symbolisation of the 'feminine'.

[470] {p. 9}
[471] {p. 319}

one would take this type of argument to its logical conclusion, it seems that for women the desire to master this kind of technology is of a different nature. The notion of masculine 'anxieties about the apparent excess of the maternal in a feminised contemporary culture characterised by replication'[472] [Lury, 1993] can not be applied to the feminine, although not necessarily female, subject. For this type of subjectivity, which does not have a masculine identity as informed by patriarchal sensibilities, there is no drive to be occupied in a technocratic manner in a bid against a potential loss of power.

Like other traditionally marginalised social groups, feminised, feminine and female subjects have begun to gain a recognised place in the network of power relations. The possibility of making one's own aural, textual and visual creations, utilising reproductive technologies within a DIY structure[473] is a cause for celebration, without a need to be driven by the desire to fetishise the technology involved. Whether one fears the loss or embraces the gain of power, the use of reproductive technology gives a pleasure of having a sense of creative control which is shared by all persons involved.[474]

Conclusion

Since the early 80s the production of house music has been made accessible due to the relatively affordable quality of (often Japanese) electronic musical instruments and the 'user friendly' manner in which they can be operated. The accessible production methods of house music, as well as the relative 'independence' of these productions from the major record industry, have given many small house music productions a type of DIY character. House music producers seem to have an uneasy relationship with large and financially powerful institutions within the record industry as well as with the state in the form of copyright law.

In a discussion of the concept of 'authorship' and of the production of meaning, I have suggested an inquiry into house music by viewing

---

472 {p. 213}

473 In addition to music making, computer technology has enabled the expansion of small press, poster and flyer manufacture, the creation of web pages, etc.

474 For further reading on the implications of the use of computer technology on the sense of self, see Haraway [Haraway, 1989], Poster [Poster, 1990], Springer [Springer, 1991], Dery [Dery, 1993a], Bukatman [Bukatman, 1993] as well as Baudrillard's theoretical writings from the 80s onwards, which have a contemporary science fiction quality.

it as a text which does not objectively produce an explicit meaning. Rather, its musical meaning depends on the way it is used, on the type of tracks which are combined by the DJ in a particular manner and on the place of its consumption. House music is a functional type of music which is made for and by DJs, to be played at dance parties and in night clubs. Only there, at a place where an opportunity is provided to engage with it in a physical sense and when it has been amplified enough to become a tactile-acoustic event, does house music become complete within the movements of the dancing crowd. Its musical interpretation shifts with each movement, which in its turn is related not only to the rhythmical stress of house music, but also to its quality of radical intertextuality, giving each beat a slightly new (cultural) space in time. In this process of 'listening' with the body a sense of bliss can be achieved. Added to the often sexually charged word-bites and lyrics, this bliss can give a sense of being unified with the tactile-acoustic space within the specific moment of consumption.

The use of electronic studio production technologies, such as samplers, has added to the construction of specific manifestations of desire, which can be linked to the construction of identities, in the context of post-modernist, post-colonialist, and feminist per-spectives. Hereby, desire comes into being from an urge to be in control, which creates pleasure. From a post-modernist perspective, 'the other' seems to have dissolved in the surface play with a many fold of possible simulated identities. From an African-American post-colonialist perspective, whilst honouring and recuperating cultural 'ancestors', cultural history is rewritten every time it is retold in order to establish a sense of rooted identity for a historically uprooted community. From a (psycho-analytical) feminist perspective, it seems that within patriarchal society, masculine men have a lot of interest invested in their seemingly established, although unstable, identities and therefore have a great desire to gain control over electronic technology which potentially could either threaten or enhance their social position. The latter type of desire may be one of many explanations of why, at the time of writing in 1994, more men than women were involved in the production of house music.

When consumed on the dance floor, the process of the continuous production of a fluid kind of meaning of house music could lead to a sense of total submersion without producing any rational sense at all. Thereby a type of untying 'the self' may result in a sense of (perhaps frightening) bliss. This idea of untying 'the self' will be further explored in the following chapter, which will focus on the spaces and technologies of consumption of house music.

7 Spectacular disappearance

We must produce our own dream[475] [Taylor, 1985].

The layers of music built up around them, like a sticky web that enmeshed its captive listeners, all entranced by a symphony of drugs, heat and the company of like-minded souls[476] [Geraghty, 1996].

We no longer partake of the drama of alienation, but are in the ecstasy of communication[477] [Baudrillard, 1988a].

Spectators see only the surface, but the ravers are already part of the scene, in the machinery. Beyond the spectacle lies total immersion; the end of the spectacle[478] [Plant, 1993].

Introduction

In order for a house production to be successful, not only is it necessary to have it played in sequence by a skilled DJ, but it also needs an appreciative audience in a space where people can gather to dance and where dance club technologies can be utilised. Since house music and its related musical forms are mostly functional,[479] they are best enjoyed in the settings for which they have been produced. In the

---

[475] {p. 209}
[476] {pp. 31-32}
[477] {p. 22}; italics by Baudrillard.
[478] {p. 7}
[479] See Chapters 5 and 6.

context of the disappearance of a clear homology between social identification and music, cultural theorist Lawrence Grossberg has noted that a different way of consuming dance music has developed:

Rather than being the affective center and agency of people's mattering maps, music's power is articulated by its place on other mattering maps, by its relation to other activities, other functions. *Rather than dancing to the music you like, you like the music you can dance to.* Thus the music's popularity depends less on its place within specific alliances than on the construction of hyperalliances as venues for other sorts of affective relations and activities[480] (my italics) [Grossberg, 1994].

In the context of house music, these 'affective relations and activities'[481] are, amongst other things, a forging of (temporary) 'communities' based on the sharing of a space and of a 'feeling' which will be described and discussed in this chapter. It is at its moment of consumption, at a house party in its many different guises, that the medium of house music is complete. 'Medium' is meant here in an unconventional 'intangible, diffuse and diffracted'[482] sense [Baudrillard, 1983]. This notion of the medium is to be understood as something which enables the articulation rather than a simple 'channelling' of an idea or a sensibility. In the case of house music, and indeed all club music, this includes recording technology; music technological skill; the structure of the music; the qualities of carrier which is vinyl; the skills of the DJ; the dance space and its technologies; and the physical abilities of the dancers. As Marshall McLuhan puts it: '... it is the medium that shapes and controls the scale and form of human association and action'[483] [McLuhan, 1994].

One could say that the different forms and sensibilities that house music has acquired have been negotiated between, on the one hand, the parameters of technology ('the medium') and, on the other hand, a variety of historically formed social and cultural structures. During my ethnographic research, I found that there were local differences in cultural production and consumption of house music, as has been described in the three chapters on Chicago, England and the Netherlands. However, in addition, I found not only similarities in

---

480 {p. 56}
481 See quote above.
482 {p. 54}
483 {p. 9}

technologies of production, but also in dance spaces and their specific technologies and, at times, even similarities in the resultant subjective experience to the dancer in the shape of a sense of abandon, of loss of self, where the sensual, the spiritual and a sense of community come together.

The first part of this chapter will discuss the spaces of consumption which most house events have in common. An example of these is the dance club, the social function of which is mainly that of a meeting place where, traditionally, one can play the ritual of mating on an uncommitted physical level and where one can forget one's daily realities. As the sophistication as well as availability of new technologies has increased, club environments have become more successful in fulfilling the latter function.

The second part will describe some of the recreational chemical intake by participants which is conducive to their quest for 'losing it'.[484] Dance drugs as a body technology have not only contributed to the way house music is consumed, but also to the production of particular formal aspects of this music. As argued in Chapter 6, production is not isolated from consumption; rather, cultural products such as house music develop and mutate as part of a dialogue between performer and audience. With the involvement of both DJs and dancers in the production of house music, who often release material independently without the delays which are caused by corporate structures of the major music industry,[485] the reaction to local popular taste can be rapid. Therefore, the popularity of a particular drug in a prominent dance space can lead to the incorporation of its psychological and physiological effects, such as fragmented perception[486] or an increased heartbeat,[487] into its soundtrack. However, it must be stressed that a physiological condition does not determine a cultural effect. Rather this condition is interpreted and given a meaning within a specific cultural framework. Therefore, house music as a medium within a certain cultural setting provides limits and conditions within which, for instance, effects of dance drugs can be articulated. Since different drugs do have different effects, the more prominent categories will be briefly discussed separately in the context of dance music.

---

[484] Losing both an awareness of daily social realities as well as a sense of alienated self.

[485] See Chapter 6.

[486] As can be due to an intake of LSD; arguably, this influence can be traced in Acid House.

[487] This may be due to the use of amphetamines and/or the physical effort of dancing; listen to, for example, the fast beats of Gabber House.

A discussion of what place can be given to club culture based on house in the context of subjectivity, spectacle, festival and surveillance will close this chapter. During the 80s, English club culture as a spectacle seemed to turn in on itself. Flaunting had no other purpose than to flaunt, dancing had no other purpose than to dance. By 1987, at the same time as house music gained popularity in England and other places outside of Chicago, it looked as though this process accelerated. Especially in England, specific environments were created,[488] where the ritual of mating transformed into a form of anonymous celebration of togetherness as a community. This was enhanced by the use of dance drugs such as the entactogenic drug ecstasy. The term 'entactogenic' indicates an effect of increased tactile awareness; since tactility can be sensed by the entire body, this means that, subjectively, one has a many-sided empathic relationship with the environment. If, in contrast, one would have an increased visual awareness, this could result into a one-sided relationship between the self and the object at which the gaze is directed. In addition, the spaces for which house music has been designed, emphasise a tactile space since they contain sound systems which are so loud that the drums and basslines can be felt by the body, while, at the same time, the visual space is disrupted by special effects. In a tactile rather visually emphasised space,[489] the place of the observer, who used to be part of the audience in search of social and perhaps sexual partners, becomes that of the outsider. To be part of the 'club', during the heady times of house and rave parties, meant to be immersed [Plant, 1993]. As clubbers lost their selves into the raving mass, so their mastering gaze disappeared together with the ability to 'make sense' of it all [Melechi, 1993; Rietveld, 1993]. The meaning of the spectacle, seemingly so 'obvious' to the observer, changed within the perception of its participants, since at the height of the night spectator and spectacle became one. Dayan and Katz have proposed that the opposite pole of the spectacle is the festival, which they have described as follows:

Festival (...) is diffuse in focus. No simple picture or pageant imposes itself monopolistically on participants[490] [1985].

---

488 First called acid house parties and later raves; see Chapter 3.

489 An interesting, although speculative, discussion on tactile-acoustic space by McLuhan can be found in Chapter 3 of *The Global Village* [McLuhan and Powers, 1992].

490 {p. 17}

Like a carnivalesque festival, a house music event is very much dependent on an 'unregimented'[491] interaction between its participants. Therefore, regulating licensing laws as well as increasingly sophisticated methods of surveillance by the state and a growing information industry can be conceived of as an over-production of interference with a festival 'spirit'. Baudrillard suggests the following in the context of culture in the westernised world at the end of the twentieth century: 'Saturated by the mode of production, we must return to the path of an aesthetic of disappearance'[492] [1988a].

In the case of some house parties, the 'disappearance' of both the actual event (from the surveying gaze) as well as the disappearance of a sense of alienated self (which is linked to its own 'mastering' and objectifying gaze), became an aesthetic as well as a tactic to find a release [Rietveld, 1993] from the 'obscenity'[493] of the 'immediately transparent'[494] gaze [Baudrillard, 1988a].

Dance space technologies

In the previous chapters on Chicago, England and the Netherlands, it has been shown that in addition to the more traditional dance club environment, there have been a tremendous variety of physical spaces in which house music has been enjoyed with a similar range in their legal status. In summary, for instance, in the USA there are the so-called rent parties, where one gives a party in one's own house and charges guests in order to be able to pay the rent [Blanchard, 1992]. In the Netherlands, conference centres and sports halls were used for legally organised dance 'marathons', such as MTC in Rotterdam in 1991. In England, popular spaces were those provided by deserted structures of post-industrial and of post-aristocratic society as well as empty EEC subsidised farmer's fields and British hippie festival circuits. In all three locations squatted premises were used for non-legislated events on a temporary basis, such as deserted industrial work spaces and warehouses (often on the outskirts of city

---

491 'Unregimented' in the sense that no formal rules have been designed by an agency of institutional power. However, within the events themselves there are implicit 'rules' and structures, which will be discussed in this chapter.
492 {p. 71}
493 {p. 21}
494 {p. 21}

centres in order to prevent detection) or inner city residential spaces. One-off events of various degrees of legal status often took place far away from any densely populated area. In England, since the introduction of the Entertainments (Increased Penalties) Act, 1990, which requires that dance parties need a licence for charging an entrance fee, some of these outdoor events have been free for all, such as the Rave In The Cave events in the North West of England between 1992 and 1994. At the other end of the commercial scale, there have been pay parties which were organised to different degress of sophistication and legality; for example, at some English commercial parties, such as Live the Dream and Sunrise in 1989 (which attracted ten thousand or more ravers), lawyers were present on the premises to deal with police threats of closure and confiscation. More up-market premises were hired for private parties, such as marquees on the grounds of an estate or castles, like the Boy's Own parties of 1988-89. River boats were also used as house party spaces for more exclusive gatherings, which were especially popular in the Netherlands and, to lesser extent, in England. Other types of physical spaces were roller-discos, such as Radioactive and Twilight Zone in London in 1993, as well as (ex)trade centres, such as Leeds Corn Exchange for Soak, 1992 to 1994.

In addition, since 1989 in England, legal parties or 'raves' took place which resembled theme parks. They offered several marquees with different styles of dance music (mainly variations of house music) and attractions such as bouncy castles, dodgem cars, carousels or other fairground attractions. Not only farm fields such as those used for Joy in Rochdale in 1989, but also car racing tracks were used as premises for such events, like for instance Perception at The Speedway Stadium in Norfolk in 1991. This trend was in line with the developments of outdoor entertainment in western affluent capitalist society during the mid 80s, when complete hyperreal worlds were created such as Alton Towers, the Robin Hood museum and the Yorick centre in England and much earlier on, Disneyland and the many waxwork museums in the USA, which incidentally, like rave parties, all depended on private transport by car for access [Baudrillard, 1983; Eco, 1986; Tomlinson, 1990]. Although seemingly unaware of this particular development during the 80s, The Henley Centre for Forecasting has made the following forecast for British leisure activities in the 90s:

We believe that out-of-home leisure will make a come-back in the 1990s — but activities which can most easily be replicated in the home remain vulnerable. Venues should therefore concentrate on offering a 'total experience' that the television cannot match [Veares and Woods, 1993].

Perhaps one could call these huge kinds of English raves 'the theme parks of the outlaw' [Eshun, 1993], a carnivalesque festival re-packaged and sold back to a crowd which desires the illicit celebratory experience of the grotesque body [White, 1989].[495] It is of interest to note in this context that since 1989 many British free (travellers) festivals took place on the edge of legality which sported sound systems which played music related to house like techno, trance or jungle. These (perhaps) counter cultural occasions [Rietveld, 1993], as well as other open air raves, have acquired an increased outlaw status when the draconian new Criminal Justice and Public Order Act, 1994, was implemented [Platt, 1994; Hutchings, 1994; Kingston, 1994; Stone, 1996].[496] The organisation of most of these free festivals is traditionally akin to a non-hierarchical 'organic' web, involving a network of many people operating small ventures[497] rather than the hierarchical set up of commercially organised events [Collin, 1991; Marcus, 1993; Lowe and Shaw, 1993; Champion, 1993].

It is clear from the above that the physical spaces and organisational structures for house related events can vary enormously. Even though there are a great number of private and public parties with or without the required licences (which vary for

---

[495] See discussion at the end of this chapter.
[496] By Autumn 1995, some sound systems have been confiscated under the new CJA. For instance, in the weekend before the examination of my PhD, on 8 and 9 July 1995, a Freedom Network Festival, The Mother, was organised in defiance to the new legislation at a secret location on an airfield in Devon, where the police confiscated equipment which had arrived earlier than their alert and also blocked the few access routes. As a result the party was reduced to a few hundred people without sound systems, who, according to eye witness reports, had a good time anyway. However, on that occasion, the medium of house music, its multitude of technologies, was disabled by police action based on a certain interpretation of the CJA. Thereby techno trance, a certain hybrid of house music, acquired its oppositional status in relation to the state.
[497] Such as selling foods, drinks, accessories or playing music.

each geographical area),[498] most dance music has been, and still is, consumed in dance clubs. These spaces have been specially designed for dancing, are often in easy reach of city centres and are licensed according to local regulations. This means less risk for the organiser. However, the profit margin, which may increase with risk, will also remain smaller, since for the punter there is a certain excitement in attending a party at an unusual location; in addition, perhaps the less strict ruling on drug use may make some of the illegal parties a bit more energetic. Having said that, for a large proportion of the dance loving audience, clubs are more comfortable to attend; the sound system has been designed to suit the dance space; there are facilities for refreshments; seated areas have been provided; sometimes air-conditioning or other cooling systems have been installed; and there are legally prescribed quantities of toilets and fire exits [DJ, 1993].

Whatever physical space has been chosen, the basic requirements for a house music party are to have a space to dance; to have some 'other worldly' visual effects; to have a sound system with sufficient amplification; to have a DJ who is able to mix records between two or more record decks; and to have a crowd which is willing to enjoy its company and the music with a certain intensity of celebration. Despite geographical and social differences, judging by the many parties at which I have been present and taking into account both oral and written descriptions, it seems there are definitely similarities in which the variety of physical spaces have been used: the total abandon with which people dance; the frenzied sense of hedonist escape; the sense of a disappearance of daily rationality, the heat generated by sweating dancing bodies (when the event takes place indoors); the booming bass drum in a steady four quarter beat; and the artificially produced smoke and the disorientating light effects are all aspects of a typical house music event, which thereby define a cultural space. A Dutch eye witness report from Spring 1989 sums this up very well when describing, as an outsider, an acid house party at a club in Amsterdam. There, at that time, (acid) house as a musical form and as a pattern for a social gathering had been distilled to some of its 'essential' elements:

---

[498] For instance, one may need a licence to run a club or a paid party, another licence to be open to the public at certain hours or to sell liquor or to dance; there needs to be approval on the amount of available fire exits and toilet facilities while the fire brigade has to judge how many people can be safely allowed inside a party space. Also, the police need to be satisfied that no illegal activities take place on the premises, such as the selling or using of illegal substances (i.e. most dance drugs).

Een diepe, zware bas-dreun komt ons al van heel ver tegemoet. Door een lange gang, spaarzaam verlicht door enkele blauwe en rode lampen, lopen we in de richting van waar de muziek vandaan komt. Overal schuivelen mensen voorbij, de armen omhoog en zich voortbewegend op de maat van de muziek. In de lage, overwelfde zaal is het broeierig en benauwd. Met zijn '120 beats per minuut' beukt de muziek in op de bezwete hoofden. De zenuwachtig flikkerende stroboscoop-lichten maken dat je nauwelijks recht kunt blijven lopen. Iedereen is in beweging. De zaal, op het podium, zelfs aan de bar 'kicken' de mensen mee op het snelle ritme van de muziek. Het is feest. Bijna iedereen lacht en schijnt elkaar te kennen. (...) De temperatuur in de zaal heeft inmiddels het kookpunt bereikt. De lucht is zo vochtig dat er straaltjes water langs de marmeren zuilen naar beneden komen druipen[499] [de Lange, 1989].

(Eng. trans.) A deep, heavy bass booms towards us from a long distance. We walk in the direction from where the music comes, through a long corridor which has been dimly lit by some blue and red spots. Everywhere people shuffle past us, arms raised, moving in the rhythm of the music. In the low vaulted hall the atmosphere is sweltering and sultry. With its '120 bpm' the music batters onto the sweat covered heads. The nervously flashing strobe lights cause one to be hardly able to walk straight. Everyone is in a state of mobility. The hall, on stage, even at the bar people get a 'kick' out of the fast rhythm of the music. It's party time. Nearly everyone laughs and seems to know each other. (...) In the meantime the temperature in the hall has reached boiling point. The air is so damp that condensation runs down along the marble columns.

At these types of events, the participants are preoccupied with the all embracing sound of the music which, if the promoter gets it right, is amplified and reproduced through speakers which have the potential to create such a loud bass sound that it makes the body vibrate. This boom of the bass drum is often the first thing one notices when looking for a club or (perhaps obscured) party where house music is being played. For instance when driving around the countryside the windows of cars transporting party people were

---

[499] {newspaper}

opened in order to hear in which direction to drive. Another example are parties which took place in English tower blocks on council estates which looked deserted at night, where it was the bass drum which guided the partyhead to a dance occasion which may be on the eighth floor of one of three tower blocks.

It is the pace of this bass drum which dictates the movements of dancers. The Dutch article above mentions that 120 bpm is a fast rhythm. Perhaps this was the case in comparison to electro, hip hop, funk or the dance music played at New York clubs like Paradise Garage in the early 1980s.[500] However, some disco tracks or the 'white' 'gay' HiNRG have been produced at faster speeds. During the mid-1990s, despite efforts by connoisseurs of 'classic' house to keep the pace down, 120 bpm was generally considered by contemporary dance audiences as too slow. By 1996, gabberhouse had reached 'devilish' pulse speeds of 200 bpm and higher [Carvalho, 1996].

When judging a club, the lighting system is not often talked about in the large range of dancezines[501] which are available; they rather discuss music, DJ-personalities and club people as well as drugs which, for example, improve tactility. However, professional club magazines like *Disco Mirror* or *DJ* do supply reviews of the newest developments in visual technologies, which are able to create a dream space out of any physical space. Together with the music this enables the crowd to be 'transported' to a different world; the most important requirement of club and party lighting is that 'normal' visual perception of space is ruptured in a way that pleases or arouses the crowd, so that the tactile and acoustic space, created by a loud sound system with a sensuous bass sound, is accentuated. For example, grim looking concrete walls could be made to disappear by bathing them in a luscious coloured light; by hiding them behind projection screens; by being painted black whilst props are highlighted or by being veiled by a curtain of smoke. Pubs could be turned into psychedelic dens by covering the walls with white cotton sheets and using these as projection screens for whatever is seen to be conducive to the spirit of the night. Small basements as well as large warehouses lost their visual dimensions and the view of their occupants when acid house parties set the tone, which required

---

[500] Music in the style of Paradise Garage 'classics', also popular at New Jersey's Zumbar club is referred to as garage music; see Chapter 2.

[501] See Appendix C.

spaces filled with smoke and only a strobe as light source (fragmenting one's perception of movement and thereby one's sense of time giving a sense of timelessness). Large soap bubbles, specially designed for dance floors, which submerge the crowd have been used with an effect of temporary visual disablement, initially in custom built places such as can be found in the Balearic island Ibiza[502] [Alvarez and Santander, 1993], but since 1991 imported for special one off events by clubs like Parkzicht in Rotterdam and The Haçienda in Manchester. Together with set design, some of the more exclusive or established events can use visual effects to create a theme. An example of this was Shiva night in The Haçienda in 1990, which incorporated sets with polystyrene statues of Buddha and Shiva, as well as a particular lighting which was bright orange and deep violet reflected onto artificial smoke; the effect was like a temple shrouded in incense. In contrast, in 1988, the same space looked like a holiday in the sun on its legendary HOT nights, due to a yellow sunny lighting, a little pool and many other props such as beach balls, ice sticks as well as the club audience wearing their beach outfits.[503] Although one can hire excellent up to date lighting and projection equipment for a one-off event, these technologies can be improved upon in a club to the advantage of the specific space. In the end it is very much dependent on the management if such improvements are made. Sometimes a club can thrive on its past reputation although the equipment has become inefficient, while a one-off event needs to sparkle with the best it can afford in order to advertise itself and thereby make the next event yet more successful.

In addition to being a culturally designed physical space, a club is a socially defined space where a crowd can make or break the occasion. For this reason, a form of selection takes place as to who is allowed to enter this space. This can be achieved, for example, through the use of flyers which have been designed to announce an event or a new club night [Rose, 1991; Rietveld, 1992b; *Ravescene Magazeen*, 1992]. Through the appeal of the design and the information it gives,

---

[502] In August 1995 I finally made it to Ibiza. My experience of a foam party at dance nightclub Amnesia was one of bewilderment, especially since I had only just arrived on the island and, more importantly, I was a female on her own. The attitude of the crowd was unlike the British raves and house parties I had attended; most girls escaped the dance floor when the foam came down from the soap canons on the balconies and the boys roamed around to grope and snog whatever female dancer was left in the middle of the confusion. This was an event at the height of the holiday season, where conventional club attitudes, such as finding a sexual mate, were foregrounded.
[503] See Chapter 3.

a certain crowd is hopefully drawn which identifies with the same taste [Thornton, 1995]. Apart from the name of a particular night, the design, the promises of particular facilities and sometimes of a certain type of music, it is also the name of a (guest) DJ which will attract a specific crowd. However, in England and elsewhere in the early 1990s, the focus seemed to shift temporarily from the cult of the DJ to the cult of the organisation which puts on the night. Therefore in England, sound systems and DJ collectives like DIY from Nottingham or Spiral Tribe from the free festival circuit have a following which is just as loyal. Also, party organisations, such as Soak in Leeds, or club nights, like Renaissance in the English Midlands, have attracted a regular audience across several venues, in the same way as a 'name' DJ, such as Norman Jay, can have a loyal following. Similarly, both in the Netherlands as well as in places like Chicago and New York, party organisations have attracted regular crowds at its events despite the use of different locations and even, at times, different DJs. It is publicity generated by techniques such as word-of-mouth, reviews, posters and, especially, flyers, handed out at specific parties and record shops, which gives an overall public image to these organisations.

So, apart from the design of the flyer, the place where one receives the information is of importance to define a crowd. At the end of a party with a certain type of music or theme, flyers are given outside the venue in order to attract that crowd to similar events. Adverts for parties with a bias towards house music will not be available at record shops specialised in rock or mainstream pop. In a similar manner, adverts are placed in magazines with the right target audience. If a party is underground for whatever reason, then word of mouth is usually the route of communication; in this way only a certain, often small, social circle will be part of the crowd. An example of a very large crowd drawn through this method was the Avon Free Festival near the English town of Castlemorton in June 1992, which attracted 25,000 people despite the fact that the site was unknown, even to the sound systems, until 24 hours before it began [Marcus, 1993; Lowe and Shaw, 1993]. The mobilisation of party people on a large scale in such a small time span is possible through a network connected by modern private communication and transport technologies, such as telephones, fax machines, portable phones and cars. These technologies have been used throughout the time that there were many large scale illegal parties in both England and the

Netherlands during the late 1980s and early 1990s. Since around 1992 the world computer net has provided bulletin boards for raves and house music events. Initially an American feature, since 1994 several British bulletin boards have been made available for dance parties [Mixmaster Morris, 1994].

Another manner in which to create a certain crowd is by using the procedure of a social filtering system at the entrance of a dance space. Clubs and some of the larger parties employ security teams, or bouncers, in order to prevent 'trouble' both at the entrance as well as inside in order to pick the type of person who would have a positive effect on the sensibility of a particular night [Humphreys, 1990; Bonsu, 1991; Bunyan, 1991; Loehnis, 1991, Campbell, 1991]. 'Trouble' could be aggressive or disturbing behaviour of clientele, but in licensed spaces 'trouble' is also defined as the selling of illegal drugs. Apart from this internal policing, at the more exclusive occasions there is also a 'host' or 'hostess' at the door who will decide who will be allowed entry on the grounds of 'attitude' (like friendliness) and dress sense. Other criteria may be gender ('single ladies free'), sexuality (of importance to 'gay' clubs), race and/or class hidden in dress codes such as 'no trainers', as well as, in some cases, whether one knows the organisers, security, DJs or other staff at the event. At many raves in England during the late 1980s criteria of gender, sexuality, race and class seemed to be largely subdued. When the people inside a club feel like they belong to 'The Club', a dance event will gain a special quality, which gives a sensation of 'stepping' out of one's 'ordinary' way of experiencing the self. A fragile moment of a sense of belonging to a community is thereby set up, which needs protection. Selective advertising and door policy as well as a certain choice of space (neighbourhood, accessibility and visual design) and music (mellow or fast and aggressive) can add to the prevention of this temporary community falling apart. Sometimes a common choice of dance drugs can also add to a sense of cohesion, which will be discussed in the next section.

Dance drugs

Dancing at a pace which is demanding combined with flashing lights and a loud thumping pulsing sound has physiological effects, which are calming (due to the painkilling substances produced by exercise), exciting (due to the speed of the music of at least 125 bpm), dehydrating and disorientating (due to the visual effects as well as to the music not always being synchronised with the body). Perception is affected by the music and the space in which it is consumed. However, it is also influenced by physiological processes which are not auditory or immediately social. Body technologies are the devices which can alter and enhance these processes. This part will discuss various devices which are used by partakers of house music events in order to enhance a feeling of 'other worldliness' and of escape from daily reality. Although for some the music without additives is enough to 'transport' the dancer, much has been reported in England and the Netherlands about the dance drugs taken at these occasions [Newcombe, 1991; Lifeline, 1993], especially the drug 'ecstasy' [Adelaars, 1991; Korf et al., 1991; Saunders, 1993]. Other drugs most commonly used are amyl-, butyl- or isobutyl-nitrites (poppers), amphetamines (speed), LSD (acid), cocaine (coke), cannabis (draw and grass), [Newcombe, 1991] and alcohol, as well as caffeine and sugar contained in drinks and sweets and plenty of tobacco in the form of cigarettes.[504] In this context, I use the word 'drug' not to distinguish between what is legal and what is not; rather the word 'drug' refers to a substance which affects the user in a physiological manner, with noticeable results to the user's mental state. The drugs taken enable the user to last through the night and to make it an ecstatic experience. Some drugs cause the user to want to be entertained at a more surreal level, to keep up with the chemical intake. Therefore, the music produced for house parties, acid house parties and raves do often have drug related or drug influenced aspects. In turn this may cause the listener to get a kind of 'druggy' feel, even when not taking drugs at all.

Many HiNRG, disco and house records often have an instrumental break about two thirds into the track which carries a lot of echo or flanging effects.[505] This sounds as if the song is rolling around in one's head akin to the effect of a moment of change in blood pressure, for instance just before fainting or perhaps of having a high fever. This break may be called the 'popper bit' of a record [Savage, 1993b].

---

504 Other drugs, such as smart drugs (legal substances such as herbal teas and other cocktails) and 'liquid E' have been identified [Maughan, 1994], but are marginal to the story of house music and, to date, have not had a major influence on dance music's formal aspects.

505 Both echo and flanging are ways of processing a sound. With an echo the sound is repeated, with flanging the higher frequencies of a sound are compressed and then expanded, giving an effect like a white noise on the radio which is altered when tuning between stations.

Existing in the forms of amyl-, butyl- or isobutyl-nitrate, poppers are a drug which affects the flow of blood and which, despite some claims of related fatalities [Alcorn, 1994; Bowen et al, 1992; Biol et al., 1994], is legally available in Britain.[506] However, since February 27th, 1991, it has been put on the list of illegal narcotics in the USA [Editorial: Capital Gay, 1991]. Like glue or other evaporating substances, it is used through inhalation and the effects of a sniff last only for a few minutes. Its main sales points have been clubs and shops which cater for a male 'gay' clientele. It is claimed that apart from enhancing the experience of sex because of its heady rush effect, it also helps to relax the sphincter of the anal orifice, thereby being a useful substance for people who practice anal sex. Poppers have entered dance clubs via the male homosexual dance scene and are used on the dancefloor in order to recreate a sense of sexual 'rush' and to feel 'at one' with the tactile-acoustic environment. Amongst the interviewees in Chicago it was common consent that in its heyday the floor of the Warehouse was mopped with poppers to give its clientele a rush of excitement. In New York and London, 'gay' dance clubs have spiked their air conditioning systems with poppers for the same reasons. The sense of a dizzy sexual rush caused by poppers is carried on in formal aspects of house music, for instance in parts of a contemporary dub mix by New York based house DJ David Morales of *Throb* by Janet Jackson (Virgin, 1994). Between 1979 and 1994 in both the Netherlands and England I have witnessed many non-anal sex inclined persons using and abusing poppers. In England it has been and still is very popular amongst ravers, perhaps because it is legal and relatively cheap. In the early to mid-90s it sold at £5 for a small bottle, which may last several nights, depending on how many people ask for a whiff from it.

LSD or 'acid' is used by members of the dancing crowd [Newcombe, 1991] in order to get a giggly high and to have an experience of being submerged in the sound, lights and social company of dance events. It is an orally taken hallucinogenic drug which loosens and at higher dosages even dissolves habitual structures of perception [Stevens, 1989; Siegel, 1989]. In Britain it is listed as a Class A drug under the

---

[506] When sniffed in large quantities, a lowered resistance to illness has been reported by its users, as well as a risk of haemorrhage due to the widening and narrowing of the capillaries or perhaps cardiac arrest. Some deaths in connection with amyl- and isobutyl-nitrate are known, but it is difficult to prove that these fatalities can be solely attributed to the (ab)use of this substance [Alcorn, 1994; Bowen et al., 1992; Biol et al., 1994]. Many users who insist on frequent deep inhalation end up with a hangover headache the next day.

Misuse of Drugs Act 1971, thereby 'attracting the highest penalties' [Newcombe, 1991]. Even so, it is relatively cheap; in the late 1980s and early 1990s it cost around £5 for one 'tab' and for the purpose of dancing this could be shared between four people, whereby its physical effect lasts between six to twelve hours. Taken in a party environment, it ensures a complete sense of escape from daily realities. It also causes the dancer to allow the music to take over the will to move the body in a rationally controlled manner. As the music gets wilder, so will the dancer without any sense of social reserve. Certain fluctuating sounds have been incorporated in house music which take the acid user to an even further state of incoherence of the mind. In 1987 the term acid house was coined in Chicago when Phuture produced, *Acid Tracks* and *Your Only Friend* by Phuture (Trax, 1987):[507]

> (...) Acid House has a rather schizophrenic and psychedelic 'feel', not unlike Acid Rock. The texture of the bass-line continually changes and voices and other fragments of stolen sounds make a 'disembodied' appearance. The 'Acid' (the wobbly random synthesized sequence, originally produced by a Roland TB303 which had lost its memory) is secured by a 'frame' of an insistent four quarter beat at around 125 beats per minute, which in effect enhances its hypnotic appeal[508] [Rietveld, 1993].

Larry Sherman, the owner of Trax claimed he wanted to call this music Acid Tracks because it reminded him of the psychedelic madness in acid rock [Sherman, 1992]. One of its composers, DJ Pierre, said he felt inspired by the dancers in Chicago club the Music Box who he believed took acid [DJ Pierre, 1992]. The name most certainly inspired the popular imagination in Britain and resulted in a populist mass marketing of house music [Rietveld, 1993].[509]

Rather than addressing the subject of 'acid', the actual lyrics of *Your Only Friend* (Trax, 1987) discuss, in an ironic manner, the negative social effects of the drug cocaine. Cocaine is an illegal substance in all of the three researched locations and is listed in Britain under Class A in the Misuse of Drugs Act 1971. In the house party scene it is usually taken in the form of a powder, which is sniffed into the nose

---

[507] See Chapter 5.

[508] {pp. 54 - 55}

[509] See also Chapters 2 and 3.

178

'snorted') or rubbed on the gums, rather than the smoking of cocaine ocks (crack). Its effect of exuberant and confident behaviour lasts for around 25 minutes; it numbs the nervous system in such a way that he user feels no tiredness [Snyder, 1986]. For some people this extra ittle 'push' in the direction of movement may be enough to get going and stay on the dance floor, but for others there is a need to take nore, since the body has exerted extra energy and may announce its exhaustion at the end of the effective period. In the track *Your Only Friend* (Trax, 1987) a voice personating cocaine warns that one may end up with no friends at all except for cocaine itself. Cocaine may ake control of the user because it can be addictive if taken in large quantities at regular intervals [Snyder, 1986; Washton, 1989] while at he same time it is relatively expensive at around £50 a gram; its effects may last 30 minutes when sniffed, but when smoked its effect only lasts for 5 minutes [Lifeline, 1993]. Cocaine powder, which is not as addictive as crack, is therefore often found at more exclusive social gatherings of people from a higher income group.

A cheaper and longer lasting alternative is amphetamine which house party goers may 'snort' in a powder-form called 'speed' or 'sulphate'.[510] In England it currently sells 'on the street' at between £8 and £12 per gram, which can take, depending on the person who takes it,[511] at least one night to finish off. In Britain it is listed as a Class B drug under the Misuse of Drugs Act 1971, 'attracting medium penalties', and in schedule 2, which means that it can be prescribed under certain circumstances [Newcombe, 1991]. Amphetamine keeps the dancer awake and moving all night long; its effect of a feeling of never ending energy after the last intake lasts up to eight hours. Its chemical structure and the way it affects the body is akin to the hormone adrenaline, which is produced when one is in a state of stress, anxiety or anger [Snyder, 1986]. For that purpose energy reserves are tapped. It is possible to move at a faster rate than would normally be possible. In Newcombe's report on dance drugs it is said hat:

---

[10] Less common are amphetamine tablets, which used to be prescribed to tired or to dieting persons by their GP. For example, as mentioned in Chapter 5, in England in the 70s Dexedrine or 'Dexies' were popular. Injection of amphetamines does not seem to be popular at all on the dance scene, indicating, in my opinion, a recreational use, rather than serious physically addictive abuse of this substance.

[11] Depends on the body weight and metabolism of the user as well as on the frequency with which it is used. The body does build up a dependency, which means that frequent and prolonged use results in the user needing more speed to get the same effect.

... occasional checks revealed that pulse rates of up to 150 beats per minute are common at raves, though this may be true of dancers at other kinds of parties and nightclubs[512] [Newcombe, 1991].

This then calls for a faster music, which in the case of gabber house could reach a speed of 160 bpm and higher. In its turn this has inspired Northern European pop dance acts to speed up as well, such as the 149 bpm part of the 'Techno and Champagne'-version of Capella's *U & Me* (Internal Dance, 1994).

Most frequently discussed in the context of house music is the drug 'ecstasy' [Adelaars, 1991; Redhead, 1993a; Saunders, 1993],[513] which the British abbreviate as 'E', the Americans as 'X' and the Dutch as 'XTC'.[514] Initially, this name was given to MDMA, a form of amphetamine which has an empathic and entactogenic effect [Nasmyth, 1985; Jellema, 1991], which makes it an excellent drug for gatherings of people who want to explore aural and tactile space. Like LSD and cocaine, MDMA is a mood enhancer. It lasts for around four hours, which makes it ideal for British legal club nights which, during the late 1980s, lasted between four to a maximum of six hours only. Its price between 1988 and 1994 has fluctuated between roughly £10 and £25 depending on demand and availability. In Britain it is categorised under the Misuse of Drugs Act 1971 as Class A and Schedule 1, which means that in this country it can not be prescribed and dispensed [Newcombe, 1991] or used for research [Haughton, 1991]. It affects the body in its chemistry at nerve ends; it causes serotonergic nerve ends to secrete serontonine, a neuro-transmitter which affects one's mood [Jellema, 1991]. When a high amount of this is active in the body, this results in great euphoric happiness; on the other hand, a low amount, for instance due to a too frequent use of MDMA, causes depression [Korf et al., 1991]. In a similar manner to that of a person in love, the user can feel in a state of mind which if one feels emotionally insecure can make one's world fall apart, but which if one is in a state of equilibrium and in a

512 {p. 11}

513 The amount of references in press, drug advice leaflets and academic literature is enormous; many of these can be found in Nicholas Saunders' update on his book on 'E', where he has attempted to catalogue what has been published about house music events and MDMA [Saunders, 1995].

514 The connection between dance parties and ecstasy has been an ongoing worry to the Dutch and British authorities. This connection has also been a reason for the popular press to sensationalise the 'dangers' of house music parties and clubs.

conducive sensory environment can make one soar to a state of near religious ecstasy. The gospel inspired lyrics of American house music and garage music, which speak of unity and community, such as *Promised Land* by Chicago based Joe Smooth (DJ International, 1987), fit the state of mind which accompanies a sense of (religious) ecstasy perfectly. Within the context of the ancient religious practices of Shamanism and magic, serontonine is mentioned as a substance which will 'open the mind' to a transcendental spiritual world [Taylor, 1985; Taylor, 1994]. For instance, this sensibility seems to be touched upon in the dance track *Voodoo Ray*, composed by the Mancunian artist A Guy Called Gerald (Rham!, 1988).

Its empathic quality means that one can lose one's identity in the music and in the social space; for this reason, when under the influence of the drug ecstasy, this purpose-made music of loss and escape is perfectly 'understood' on a subconscious level[515] by those who would not normally enjoy house music. The combination of house music and the drug ecstasy has worked so successfully, that for both clubbers and the authorities the words house and ecstasy seem to have become synonymous. Taking into account numerous articles, eye-witness accounts and remarks by both English and Dutch interviewees, it may be claimed with a high rate of accuracy that the drug ecstasy has been an important factor in enabling the huge success of house music in England in 1988.[516] As an entactogenic drug, MDMA makes the skin subtly sensitive, creating a higher sense of tactility. This may affect the user's sexual feelings, which in Freudian terms may best be described as being polymorphous, having returned to the mental state of an infant which can not yet speak [Rietveld, 1993]. For example, here is a remark from the dancefloor (i.e. clubber's discourse):

> The best clubs are packed with people enjoying childhood regression to the full. I mean, baby's dummies on the dancefloor?! Draw your own conclusions[517] [King, 1992].

Its effect of the loss of oneself into the 'community' and of its effects of feeling child-like will be discussed in more detail in the next part of

---

[515] Many (mostly American) house tracks refer to the idea of 'a feeling'; 'understanding' house music means that one can 'feel' it, both emotionally, as well as physically (through the vibrations made by the amplified sound).

[516] See Chapter 3.

[517] {p. 4}

this chapter.

Adelaars has described how in the 1970s for its earlier yuppie[518] users in Dallas, Texas, a leaflet was provided stating that the drug should only be used in a peaceful environment whilst listening perhaps to classical music [Adelaars, 1991]. However, by the mid-1980s it was also used in the 'gay' bars of Dallas [Nasmyth, 1985]. In 1983 I witnessed its use by the people who attended New York's 'gay' club Paradise Garage. In 'gay' dance clubs in Ibiza it gained popularity during the 1980s as well. With the arrival of acid house in 1988 ecstasy was successfully adopted, probably via the Ibiza club scene, by the English dance crowds [Adelaars, 1991; Rose, 1991]. In this way, it became the main drug associated with house music and its related frenzied festivities. As with LSD, which could potentially be used for a therapeutic form of introspection, MDMA was recreationally used to lose oneself in the crowd, the music and everything else which makes a house party tick. Dance tracks have been produced with references to ecstasy or 'E', especially in England, such as *everything starts with an 'e'* by e-zee possee (More Protein, 1989) and Shades of Rhythm's *Extacy* (XTT, 1991). Sometimes the words 'E' and 'acid' were interchanged, collapsing its meaning such as D-Mob's *We Call It Acieed* (FFRR, 1988) where in the popular imagination acid house referred to nothing else but the combination of 'E' and house music. Other tracks, mostly American, which mention words associated with a feeling of positive ecstasy (as opposed to feeling lost in chaos) have been adopted in Britain and elsewhere in Europe as anthems, almost like odes to the feeling of being under the influence of 'E', such as Ten City's *Devotion* (WEA, 1987) and *It's Alright* by Sterling Void (DJ International, 1987).[519]

Due to its illegal status, MDMA is not easy to produce. For the same reason, there is no quality control on the production of ecstasy tablets and capsules. Therefore, ecstasy tablets do not always contain MDMA proper. Instead one can find chemical cocktails which at times have been identified as mixtures of speed and LSD, MDA or sometimes the strongly hallucinogenic anaesthetic ketamine. Also the dose of MDMA is not always the same. Since the user does not always get the effect as expected, this could then lead to various types of casualties. In order to prevent these from occurring, in the

---

518 A 'yuppie' is a Young Upwardly mobile Person; motivated to earn money and to have a career.
519 This was covered with success by The Pet Shop Boys in 1988.

Netherlands drugs advice organisations such as Adviesburo Drugs operated by August de Loor have made it possible for users to have their pills and capsules tested at a small selection of parties and clubs [de Wolf, 1992]. Due to its particular status in British law, this service cannot be provided in Britain, resulting in high risk drug taking in the British Isles with subsequent occasional fatalities.

Few deaths have been recorded due to either an allergic reaction or otherwise as a result of internal bleeding [Newcombe, 1991], which may occur due to the sudden dilation of capillaries in the MDMA user [Haughton and Rietveld, 1992]. This could happen when one takes too much in a short time [Newcombe, 1991]. To most users this dilation gives a mild sensation of a 'rush' to the head and body in a similar manner as caused by a whiff of poppers. In the Netherlands the main worry is the deep depression which some abusive users can sink into. Also it has been found in test animals that higher doses can cause long-term damage to the serotoninergic nerve endings, although this effect has not yet been demonstrated with human subjects [Jellema, 1991]. In England, a main concern amongst health workers is that enthusiastic (over-)stimulated people tend to exert themselves physically, which could be lethal in combination with dancing with a similarly overheated crowd. Some unscrupulous organisers of parties or clubs abuse this situation by turning off the water taps in the toilets, so that people are forced to buy drinks from the bar at highly inflated prices. Dehydration and overheating through excessive body movements in a badly ventilated space, combined with a lack of fluid replenishment, is probably the largest cause of casualties at any of these events [MDTIC, 1992; Lifeline, 1992; MDPI, 1993].[520]

Air conditioning and the availability of plenty of fluid as well as sugary and energy generating substances are needed to sustain the body. Lemonade, iced lollies and fruit are popular at house parties to combat dehydration and over-exhaustion. In the Paradise Garage in New York in 1983 there used to be a free supply of fruit, water and donuts. In the late 1970s The Warehouse in Chicago used to have a fruit juice instead of an alcohol bar [Knuckles, 1991]. In 1988 The Haçienda in Manchester gave away ice bars. Many other clubs and parties will have variations on the theme:

---

[520] Ironically, since 1995, after clubbers had been warned to keep dehydration in check, some casualties and even deaths occurred when some ecstasy users overflooded their kidneys due to repetitive water drinking. Water requirements are relative to physical exertion; general advice is that a pint of water per hour is sufficient for a dancing person.

High sugar soft drinks are preferred to alcohol at raves because they provide energy and prevent dehydration. Many ravers report losing over 10 pounds in weight in a single night (mostly through perspiration)[521] [Newcombe, 1991].

The iced lollies help against over-heating. Caffeine containing drinks such as cola help the nocturnal dancer to stay awake. Vicks rub was popular in England in 1990 and 1991, since it makes the skin tingle, which for an ecstasy user is perceived as a sensation of cooling bliss. Also chewing gum, which keeps the amphetamine and MDMA affected tendency of facial 'gurning'[522] at bay, and a variety of other props and sweets have been in fashion:

Imagine the best point in the evening. That song has just come on, your spine is tingling, your eyes are moist with tears of joyousness and your best friend has just given you a hug. Crunch! You bite through your Refresher and a wave of exquisite sweetness — just like when a Locket bursts — is shot through your mouth, your head, your whole body even. You've had the bobble hats, Vicks and blow-up guitars. Now forget the tooth rot and go for the irresistible appeal of the sugar fix[523][King, 1992].

The above quote gives some sense of the attitude and atmosphere of a house party; hedonism at its most innocent, infantile, 'regressive' and uncaring level. An educated guess would suggest that this sensibility is due to an attitude generated by the use of 'E'. The physical effects of 'E' and child-like state of mind of the user are articulated on English rave tracks, such as *Charly* by The Prodigy (XL-Recordings, 1991), which has a sound which seems like a face gurning voice[524] and a sampled voice of a child which paraphrases

---

521 {p. 15}

522 An involuntary movement of the face muscles, caused by tightening jaw muscles. Sometimes it is an exaggerated expression of one's mood or of what one hears in the music. Most other times it seems more a random type of movement. For an illustration, see *Mixmag* March 1993 [Barden, 1993].

523 {p. 4}

524 Try this gurning excercise; repeat: 'eeoooouuaaawwweeeoowwaawwoouuweeeea'.

Charly's advice to tell your mother about your whereabouts.[525] The trick in this sample is that the latter advice is exactly what teenagers, in their rite of passage to independence, would like to ignore. Listening to it in places of which their mothers would hopefully not be aware, became an act of defiance to parental control. It was a track par excellence for the teenager in general, who may be inspired by 'E'-culture, but who would not necessarily be an 'E' user. Without intending to have this effect, this initially underground rave record charted in England and made rave a pop event [Phillips, 1992].

Cannabis is often smoked at dance occasions, depending on its status within the local legal system, whereby non-surveilled spaces are more likely to ignore legislation with regard to its consumption. Both in the USA and the UK it is still illegal; in Britain it is listed under Class B in the Misuse of Drugs Act 1971. In the Netherlands, although also illegal, both the law and the police have a very relaxed attitude to its recreative use as opposed to selling. In late 1993 the discussion to legalise this substance flared up once again in Britain [McDermott, 1993]. It has long been claimed that it enhances one's perception of music and colour [Siegel, 1989]. It is used during a moment when one takes a break from dancing, perhaps for a refreshment, to rest the body and to get some air. It is popular at the end of the night when a group of people may go home or to a quiet place together, in order to slowly recuperate from a night filled with dance and the possible use of stimulating, entactogenic or hallucinogenic dance drugs. Such breaks have been named a 'chill out'. As house parties in England have been refined in style, the chill out has become a style of 'laid back' entertainment with its own music called ambient house.[526] One of the early examples of this slower atmospheric style of music can be found on the Italian compilation *Ambient House* (DFC, 1991), which contains, for instance, productions by The Orb and Sueno Latino. In October 1993 the first

---

525 The samples were taken from a British television advert which warns children not to take sweets from strangers or to go home with them. Because of its new context, its original sinister references have been changed into something that is fun. For those that remember the advert this may seem quite subversive. The gurning sound is constructed from a sample of the cat Charly in the advert, who tells the child that it should be careful when out alone. Teenagers who grew up with the advert do not want to tell their parents anything about their activities in an attempt to become independent; during their 'rite of passage', they defy the Bogey man. This example does show how the act of sampling can recontextualise and alter a meaning of a sound bite. Coincidentally, 'Charley' is a user's nickname for cocaine, which causes some amount of gurning but not as much or intense as 'E' does.
526 For a broader discussion of the concept of ambient music, see David Toop's *Ocean of Sound* [Toop, 1995].

Ambient Weekend was held at the Amsterdam club the Melkweg (Milky Way), a clubbing space which thereby turned full circle, since it initially had started as a place for cannabis smoking hippie gatherings more than two decades before. There was barely any sign of frantic dancing during both days, where some Dutch, but mainly English DJs such as Mixmaster Morris entertained a crowd which was largely English [DJ White Delight, 1993].[527]

Tobacco in the form of cigarettes is still popular amongst those who frequent house events, even though it seems that less is currently being smoked than in the 80s. Despite adverse news reports on the damaging and eventually carcinogenic effects of tobacco smoke as well as the increasing trend to make public places non-smoking zones, it is still legal in all of the three researched localities. Tobacco contains the lethal toxic substance nicotine as well as alkaloids such as harman, which affect the brain. According to Ronald Siegel, it has a stimulating as well as a hallucinatory effect, inducing a type of trance when smoked in high doses. It was therefore used by the earliest American Shamans as an aid to rituals of magic and religion [Siegel, 1989]. Unlike the Shaman's pipe, which allowed luscious clouds of smoke to be (re)inhaled, cigarettes do not allow for a high dose at once. Nevertheless, its effect as a stimulant, as well as a way to stabilise one's mood-swings, is appreciated during, but more so after, long exhausting nights of partying; to run out of cigarettes on a night out may seem like a total disaster to some. This is confirmed by the high number of occasions on which party people passionately and incessantly beg each other for their last cigarettes. Although perhaps the cigarette-blagging,[528] exhausted, blurry-eyed, close to speechless party person may seem like a long way removed from any self-respecting Shamanistic practice, in the next part of this chapter it will be attempted to make this connection in a metaphorical and secular sense; to Shamanism proper, 'being at the end of your tether'[529] is an important part of its ecstatic ritual [Taylor, 1985].

Ecstasy is a subtle drug and its effects can be subdued or altered not only by one's state of mind, but also by the use of other drugs, since it is what is commonly called a 'mood enhancer'. Combined with LSD (called a 'candy trip' in the USA) it makes the user mentally walk into

---

[527] See Chapter 4 for a discussion of the use of Amsterdam by British party lovers because of the Dutch liberal attitude towards sex, drugs and music. One could predict from past events that The Ambient Weekend will spawn a new 'hyperreal' hippie community in the Netherlands.

[528] See introduction of Chapter 5 for the verb 'to blag'.

[529] {p. 13}

a mad cartoon-like world, with the odd visual hallucination of kaleidoscopic, almost digital looking, fragmentation of light. Combined with speed it enables the user to continue an ecstatic dance mood for hours without much of a pause, which seems useful since MDMA tends to work in a series of 'waves' which stop and start the body in its desire to dance; a problem may be that the user can collapse from exhaustion and dehydration. Combined with cocaine dancing can be continued as well [Korf et al., 1991]. Combined with poppers the initial sensual rushes caused by ecstasy can be enhanced or extended. Combined with cannabis it calms the user down and prolongs 'a sense of mutual solidarity' [Korf et al., 1991]. Tobacco gives the user a sense of 'putting one's feet on the ground', which at some moments in combination with perception-affecting drugs may lead to temporary enthusiastic chain smoking, especially since sometimes 'E' can cause obsessive repetitive behaviour.[530]

Combined with (the legal drug) alcohol however, the empathic effect of 'E' may be nullified. The numbing effect of alcohol makes the user single-minded, which is the opposite of the openness of an ('E' induced) empathic state of mind. Alcohol interferes with body co-ordination, accelerates dehydration and, after an initial sense of stimulation, becomes a sedative which causes the drinker to slow down considerably [Hofman, 1983]. Although it can give the user an initial energetic 'alcohol-rush', it is not of much use at dance marathons which may last between four to twelve hours. However, combined with amphetamines the drinker can keep going for a much longer time. In this combination, drink like beer may cause a sensibility which suits the extremely aggressive, hard hitting and fast versions of Belgian and German techno, British hardcore and Dutch gabber house. *Feyenoord Reactivate* by Rotterdam Termination Source (Rotterdam Records, 1992) is a gabber example of what seems to me an amphetamine and alcohol inspired track which is a contemporary ode without conventional song structure to the local top division football team. Alcohol is available at clubs and parties but as long as a proper standard of quality was maintained in the production of ecstasy (meaning that it actually contained MDMA rather than other substances) the consumption of alcohol was on a low if non-existent level amongst (the early English and American) house music crowds. It has only been the 'hardened beer boys' who

---

[530] A wonderful insight into combined drug use in practice during the heady British rave days can be found in *Disco Biscuits*, a collection of stories by people from that scene (Champion, 1997).

would not be able to leave their beer alone[531] [Lifeline, 1991].

However, in general fights are rare at house parties,[532] except if drug trade or other gang related warfare is brought into a club. During 1990 and 1991, Manchester in particular provided a good example of this pattern. Having enjoyed being a partying city during 1988 and 1989, which earned it the nickname Madchester, it then gained another nickname, Gunchester. Several gangs attempted to gain a 'patch' in different dance clubs to profit from the lucrative drug market these spaces provided. At the same time within a gang from North Manchester there was a competition over leadership. This was fought out in the clubs over which they tried to gain power. Not only free entry, but also free drinks were demanded while they forced some clubs to change their security staff so total control could be gained. Local police were worried and revoked the licenses of several dance clubs, such as The Gallery and Konspiracy. In January 1991 The Haçienda celebrated its legal victory to keep its licence, only to close down a couple of weeks later on the initiative of its own management, after a member of staff had been threatened with a gun. The Haçienda closed down for several months and reopened in May 1991, after which occasional spells of violence became less frequent [Rietveld, 1992a; Redhead and Rietveld, 1992; Park and Wainright, 1993]. This shows that an efficient security system as well as other social filtering procedures are necessary to keep a fragile 'virtual' community intact.

The festive spectacle of disappearance

In order to represent subjectivity on the dance floor of a house music event I am relying on several comparable metaphors. A variety of approaches can be found elsewhere, from discourses on African-American cultural identity [Berry, 1992] to European theories of cultural resistance [Redhead, 1990; Rietveld, 1993; Plant, 1993]. In the previous chapters notions of racial and sexual identity, bohemian elite and of youth culture, as well as reactions by different authorities have been touched upon. The last part of this book will provide a closer focus on the experience of house music on the dance floor.

---

[531] For example in the case of the Rotterdam club Parkzicht, the resultant aggressive attitude would lead to fights [R. Rietveld, 1992].

[532] See for example the observation made by DJ Ardy Beesemer on gabber parties in Chapter 3.

When a dance night is at its height, somewhere in the middle of the cyclone of sensory overload, the dancer communicates with the music, space and fellow dancers in a specific manner which seems, if not unique, at least special. None of these metaphors proposed in the following equal this experience exactly. They are approximations which have been borrowed from disparate disciplines, such as anthropological sources on Shamanism and trance dance, as well as European critical theory and philosophy. Some metaphors have been appropriated from a philosophical line of thought which is based in a Modernist tradition, employing terms such as 'infantile' and 'regression'. This should be interpreted with a sense of irony, since a house event does not fit within a world view that puts a hierarchical importance to these terms (which could imply notions of 'progress' and 'maturity'). It is important to note that the metaphors which are proposed have been chosen due to a lack of a more suitable representative language.

This void was demonstrated during my research when dancers at raves and other house events were asked what it was like, most of them had problems in articulating this verbally. English participants in the Manchester area produced minimal comments, such as: 'it was wild', 'great', or 'absolutely unbelievable, there wasn't anything like it'. I also came across the following: 'this is not dancing, this is a religion' [Rietveld, 1993].

In previous chapters, similar sentiments were expressed by African-American participants in the American city Chicago. DJ Keven Elliott said: 'I dance until the walls around me fall away' [Elliott, 1992], while producer Marshall Jefferson once exclaimed that 'You may want to seek religion afterwards' [Garratt, 1986].

A crowd which dances to house music is bound on a route to pure escape[533] whilst at the same time celebrating a sense of community which has been forged at the moment of interactive consumption. It is therefore of major importance that a crowd is able to 'gell' together. The sensory overload of theatrical psychedelic trickery of visual and audio effects drown out many social differences which a crowd selection cannot control completely. As mentioned above, for many members in the crowd at a rave or house party drugs (such as the empathy generating and tactility stimulating MDMA) have an effect of unstructuring a daily rationalist pattern of thinking. This supports

---

[533] In the discotheques, dance clubs and dance parties of both the USA and Europe [Joe, 1980; Rietveld, 1993].

the radical effect which the incessant groove of house music has on the dancer. In this context, I came across a remark by British musician and counter-cultural practician Genesis P. Orridge who was quoted by pop journalist Simon Reynolds as saying:

> ... it's got something to do with the speed of the beats. It's hypnotic, tribal and primal. That particular speed has worked for thousands of years, which is why you can spin in Arab music, Bhangra music, Aboriginal music ... You can take all these different cultures and find the same beat, between 125-130 bpm. It's there in ecstatic, trance music, where people shake and spin until they reach a state of hyperventilation and psychedelic alpha-wave experience. In a sense, acid (house) is regressive music. You're going back to the roots of why music was invented: to reach ecstatic and visionary states, in a communal tribal celebration[534] [Reynolds, 1990c].

Orridge's comment is a good pointer to some of the ideas which in a sometimes confused and often self-conscious manner have been adopted by some producers and consumers of European genres in dance and trance music.[535] In his book *Music and Trance*, ethnomusicologist Gilbert Rouget has proposed that trance-like states are part of the potential of human experiences, but that their manifestations depend on their cultural context. He has also made an attempt to prise apart different meanings of the words 'trance' and 'ecstasy' even though confusion exists in its various practical uses; Rouget defines trance as a type of possession [Rouget, 1985]. Biomusicologist Nils Wallin picked up on Rouget's ideas and explained that trance, a type of communally induced dream like state, can be caused by overstimulation such as music and dance, as well as by noise and hyperventilation; while, in contrast, in his terminology,

---

[534] {p. 184}

[535] In England between 1993 and 1995, the psychedelic trance aspects of acid house and techno have been embraced in a self-conscious manner by a mostly 'white' urban hippie scene, to be heard at, for example, the nationally touring Megadog events, The Herbal Tea Party in Manchester or Return to the Source in South London. On the day I re-edited this chapter, 23 October 1995, it was, for lack of a better word, officially declared as Goa trance. Goa refers to the old hippie hangout in India, while with 'official' I mean that it was announced on English television Channel 4 News. In addition, as shown in Chapter 4, since the arrival of house music on its shores, the Dutch have focused on its trance qualities. In the USA, DJ Pierre's Wild Pitch mixes and acid house productions have been exemplary of trance inducing productions, although philosophically, he is not as self-conscious about it as his European counterparts.

ecstasy, a state of non-discrimination and characterised by the neural discharge of alpha-waves, is achieved by deprivation, such as meditation in silence or when one is just about to fall asleep. However, Wallin admitted that this neat distinction is confused when one considers that in the practice of tantric yoga a state of ecstasy does seem to be achieved through arousal. One may conclude from Wallin,[536] that the physiological state of the dancer to house music in its intended setting is akin to that of a state of trance, which according to Wallin is a socialised form of mobilised REM[537] (active dream) sleep and which is generated in an older (in evolutionary terms) part of the brain, the mid-brain. This then results in the elimination of the ego of the individual 'I' in favour of the ego of the community. Wallin commented that the combination of dance and music in tribal social events can induce this state of consciousness, which is expressive and active, rather than introspective (the latter generates alpha-waves) [Wallin, 1991]. So, events of trance dance could in principle be as old (and 'traditional') as pre-historic human society [Natale, 1995]. Perhaps confusingly, as far as the above technical definition of the term 'ecstasy' is concerned, I have stayed close to current everyday English use of this word, as well as to its use by French critical writers such as Baudrillard and Barthes (and their various translators) [Baudrillard, 1988a; Wiseman, 1989] and by different anthropological sources on Shamanism [Kalweit, 1988; Lewis, 1989; Taylor, 1985]. Therefore, I have used the word 'ecstasy' to indicate a sense of (elated or bewildered) arousal as well as of loss of self, in the way that Rouget and Wallin have proposed to use the word 'trance'. The latter term I have only used in this type of meaning if and when it is mentioned by ethnographic sources in the context of certain musical styles which are related to house music, such as Goa trance.[538]

So even though Genesis P. Orridge's remarks got me on the right track, his statement did confuse a few issues: alpha brainwaves occur during introspection or lullabys, not during a wild and communal state of arousal. A comparison of the ritual of house music consumption could be made with certain aspects of Shamanism. Rogan Taylor stressed that this 'is fundamentally an ecstatic form of religion',[539] whereby ecstasy connotes 'the idea of "being at the end of

---

536 {pp. 281 - 287}
537 Rapid Eye Movements; a stage in one's sleep when one actively dreams.
538 See the above footnote on Goa trance.
539 {p. 13}

191

your tether", "out of your mind", "at your wit's end"',540 rather than 'something of an exalted state of feeling'541 [Taylor, 1985]. In other words, within the discourse of Shamanism, to be in a state of ecstasy is to be in a 'transcendental' unstructured state of mind. At house music events dancers perform incessant rhythmical body movements; in anthropological studies of Shamanism it has been observed that habitual patterns of thought are disrupted by this type of dancing:

> It takes surprisingly little to turn human consciousness upside down or cause it to disintegrate (...) the uninterrupted repetition of an activity to the point of total exhaustion is an important triggering mechanism (...)542 [Kalweit, 1988].

In this manner awareness of an outside world can disappear. This means that there is no motivation to observe, to subject the world to one's 'mastering' gaze [Rietveld, 1993]. By not subjecting the surrounding world, the observable subject disappears. This also means that preconceptions about other people disappear to such an extent that at, for example, (English) raves social differences seemed to be of little importance to the participant:

> Friendliness, sensuality and 'body language' are valued more than trendyness, sexual displays or long conversations.543 Standard discos and parties are too oriented towards alcohol intoxication, posing, chatting, courtship rituals and aggression to be comparable, though they are cultural cousins of the rave, sharing common features of audience participation, drug taking and celebration544 [Newcombe, 1991].

A dream world is generated which does not exist outside of it. Since this is a moment of a 'perfect' community for which there is no original and which by the same token can be reproduced, one could call this an experience of a type of 'hyperreality' which is difficult to express in words: 'The hyperreal transcends representation (...) only because it is entirely in simulation'545 [Baudrillard, 1983]. At most rave

---

540 {p. 13}
541 {p. 13}
542 {p. 119}
543 {p. 6}
544 {p. 7}
545 {p.147}

parties, there was no conscious political aim in this quest for a forever 'here and now' other than the forging of a community which (may) lie outside conventional hierarchical social structures. For people who do not experience any problems from those conventional types of structures, this sense of community had no other purpose than being just that. Baudrillard's description of a simulated hyperreal world seems quite fitting for a majority of party people: '... deep down the message has already ceased to exist, it is the medium which imposes itself in pure circulation'[546] [Baudrillard, 1988a]. Forms of house music which are predominantly instrumental, such as trance and German hart house, do not specify a particular community. Although there is a lot of hugging, smiling and other displays of appreciation of the presence of fellow revellers on the dance floor of a rave styled house party, this seems to be a play of surfaces, since often this is spontaneously enacted with complete strangers without any further social commitment.

At these occasions the process of participation is foregrounded. No longer is the crowd entertained by a performer who needs to be observed. Rather, the crowd is as much responsible for what happens at this cultural event as the technicians such as the DJ and the lighting engineer. Separation between audience and performer has been eroded in the club environment. The 'Aleister Crowley maxim "Every man and woman is a star"',[547] reflected in the star motive on disco associated clothes in the 70s, can be reappropriated to this type of event, from disco [Savage, 1988] to house parties.[548] Baudrillard's ideas on contemporary subjectivity in the age of interactive information technology seem quite fitting:

> ... from the required passivity to models constructed all at once on the basis of the 'active response' of the subject, on its implication, its 'ludic' participation, etc., towards a total environmental model made out of incessant spontaneous responses of joyous feed-back and irradiating contact[549] [Baudrillard, 1983].

---

546 {p.23}
547 {p. 66}
548 Aleister Crowley, British occult existentialist who wrote his ideas in the first half of the twentieth century, has said that every person must follow his/her own path in the way that a star in the universe follows its own trajectory [Crowley, 1991]. This means that one does not follow a leader but rather, one's own 'inner' guiding ... whatever that may mean ... .
549 {p. 139}

Ironically perhaps, it is the club technicians who are put in the position of the spectator, the accidental audience of the unintentional spectacle of the swaying elated crowd. The DJ interacts with the crowd to make the sentiment affecting sound track of the evening work. The skill and art of the DJ are based partly on an ability to be attuned to the moods of people and to play with those emotions, until the crowd allows itself to be taken on a trip of rhythms, sound bites, audio textures and lyrics. If one record is played which seems to be out of place this fragile moment of magic could be ruined and the crowd will vote with its feet. One may therefore speak of 'the great festival of Participation',[550] a concept which Baudrillard expands as follows:

> Here comes the time of the great Culture of tactile communication, under the sign of the technico-luminous cinematic space of total spatio-dynamic theatre[551] [Baudrillard, 1983].

The metaphor of a 'theatre'[552] seems to stem from a different conceptual world. Visual space produces an object to be viewed which in turn induces hierarchical thinking; on the other hand a tactile and acoustic space dissolves the separation between object and subject [McLuhan and Powers, 1992]. In an article on English contemporary club culture in relation to European avant garde ideas such as Dada and Situationism, cyber philosopher Sadie Plant observed that:

> For those exposed to the strobes and rhythms, hooks and speeds of the rave scene's nights, autonomy is no longer the issue. Spectators see only the surface, but the ravers are already part of the scene, in the machinery. Beyond representation lies total immersion; the end of the spectacle[553] [Plant, 1993].

Dancers often seemed to be dancing with themselves, in a trance, locked into a private mind-altered state, whilst at the same time feeling empathically connected to the surrounding bodies. With the disappearance of a sense of 'the other' (i.e. what is not oneself and therefore considered outside of it), a sense of self also disappears, since 'the self' is defined by its sense of difference. Baudrillard defines

---

550 {p. 139}
551 {p. 139}
552 See quote above.
553 {p. 7}

this state of subjectivity as one which is ecstatic, whereby: 'Ecstasy is the quality proper to any body that spins until all sense is lost, and then shines forth in its pure and empty form'[554] [Baudrillard, 1990]. At that moment, there is no separate inside or outside world; there is simply a sense of being 'here' at the present, with nothing else but the music, with its repetitive rhythms and many soundbites put into sequence by the DJ, to 'flow' through one's being. The DJ could thereby be represented as the Shaman who leads the dancing community through a 'hell' of loss and back again, ideally finishing the experience of total loss with a 're-embodying' anthem which speaks of love and togetherness and which facilitates a 'rebirth' of 'the self' [Taylor, 1994]. Alternatively, the punters 'pull themselves together' in a chill-out setting.

The state of trance of the dancer is like a secular version of a religious experience [Lewis, 1989; Clark, 1993]. Both the European types of sparsely vocalised house grooves which are designed to induce the crowd into a trance and the African-American versions of house which represent an uplifting spiritual sense of community in their gospel influenced vocals, can fit in with this idea. As has been argued in Chapter 5, house music has historical connections with disco, of which Walter Hughes has commented the following:

> At their best, disco singers draw on the gospel music tradition, where vocal repetition empties out language in order to open the self to divine inspiration, expressed in heightened emotive renderings of the repeated phrase [Hughes, 1994].

One may even go so far as to call a dance space, which involves the consumption of house music, a kind of night-time 'church', where an experience can be achieved of a self-effacing identity which becomes part of a community.[555] Surrealist philosopher Bataille says of the sacred that:

> (it) is only a privileged moment of communal unity, a moment of the convulsive communication of what is ordinarily stifled[556] [Bataille, 1985].

---

554 {p. 9}
555 An expression amongst ravers for being in a drugged state is to be 'off your face', or shorter, to be 'off it', which signifies a loss of the face, the daily mask, one's daily identity.
556 {p. 242}

195

In a capitalist society which alienates the individual from the larger social fabric, a celebration of a temporary community can lead to an intense, yet temporary, experience. An alienated sense of self is thereby lost, since the entranced dancer in a state of ecstasy has an experience of being decentred. The concept of self has been untied, losing its socially constructed identity like some unnecessary luggage. One could call this a kind of death of 'the self'. As Sadie Plant puts it:

> What should have remained the impossible experiences of a mythical future are becoming real: a dissolution which should be known only as death becomes a weekend routine[557] [Plant, 1993].

Hence this is a spectacular disappearance of the ability for the subject to represent itself and its cultural activity. Afterwards a person may feel spiritually 'reborn', especially after a first experience of a long night dancing to a house groove, with or without the aid of drugs.

Although in practical terms, one of the main functions of the DJ is to present a certain taste of music to the audience, it may be also be useful, in the context of the notion of 'rebirth', to represent the DJ as a mother figure who, with the use of rhythms, textures and positive lyrics, rocks the dancing crowd like a baby in the safe, warm and moist womb-like environment of the club. Like a mother, a good DJ takes control, but is at the same time empathically responsive to the needs of the dancer-'infants'. The crowd is placed in a 'masochistic' subject position rather than a narcissistic one (i.e. one that likes to stay in control). Film critic Ros Brown-Grant explains: '... the enjoyable, suspended pleasures of pre-phallic, pre-Oedipal re-fusion with the all-powerful mother figure'[558] [Brown-Grant, 1988].

At intense dance events, this psychological state seems fitting. The inability to put the experience into language, to represent what is happening could be due to a return to a mental state which stems from before the acquisition of language. Where house music does have lyrics, these often indicate a sense of love, desire and a sharing of feelings, suggesting a basic emotional relationship like that

---

557 {p. 7}
558 {p. 6}

between mother and infant.[559] A regular 4/4 beat, like that of house music, seems to resemble a heartbeat [Middleton, 1990]. As has been mentioned before,[560] taking the womb-like qualities of the full dance floor into account, it may even resemble the heartbeat of the mother of the (unborn) infant. As the pace of the beat changes, although it does not synchronise exactly, so does the heartbeat of the dancer-'infant' in an empathic system of 'symbiosis'.[561] At the same time, other rhythms, based in various cultural traditions, such as Salsa and Samba, syncopate with this 'heartbeat' and thereby recontextualise it, defying a rationalist logic of representation. A similar defiance can be noticed in the stress on sound textures in house music. In more unstructured house genres, such as trance, DJ tracks, acid house, wild pitch mixes, tribal house and jungle techno, rhythm and sound textures take on prime importance. One could therefore argue that these types of house music celebrate a pre-linguistic and therefore 'infantile'[562] state of mind. In addition, the way the body is related to in a sexual sense is one that is tactile rather genital, pointing to an 'infantile' or not-yet-structured stage in the development of sexuality [Freud, 1977]. This metaphor of the raver as 'infant' has also been mentioned above in the context of the drug ecstasy, which is conducive to this state of being. Combining a loosely structured and repetitive dance music like acid house with the drug ecstasy is therefore a successful formula.

In his inquiry into the subversive aspects of the unconscious in Freud's system of thought, cultural philosopher Marcuse has argued that to regress to a state of pre-linguistic infantility could be seen as progressive in the context of a repressive society:

---

559 Except in the often more 'demonic' or negative death inspired lyrics of Dutch gabber house, known in the English speaking world as gabba house, which may for that reason have more in common with the seminal Siberian Shamanic ritualistic tradition of leading the crowd into a disintegrating 'underworld'. However, gabber events do not provide a return to the 'middle world', which has to be provided by the punters in their own private settings. Gabber house events have inspired Dutch Evangelists to declare that house is Satan's music; it does not aspire to the 'upper world' in the way that gospel inspired house music does. An example of a reaction to the notion of love and empathy may be found in the dance compilation *None of these are love songs* (Caustic Vision, 1994), which provides tracks that can, however, still make the dancer lose a sense of everyday reality.
560 See Chapter 6.
561 The notion that the beat of the music may in any way empathically form a system of 'symbiosis' with the dancer cannot be upheld in the context of some gabber house and related events on both sides of the Atlantic, where the current rate of the speed of tracks is a relatively 'slow' 140 bpm to a symbiotically useless, but in 1994 very much favoured, 180 bpm.
562 The term 'infantile' will be qualified later in this chapter.

Regression assumes a progressive function. The rediscovered past yields critical standards which are tabooed by the present. (...) The liberation of the past does not end in its reconciliation with the present. Against the self-imposed restraint of the discoverer, the orientation on the past tends toward an orientation on the future. The *recherche du temps perdu*[563] becomes the vehicle of future liberation[564] [Marcuse, 1987].

One could argue that a state of total innocence, of a Garden of Eden, is a myth typical of cultural discourses which have been influenced by the Old Testament; that it never existed in the first place, since we are born into a certain social structure, so one cannot return to it. Within the tradition of cultural studies it is argued that one's identity comes into being as a negotiation within the parameters of a certain society and culture. Yet, whatever metaphor one would like to use, the loss of that structured sense of self, however temporary, can shake a static sense of identity and awaken different manners of perceiving the world, as though it were all new, as though one looked upon it again as when one were a toddler and ask that question so many children ask: 'why'? In this sense, by finding 'lost times', a critical awareness of the surrounding world, as well as a feeling of bewilderment, could, in principle, be triggered.

For example, especially in New York, house music is defined as the soundtrack for 'gay' clubs. Here people celebrate sexualities which defy the rules of gender identities which are inscribed in patriarchal language and in discourses which defend procreation within nuclear families. Thereby those people with 'queer' identities and sexualities benefit from the celebration of an 'infantile polymorphously perverse' state of being. Sexuality of this kind ignores gender differences; the masculine and feminine aspects of sexuality are made irrelevant at these types of occasions. Thereby, the loss of the traditionally inscribed subject could become a radical event.

However, a person in this state of mind is quite vulnerable. In contrast to the above, one could put a slightly different emphasis on the metaphor of mother-child relationship between DJ and dance crowd and argue that within a patriarchal discursive context the dancing crowd is (symbolically) 'feminised', rather than 'infantilised'. In this scenario, as the crowd is submerged in the sensory experience

---

563 {Eng. trans.}: to find lost times, the state of being one has forgotten.
564 {p. 19}

of a house music event in an empathic manner, the DJ has 'masculine' rather than motherly traits and is the person who has the overview of, and control over, a totality and who subjects the crowd to 'his' control. This may explain the dictatorial aspirations which some DJs seem to adhere to and which, for instance, have been parodied in the comic *Moody DJ* [TBC and Browne, 1992]. A potentially radical event could thereby be contained and controlled in a particular space and time in order to accommodate a hegemonic status quo.

In addition, if a person escapes mentally in such an intense manner during the weekend in order to re-enter the same routine, this type of subjectivity would have a conservative effect. An event which requires a lot of human energy in order to facilitate a temporary escape, allows people to let off steam without affecting the overall hierarchical structures of society. To return to the metaphor of religion, a Marxist maxim is that '(r)eligion (...) is the opium of the people'[565] [Tucker, 1978], subduing those who are subordinated economically and socially by the effects of a hegemony. Cultural interventionist Stewart Home has bluntly stated, that the 'loss of self is the triumph of authority'[566] [Home, 1989a], since a state of non-being interrupts one's critical faculties to analyse and fight against hierarchical social structures. In the USSR, in 1929, a similar argument was raised in the context of folk festivals and of carnival by commissar of enlightenment, Anatoly Lunacharsky, then in service of the Stalinist government, who felt that: '... carnival was a kind of safety valve for the passions the common people might otherwise direct to revolution'[567] [Holquist, 1984]. However, Lunacharsky's opinion 'flew directly in the face of the evidence Bakhtin was then compiling'[568] [Holquist, 1984]. The Russian literary critic Mikhail Bakhtin represented carnival as an anarchic breeding ground for a real potential cultural and political resistance, exactly because of its ambivalent quality, like that of spring's death-rebirth [Rietveld, 1993].

My argument is that the political effect of 'loss' and of carnivalesque occasions depends on its social context. On the one hand, dance clubs and rave parties have often been organised by unscrupulous entrepreneurs who could earn some fast money from the raver who is placed in a vulnerable and uncritical position at the time of consumption of those events [Rietveld, 1993] and who plays

565 {p. 54}
566 {p. 138}
567 {p. XVIII}
568 {p. XVIII}

with the seemingly meaningless surfaces of a simulated community. On the other hand, 'grassroots' events such as 'gay' clubs, (travellers) free festivals, as well as early warehouse, squatters and rave-like blues parties, have provided a different context, which can strengthen the bonding of an alternative community. In this context, veteran hippie and zippy[569] Fraser Clark attempted to affect the ecstatic state of mind in a purposeful manner. Between the Autumns of 1993 and 1994, he worked with the collectively organised weekly club night Megatripolis, in London club Heaven near Charing Cross, which attempted to resemble a new age festival event under one roof. Here the concept of 'Shamanarchy' was put into practice [Swindells, 1993]. The idea was that the temporarily deconditioned clubber was reconditioned with countercultural ideas through discussion groups, lectures and the availability of underground press. As anthropologist Taylor put it: 'We must produce our own dream'[570] [1985].

In October 1993 I visited Megatripolis for the first time. I have to admit that it was difficult to 'lose' myself or to feel 'decentred' at any moment in time; there were many talkative strangers and the zines I bought there were too engaging to put away until a later moment. According to structuralist and post-structuralist thought, language and its structures inscribe the identity of the subject. Reading and talking in a loosely critical discourse therefore anchored me in a state of critical reality, which was only the partial aim of the event. Using post-structuralist Roland Barthes' terminology, the experience was one of 'pleasure' rather than of 'bliss' [Wiseman, 1989].[571] In addition, observing the crowd at Megatripolis, despite its soundtrack of 'unstructured' house music like trance and tribal house, it did not show the signs of frenzied abandonment as had been witnessed at earlier acid house parties [Rietveld, 1993] or at London 'gay' club Love Muscle at The Fridge in Brixton which I visited only two days later on a Saturday night. Perhaps this was partly caused by the fact that Megatripolis was programmed on a Thursday night rather than at the weekend, which meant that one could not 'let go' with abandonment due to work commitments the next day. Unlike travellers' new age dance events outside of the club environment, one has to pay an entrance fee, which meant that only people with an

---

[569] See footnote 41 in Chapter 4.
[570] (p. 209)
[571] See Chapter 6.

income, and therefore most likely with a job, could afford to go. In addition, it is the deconstruction of the gendered subject when dancing to house music in an 'intensified' context which creates its sense of 'bliss', since the identity of the subject is inextricably tied to its sense of sexuality. Although historically the Shaman was considered to be androgynous and perhaps bisexual [Taylor, 1985], in a (middle class) new age and zippy context, Shamanistic ideas do not directly affect notions of sexuality; however, social circumstances combined with 'queer' politics do.

Still, English house related events, such as acid house parties and raves, have been successful in the creation of a state of radical bliss outside of the context of 'gay' politics. Radical in the sense that they undermine and indeed 'demolish serious culture'[572] [Home, 1989b], albeit without conscious intention. The body and the pure 'unadulterated' aspects of fun are forgrounded in a non-gendered sexual sense; hugging, kissing, the sharing of drinks, sweets and cigarettes with strangers and dancing in sweating unison with a mass of people have made some academic writers speculate that these events perhaps offer a 'safe'[573] alternative to finding a sexual mate and even to the act of copulation [Henderson, 1993a; Henderson, 1993b; McRobbie, 1994]. As mentioned earlier, at English and Dutch raves between 1988 and 1990 differences according to social class, various 'subcultures', gender and race seemed less important [Adelaars, 1991; Rietveld, 1993], as was the case during the old fashioned carnivals as described by Mikhail Bakhtin [Bakhtin, 1984]. At travellers' festivals, the appearance of clowns, jugglers and (again) a parody of the official culture is stressed [Marcus, 1993] in addition to the fun of dancing in the mud. Comparable to a traditional European carnival, a sweating mass of people participating 'as one' in the celebration of a 'grotesque body' can be contrasted to the:

... class pursuit of purity, and the repudiation of revelling in mess

---

572 {p. 1}

573 During the time I researched this book (1980s and early 1990s) there was a panic around AIDS, an illness which attacks the immune system of the body and which is transmitted via the exchange of bodily fluids. Taking into the account the 'bourgeois' fear of the functions of the body (especially the desiring sexual body), this disease has been fertile to the imagination of certain repressive discourses (for example by calling it 'the gay plague'). Safer sex campaigns have been launched to combat ignorance on this matter. However, some folks still copulate after dance parties, so perhaps the idea of replacement-sex at your local rave or club may be wishful thinking.

(...) (which) was a fundamental aspect of bourgeois cultural identity[574] [White, 1989].

Fun on a large scale, as well as celebrating the body rather than the mind, can have an undermining effect on any unitary belief of a particular kind of hierarchical world order:

> Folly is, of course, deeply ambivalent. It has the negative element of debasement and destruction (...) and the positive element of renewal and truth. Folly is the opposite of wisdom — inverted wisdom, inverted truth. It is the other side, the lower stratum of official laws and conventions, derived from them. Folly is a form of gay[575] festive wisdom, free from all laws and restrictions, as well as from preoccupations and seriousness[576] [Bakhtin, 1984].

Aspects of the carnivalesque can be found in the homosexual hedonistic celebrations (which attempt to forge and recuperate 'queer' identities), as well as at raves and at British travellers' festivals. In the case of 'queer' politics, the confusion of gender roles as well as the celebration of the 'grotesque', such as a camp aesthetic is of importance [Sontag, 1963]. The Flesh nights at the Manchester club The Haçienda were an example of this. Men dressed as women, women dressed as unruly boys. Although spectacular to watch, people mesh around and on the dance floor in what could only be described as a communal body. This type of event gives strength to the person who would feel like an alienated outsider in the world at large; here an organic sense of community takes shape. An example of celebration on a much larger scale is the yearly 'gay' carnival in Sydney, in Australia, called the Mardi Gras.[577]

In a socially repressed environment such as English leisure time activities in the context of licensing laws as well as homosexuality in the context of a homophobic society, these moments of Utopian freedom [Bakhtin, 1984] are celebrated with high intensity for they are short lived. House parties, especially the early acid house events

---

574 {p. 162}

575 In this case the word 'gay' is used in its more general sense rather than specifically indicating male homosexuality.

576 {p. 260}

577 Mardi Gras is the French name for its annual carnival and means 'greasy Tuesday' [White, 1989]. It is a celebration which the British only know as 'Shrove Tuesday', the day before Lent. In Catholic parts of Europe this is celebrated with extended festivities. In the Netherlands this carnival covers the entire weekend before Lent.

and raves in squatted spaces and in open fields as well as dance events on the 'gay' scene could therefore be described as examples of a temporary autonomous zone (TAZ), a concept proposed by Hakim Bey:

> The TAZ is like an uprising which does not engage directly with the State, a guerilla operation which liberates an area (of land, of time, of imagination) and then dissolves itself to reform elsewhere/elsewhen, *before* the state can crush it. Because the State is primarily concerned with Simulation rather than substance, the TAZ can 'occupy' these areas clandestinely and carry on its festal purposes for quite a while in relative peace. (...) Let us admit that we have attended parties where for one brief night a republic of gratified desires was attained[578] [Bey, 1991].

It is therefore of importance that unlicensed carnivalesque celebrations, so much part of the heart of a community and yet so threatening to a centralised government which aspires to survey all human activities,[579] are held outside of the public eye, outside of the reach of scare mongering or unveiling press: '(...) the TAZ is in some sense a *tactic of disappearance*'[580] [Bey, 1991].

People do dress for the occasion, spaces are decorated, yet press and especially photographers are not always welcome.[581] This is why the news of the time and location of events is often passed outside of publicly accessible channels, such as the 'word-of-mouth' system which with use of contemporary technology can be quite fast, using phones and fax machines; recently, e-mail has been added to a net of communications which is (relatively) free of surveillance. Reviews and inside news can be broadcasted through underground small press (zines) and flyers, which are only available at particular points of specific consumption such as record shops, clothes shops as well as at similar dance events themselves. Sometimes specialised pirate radio may advertise licensed events. Thus the public spectacle is abandoned

---

578 {p. 101 and p. 134}

579 See in Britain for example legal action in the context of S/M sex, watching videos at home, the single mother and the estranged father as well as panics over satanic rituals involving the sexual abuse of children.

580 {p. 128}

581 See for example the Rip events in Chapter 3, as well as many other instances of surveillance and interference in all three areas researched. Different British examples taken from the acid house era, together with a thesis on the subject of 'subcultural capital' can be found elsewhere [Thornton, 1994; Thornton, 1995].

and replaced by a different sense of an aesthetic:

The abandoning of the right to beauty amounts to an entry into a new world of illusion. From now on, the strategic domain extends to the very rhythm of the different disappearances ...582 [Virilio, 1991].

In the case of the vibrant communal consumption of house music, the potential 'loss' of both the subject as well as of the public spectacle is a spectacular disappearance indeed. As the visual space of the spectacle makes way for 'tactile-acoustic space' in a culture which increasingly relies on electronic communication [McLuhan and Powers, 1992] a specific form of festival for the late twentieth century has taken shape which features several processes of disappearance.

Conclusion

Although every house related event has its own qualities, a pattern of technical similarities in the uses of spaces of consumption appeared in the wealth of information which has been collected. It has to be stressed that due to the fact that most of the research on consumption has been done in England, it has been unavoidable that a certain bias towards events in that area can be found. Nevertheless, during verification with the information collected in and about both Chicago and the Netherlands, many of the general aspects (dance spaces, dance drugs and variations of the spectacle of disappearance) as described and discussed in this chapter do apply to those areas as well.

The consumption of house music achieves an intense yet ephemeral sense of community, whereby the individual may lose a sense of alienated 'self'. This is not achieved by dancing to the music alone. Technologies of consumption and of space pull a crowd together through procedures of (physical) exclusion and inclusion. Attempts have been identified to avoid surveillance by 'outside' institutions such as press or police. The amplification and foregrounding of music in combination with visual disorientation create and stress a tactile-acoustic space. African-American narrative house music, such as garage and deep house, articulates a positive sense of togetherness.

---

582 {p. 90}

Other types of house music, American and European, such as wild pitch or trance, stress its repetitive quality; when one dances to a repetitive rhythm, a sense of ecstatic trance may occur whereby one loses one's sense of self and becomes part of one's immediate social and cultural environment. The use of consciousness altering chemical substances can enhance the effects of the combination of house music and the management of space.

The spectacle which unselfconsciously unfolds to the observer seems to be one which not only heralds a disappearance from outside surveillance, but which also celebrates a disappearance on the level of subjectivity. Although the simulation of mating and the urge for a sense of community are both part of a dance party, a house music event can be a carefree ritual of death and rebirth, that is suited to a contemporary 'global' culture which relies on electronic communication technologies. This may explain why neither disco, nor its revenge, house music, have disappeared yet; a functional type of music such as house music will be sustained so long as there is a need for its function, which seems to be fundamental to a secular longing to make sense of the rhythms of urban life in the late twentieth century.

Part IV
Epilogue

8   This is our house

House music can be bold, it can be repetitive; it can be inventive, it can be derivative; it can be witty, it can be dull; it can be emotional, it can be dreary. But you can't ignore it. It is the music of our age [Stone, 1996].[583]

From the various discussions in this book it is possible to conclude that house music is a type of dance music which has gained popularity during the 80s and early 90s in clubs and at parties in West European cities such as Amsterdam, Manchester, London, Stockholm and Rome, as well as in North American cities such as New York, Chicago, Baltimore and San Francisco. Initially, formal aspects of house music included a steady, repetitive beat between 120 and 140 bpm and the use of sequencers and synthesizers. Since the mid-80s, samplers have been added to the range of production technologies. Variants of house music increased in speed during the early 90s, whereby some tracks, such as examples of gabber house, reached 180 bpm and over. Many styles of music have been assimilated within the tight 4/4 pattern of house. This has resulted in a music which includes various cultural traces, which in turn means that many people from mainly urban Western(ised) areas have been able to identify with this musical aesthetic form. Its basic effect is to 'pump' a desire into human bodies to move, to dance and 'let go'. To some people consuming house music is a form of escapism, for others it is a way of life comparable to a religion.

Since 1986 the tag 'house' has at times been used as a marketing tool. This book has tried to show that the meaning of the term has

---

[583] {pp. 11-12}

changed over time, in specific social and cultural contexts. In the first part of the 1980s, 'house' referred to a type of dance music which historically came into existence in an African-American environment, in North American urban centres such as New York and more specifically, in Chicago, where it was used to indicate a kind of urban DIY electronic disco music, incorporating a rich African-American cultural tradition which can be traced to jazz, funk, soul music and gospel music, mixed with European music styles like electronic trance and electronic pop music.[584] Although Europeans had flirted with 'black' musical styles, the European market had no tight connections with an African-American history and its politics and so, when it became successful in Europe, some of its original ethical and aesthetic sensibilities were subdued. In Europe, house music merged either stylistically into the realm of pop music or hybridised structurally in specific dance floor settings.[585] In this way house music acquired new meanings, whereby similar production technologies had been used[586] within a comparable set of rituals and spaces of consumption.[587] In this book, European examples were drawn from the Netherlands and England. It should be mentioned, however, that during the 1980s Italy had a special place in the cross-Atlantic musical dialogue of dance parties before and during the time that house music developed[588] and has continued to be an important player on the house scene.[589]

In the 90s, various forms of house music reached cities around the world such as Sidney in Australia, Cape Town in South Africa or Tokyo in Japan. Celebrating the end of this research project, I visited two specific places in 1995 which in their own way have become pilgrim destinations for dance fanatics, the Balearic island Ibiza and the north side of Indian holiday destination Goa. Both were served by charter holiday flights, both have long been part of the Western hippie trail and both have produced their own aesthetics in dance music, the Balearic mix in the former and Goa trance in the latter place. Even though the old style hippies had become like a rare species in both destinations, their legacy of psychedelic party

---

584 See Chapter 2.
585 See Chapters 3 and 4.
586 See Chapter 6.
587 See Chapter 7.
588 See Chapter 2.
589 For example, Black Box.

edonism remained.[590] A small group of mostly West European
raders and jet-setting nomads seemed to spend their lives between
hese two resorts, six months in Ibiza during the summer period and
ix months of the dry winter season in Goa, thereby ensuring a
:ultural exchange of party and fashion ideas. Nevertheless,
10ticeable differences between the two areas were apparent.

Ibiza had been a commercial holiday resort for much longer than
3oa. Its tourist industry had produced an expensive club
·nvironment, where clubs, supplied with roofs since 1993, have
nanaged to cater for a few thousand people at a time. These
·normous and spectacular dance spaces were spread between the
wo urban centres of the island, San Antonio and Ibiza Town. In
>rder to ensure that the party loving holiday maker was stripped of
1is or her last pennies which were not on the original holiday budget,
ome clubs made it possible to pay the highly inflated entrance fee
between £15 and £25) by credit card. During my visit in the high
eason, a selection of the English clubs hosted their own nights on this
sland. They cashed in on the fact that many young holiday makers
vanted to continue their home-lives, including attending their
avourite DJs, in a sunnier climate. Because of this type of tourist, a
'0s Balearic mixture of English, American and European house music
nd its more poppy variants, such as 'handbag', was foregrounded.
\1though quite a few DJs were a bit disappointing, especially after
1aving paid so much money to get into a club, some DJs had been able
o turn this type of eclectic mixing into an artful skill. During one of
1y nights out (or was it morning?), I witnessed how Ibiza's long
·espected DJ Alfredo led his dancing crowd through a wide range of
1usical moods in a baffling fluid manner, without losing his crowd's
·ttention for a moment. It was this type of attitude to dance floor
1ixing which in the late 80s had influenced the music policy of,
1itially, some London nightclubs, thereby contributing to the
ummer of Love in 1988.[591]

In Goa, which I visited four months later during the high season
round Xmas, the dance scene seemed to be less efficiently
>mmercial. The parties were held in the open air, on or near a beach,
1ostly free of charge and typically surrounded by local chai ladies,

---

[590] See Chapter 5 for the influences of a psychedelic aesthetic on former discotheques and
·ntemporary dance spaces.

[591] See Chapter 3 for references to the influence of an 80s version of the Balearic mix in England.
uring the late 80s, this musical mix incorporated Euro disco, some acid house and European
1art pop.

who held court around their tea and coffee burners and piles of home made snacks. A connection with the pagan hippie past of its party predecessors could be found in the reasons for the occurrence of these events, such as the full moon parties. DJs used portable DAT-machines[592] with speed adjusters instead of record decks. Several reasons were given for this; in the first place, the mobility of the DJ was increased since a DAT cassette is small, light and contains much more information than a vinyl record; in the second place, DAT cassettes do not scratch, which was a necessary quality in an environment where record shops were rare and the dance floor was covered with sand, which could easily have resulted in damage to vinyl records; in the third place, DAT enabled some European DJs to acquire up to date material before it was processed at the pressing plants; in the fourth place, mixing with DAT is well suited to the 'slow mix' technique[593] which house music and its trance like variant require; and in the fifth place, DJ Goa Gil, an imaginative and inspiring element in the development of Goa trance, told me that he liked the synthetic quality of DAT [Gil, 1996]. Somehow, the industrial washes of sound seemed at odds with the peaceful beaches, fringed by palm trees on one side and a luminous sea on the other. However, after sufficient sleep deprivation the music started to induce kaleidoscopic visual effects on the inner eye of yours truly, creating a mild sensation of being in a trance[594] and having the subjective effect that my body disappeared into a virtual head trip. Since the mid-90s, this particular musical trance aesthetic had been commercially known as Goa trance. In 1995, the format of these parties was recreated mainly in Amsterdam, London[595] and in certain parts of Israel.[596]

And so the story of house continues, changing, hybridising and assimilating new ideas within the margins of that machine generated 4/4 beat which never seems to stop. It would be ridiculous to single out any one particular format as the logical conclusion of house music, since there is always a new one around the corner; acid house,

---

592 Digital Audio Tape; often used for producing the master of a record, which is then sent to the record pressing plant.
593 See Chapter 5.
594 For the trance effects of repetitive beats combined with a mind altering activity, such as sleep deprivation, see the last part of Chapter 7.
595 Party organisations such as Return to the Source, Smile and Pendragon.
596 Many Israeli ex-soldiers, male and female, celebrate the end of their institutionalised lives of school and army in places such as Goa.

deep house, progressive house, gabberhouse,[597] happy house, epic house, hard bag, techno acid beats, nuhouse, there is no end to it. At the moment I would write the names of these variants, new ones emerge, others become obsolete, while some, such as drum 'n' bass and ambient house, have become genres in their opular culture, of which, for at least the last 15 years, house music has undeniably been a part.

> ... once you enter into my house it then becomes our house and our house music.
> Can-you-feel-it? [Heard and Roberts, 1988].*

---

[597] a.k.a. gabba; see Chapter 4.

Part V
Sources

Sources

Printed material

Fer Abrahams (1990), 'Hausse in House', in: *Man*, Amsterdam, March.

Arno Adelaars (1991), *Ecstasy: de opkomst van een bewustzijns-veranderend middel*, Amsterdam: In de Knipscheer.

Advance Party (1994), information sheet, July, London.

Don Aitken (1994), 'The Criminal Justice Bill: a guide', in: *New Statesman & Society: Criminal Justice & Public Order Bill supplement*, July, London.

Keith Alcorn (1994), 'Do Poppers cause Aids?', in: *Gay Times*, October, London.

Juan Luis Alvarez and Francisco Santander (1993), 'Ibiza "mon amour"', in: *Panorama*, No. 321, 19 July, Madrid.

Umbro Apollonio (1973), *Futurist Manifestos*, London: Thames and Hudson.

Paul Atkinson (1990), *The Ethnographic Imagination: textual constructions of reality*, London and New York: Routledge.

Les Back (1988), 'Coughing Up Fire', in: *New Formations*, No. 5, London.

Richard Bagehot (1989), *Music Business Agreements*, London: Waterlow Publishers.

Michail M. Bakhtin (1984), *Rabelais and His World*, Bloomington, IN: Indiana University Press.

Claudio Barbieri et al. (eds.) (1996), *Altrove #; Societa Italiana Per Lo Studio Degli Stat. Di Cozienza*, Turin.

Les Barden (1993), 'Gurning', in: *Mixmag*, Vol. 2, No. 22, March, Slough.

Marco Barelds (1994), *House-Party: Mystery, Hystery, History*, Zutphen: Walburg Pers.

Roland Barthes (1973), *Mythologies*, London, Glasgow, Toronto, Sydney and Auckland: Paladin/Grafton Books.

Roland Barthes (1976), *The Pleasure of the Text*, London: Cape.

Roland Barthes (1977), 'Death of the Author', in: *Image Music Text*, London: Fontana Press.

George Bataille (1985), 'The Sacred', *Visions of Excess: Selected Writings, 1927-1939*, Allan Stoekl (ed.), Manchester: Manchester University Press.

Jean Baudrillard (1983), *Simulations*, New York: Semiotext(e).

Jean Baudrillard (1987), *The Evil Demon Of Images*, Sydney: Power Institute Publications.

Jean Baudrillard (1988a), *The Ecstasy of Communication*, Brooklyn, NY: Semiotext(e).

Jean Baudrillard (1988b), *Xerox and Infinity*, London: Touchepas.

Jean Baudrillard (1990), *Fatal Strategies*, London: Semiotext(e)/Pluto Press.

Stephen Bayley (1991), *Taste: the Secret Meaning of Things*, London: Faber and Faber.

Jeremy Beadle (1993), *Will Pop Eat Itself? Pop music in the soundbite era*, London: Faber and Faber.

Monroe C. Beardsley (1975), *Aesthetics from Classical Greece to The Present: a short history*, Tuscaloosa and London: The University of Alabama Press.

Howard S. Becker (1963), *Outsiders: studies in the sociology of deviance*, New York: The Free Press.

Ardy Beesemer (1991a), 'Gabber op Klompen', in: *Oor*, No. 12, 15 June, Amsterdam.

Ardy Beesemer (1991b), 'Warm en Menselijk', in: *Oor*, No. 14-15, 13 July, Amsterdam.

Ardy Beesemer (1991c), 'Genitale House', in: *Oor*, No. 21, 19 October, Amsterdam.

Catherine Belsey (1980), *Critical Practice*, London: Methuen.

Walter Benjamin (1973), 'The work of art in the age of mechanical reproduction', in: Hanah Arendt (ed.), *[Schriften] Illuminations*, London: Fontana.

Glenn A. Berry (1992), *House Music's Development And The East Coast Underground Scene*, unpublished paper, Madison, WI: University of Wisconsin-Madison.

Hakim Bey (1991), *TAZ: the temporary autonomous zone, Ontological Anarchy, poetic terrorism*, Brooklyn, NY: Autonomedia.

Bilwet (1993), 'Hardware, Software, Wetware', in: *Mediamatic*, 7:1, Amsterdam.

M. Biol, S.M. Bradberry, D.A. Whittington, D.A. Parry, J.A. Vale and R.M. Whittington (1994), 'Fatal methemoglobinemia due to inhalation of isobutyl nitrate', in: *Journal of Toxicology*, 32/2, Basel.

Andy Blackford (1979), *Disco Dancing Tonite: clubs, dances, fashion, music*, New York and London: Octopus Books.

Andrew Blake (1992), *The Music Business*, London: B.T. Barsford.

Terry Bloomfield (1991), 'It's Sooner Than You Think, or Where Are We in the History of Rock Music?', in: *New Left Review*, No. 190, London.

Henk Boer (1988), 'Computer creatieve opname-machine', in: *Het Vrije Volk*, 11 May, Rotterdam.

Henry Bonsu (1991), 'Kings of clubs', in: *Manchester Evening News*, 2 January, Manchester.

Alfred Bos (1992), letter to the author, 15 April, Amsterdam.

Pierre Bourdieu (1989), *Distinction: a social critique of the judgement of taste*, London: Routledge.

D.A.L. Bowen, R. Fysh and E.R. Sarvesvaran (1992), 'Amyl nitrate related deaths', in: *Med Sci Law*, 32/2, London.

Barbara Bradby (1993), 'Sampling sexuality: gender, technology and the body in dance music', in: Popular Music, Vol. 12/2, Cambridge.

David Bradwell (1988), 'Copycat Crimes', in: *Music Technology*, September, Ely.

Christean Braut (1994), *The Musician's Guide to MIDI*, Alameda, CA: Sybex, Macintosh Library.

Ros Brown-Grant (1988), 'Sexual Politics, Visual Pleasure', in: *North by North West*, No. 4, June, Manchester.

Scott Bukatman (1993), *Terminal Identity: the virtual subject in post-*

modern science fiction, Durham, NC: Duke University Press.

Nigel Bunyan (1991), 'Security bites at "family reunion" as club reopens', in: *The Daily Telegraph*, 13 July, London.

Pascal Bussy (1993), *Kraftwerk: man, machine and music*, Wembley, SAF.

Duncan Campbell (1991), 'No jeans, no trainers', in: *GQ*, November, London.

Cleo Campert (1989), 'Acid Junks, "Ga toch naar House!"', in: *Haagse Post*, 8 July, Amsterdam.

Editorial: Capital Gay (1991), 'Why the US is banning poppers', in: *Capital Gay*, 22 February, London.

Hester Carvalho (1992), 'Wij zijn muziek arbeiders', in: *NRC — Handelsblad*, 11 November, Rotterdam.

Hester Carvalho (1996), 'De harteklop van de duivel: gabbermuziek is uitgegroeid tot jeugdcultuur', in: *NRC — Handelsblad*, 5 January, Rotterdam.

Sarah Champion (ed.) (1996), *Disco Biscuits: New Fiction from the Chemical Generation*, London: Sceptre/Hodder.

Michael Chanan (1995), *Repeated Takes: a short history of recording and its effects on music*, London and New York: Verso.

Phil Cheeseman (1993a), 'History of House DJ supplement', in: *DJ*, No. 87, 22 April-5 May, London.

John Chesterman and Andy Lipman (1988), *The Electronic Pirates*, London: Comedia/Routledge/Routledge, Chapman and Hall.

Frazer Clark (1993), 'Trance as religious experience', in: *Mixmag*, Vol. 2, No. 20, January, Slough.

Club Guide (1993), supplement of *DJ*, No. 102, December, London.

Will Colebrook (1992), *Spiral Tribe: popular culture, audience and dominant ideology*, unpublished BA essay, Cleveland: University of Teesside.

Matthew Collin (1991), 'Party On!: Soundsystems and the anarchist house culture', in: *i-D*, No. 89, February, London.

Matthew Collin and Mark Heley (1989), 'Summer of Love 1989', in: *i-D*, No. 73, September, London.

Stuart Cosgrove (1987), sleeve note to: *The House Sound of Chicago, Vol. 3, Acid House* (album), London: FFRR/London Records.

Stuart Cosgrove (1988), sleeve note to: *The History Of The House Sound Of Chicago*, Kaarst, Diepholz, Basel and Vienna: BCM Records.

Tim Creed (1993), *Social Interactions at Raves: a raver's/sociologist's study*, unpublished BA dissertation, Manchester: University of Manchester.

Criminal Justice and Public Order Act (1994), London: HMSO Publications.

Aleister Crowley (1991), *Magick Without Tears*, Phoenix, AZ: New Falcon.

Chris Cutler (1984), 'Technology and contemporary music: necessity and choice in musical forms', in: *Popular Music*, No. 4, Cambridge.

Frederic Dannen (1991), *Hitmen: powerbrokers and fast money inside the music business*, New York: Vintage Books.

David Davies (1992), 'On the Front Line', in: 'Mixmag DIY guide: how to make a record', with: *Mixmag*, Vol. 2, No. 12, May, Slough.

Daniel Dayan and Elihu Katz (1985), 'Electronic Ceremonies: television performs a royal wedding', *On Signs*, in: Marshall Blonsky (ed.), Oxford: Basil Blackwell.

Gilles Deleuze and Felix Guattari (1986), *Nomadology: the war machine*, New York: Semiotext(e).

Mark Dery (1991), 'Kraftwerk Redux: house music goes robo-rock', in: *New York Times*, New York.

Mark Dery (ed.) (1993a), *Flame Wars; the discourse of cyberculture*, The South Atlantic Quarterly, 92;4, Fall 1993, Durham, NC: Duke University Press.

Mark Dery (1993b), 'Black to the Future: interviews with Samuel R. Delany, Greg Tate and Tricia Rose', in: Mark Dery (ed.), *Flame Wars; the discourse of cyberculture*, The South Atlantic Quarterly, 92;4, Fall 1993, Durham, NC: Duke University Press.

Hiske Dibbets (1988), 'De terreur van the summer of love', in: *Haagse Post*, 20 August, Amsterdam.

Robert L. Doerschuk (1992), 'Secrets of Salsa Rhythm: piano with hot sauce', in: Vernon W. Boggs, *Salsiology: Afro-Cuban music and the evolution of salsa in New York City*, New York, Westport, CO and London: Greenwood Press.

Alan Durant (1984), *Conditions of Music*, London and Basingstoke: The Macmillan Press.

Alan Durant (1990), 'A new day for music? Digital technologies in contemporary music-making', in: Philip Hayward (ed.), *Culture, Technology and Creativity in the Late Twentieth Century*, London, Paris and Rome: John Libbey.

Richard Dyer (1992), 'In defense of disco', in: *Only Entertainment*, London: Routledge.

Terry Eagleton (1990), *The Ideology of the Aesthetic*, Cambridge, MA and Oxford: Blackwell.

Fiona Earle et al. (1994), *A Time to Travel?: An introduction to Britain's newer travellers*, Lyme Regis: Enabler Publications.

Umberto Eco (1986), *Travels in Hyperreality*, London: Picador/Pan Books.

Robert Elms (1988), 'Nightclubbing', in: *The Face*, No. 100, September, London.

Tom Engelshoven and John van Luijn (1989), 'House: muziek voor miljoenen?', in: *Oor*, 28 January, Amsterdam.

Brian Eno (1991), 'On writing space', in: *Artforum*, November, New York.

Emilie Escher and Fred Vermeulen (1992), 'De house party tegen de sufheid', in: *Het Parool*, 29 February, Amsterdam.

Kodwo Eshun (1993), 'Outing the incrowd', in: *The Wire*, No. 106/7, London.

Berry Evers (1994), *Rock da House*, unpublished paper, Amsterdam: University of Amsterdam.

Mark Farrin (1994), 'Mark Farrin investigates the use and abuse of the SL 1200/1210 series turntable', in: *DJ*, No. 110, 17-30 March, London.

Mike Fish (1992), 'Why we must destroy the music industry', in: *The Wire*, May, London.

Jonathan Fleming (1995), *What kind of House Party is this? History of a music revolution*, Slough: MIY Publishing.

Astrid Fontaine and Caroline Fontana (1996), *Raver*, Paris: Anthropos.

Michel Foucault (1980), *Power/Knowledge: selected interviews and other writings, 1972-1977*, Colin Gordon (ed.), Brighton: The Harvester Press.

Michel Foucault (1981), *The History of Sexuality, Vol. 1; an introduction*, London: Peregrine Books/Penguin Books.

Michel Foucault (1984), 'What is an author?', in: Paul Rabinow (ed.), *The Foucault Reader*, London: Peregrine Books/Penguin Books.

Michel Foucault (1989), 'The order of discourse (1971)', in: Philip Rice and Patricia Waugh (ed.), *Modern Literary Theory*, London, New York, Melbourne and Auckland: Edward Arnold/Hodder and Stoughton.

P. de Franca (1983), *Ferdinand Leger*, New Haven and London: Yale UP.

Pieter Franssen (1988a), 'House hypno', in: *Oor*, 10 September, Amsterdam.

Pieter Franssen (1988b), 'Mayday: man & machine', in: *Oor*, 10 September, Amsterdam.

Sigmund Freud (1977), *On Sexuality*, London, New York, Victoria, Ontario and Auckland: Pelican/Penguin Books.

Simon Frith (1983), *Sound Effects: youth, leisure and the politics of rock 'n' roll*, London: Constable.

Hugh Gallagher (1994), 'Gimme two records and I'll make you a universe: DJ Spooky, tha subliminal kid', in: *Wired*, August, San Francisco, CA.

Simon Garfield (1983/84), 'The producers', in: *Blitz*, No. 17, December/January, London.

Sheryl Garratt (1986), 'Chicago house', in: *The Face*, No. 77, September, London.

Sheryl Garratt (1988), 'Amsterdamage', in: *The Face*, No. 97, May, London.

Sheryl Garratt (1989), 'Keeping the faith', in: *The Face*, Vol. 2, No. 8, May, London.

Sheryl Garratt (1990), 'Was it London or Manchester invented acid house', in: *The Face*, Vol. 2, No. 18, March, London.

Geraldine Geraghty (1996), *Raise Your Hands*, London: Boxtree Ltd.

Charley Gerard and Marty Sheller (1989), *Salsa! The rhythm of Latin music*, Crown Point, IN: White Cliffs Media Company.

William Gibson (1984), *Neuromancer*, London: Ace Books.

Dave Gill and Gary Lethbridge (1994), sleeve note, for: *The Drum Album*, London: Drum Records.

Paul Gilroy (1993), *The Black Atlantic*, London and New York: Verso.

John Godfrey (1988), 'Happy daze are here again', in: *i-D*, No. 59, June, London.

Hans Goedkoop (1989), 'The big confusion: acid is dood, leve acid!', in: *Haagse Post*, 1 April, Amsterdam.

Albert H. Goldman (1978), *Disco*, New York: Hawthorn Books.

Andrew Goodwin (1990), 'Sample and Hold: pop music in the digital age of reproduction', in: Simon Frith and Andrew Goodwin (ed.), *On Record*, London: Routledge.

Andrew Goodwin (1992), 'Rationalization and democratization in the new technologies of popular music', in: James Lull, *Popular Music and Communication*, second edition, Newbury Park, London, New Delhi: Sage Publications.

Matt Greenhalgh (1994), 'The spin doctors', in: *City Life*, No. 257, 29 June-14 July, Manchester.

Lawrence Grossberg (1994), 'Is anybody listening? Does anybody care?', in: Andrew Ross and Tricia Rose, *Microphone Fiends; Youth Music and Youth Culture*, London and New York: Routledge.

Martyn Hammersley (1992), *What's wrong with Ethnography?* London and New York: Routledge.

Martyn Hammersley and Paul Atkinson (1989), *Ethnography: principles in practice*, London and New York: Routledge.

Donna Haraway (1989), 'A cyborg manifesto', in: *Simians, Cyborgs and Women*, London and New York: Routledge.

Dave Harker (1993), *Popular Song* (course handbook), Manchester: Manchester Metropolitan University.

Ross Harley (1993), 'Beat in the system', in: Tony Bennett et al. (ed.), *Rock and Popular Music: politics, policies, institutions*, London and New York: Routledge.

Damian Harris (1993), 'I'm sliding!', in: *DJ*, No. 84, 11-24 March, London.

Damian Harris (1994), 'Junior Boys Own!', in: *DJ*, No. 113, 28 April-11 May, London.

David Harris (1992), *From Class Struggle to the Politics of Pleasure: the effects of Gramscianism on cultural studies*, London: Routledge.

David Harvey (1989), *The Condition of Postmodernity: an inquiry into the origins of cultural change*, Oxford: Basil Blackwell.

Steven Harvey (1983), 'Behind the groove: New York City's disco underground', in: *Collusion*, No. 5, London.

Dick Hebdige (1987), *Cut 'n' Mix: culture, identity and Caribbean music*, London: Routledge.

Sheila Henderson (1993a), 'Fun, fashion and frisson', *The International Journal of Drug Policy*, Rotterdam.

Sheila Henderson (1993b), 'Luvdup and deelited: responses to drug use in the second decade', in: Aggleton et al. (eds.), *AIDS: Facing the Second Decade*, London: Falmer.

Sheila Henderson (forthcoming), *Dancing in the Dark: sex, drugs and the modern girl*, London and New York, Pandora.

Robert Hodge and Gunther Kress (1988), *Social Semiotics*, Cambridge and Oxford: Polity Press/Basil Blackwell.

Frederick G. Hofman (1983), *A Handbook on Drug and Alcohol Abuse; the Biomedical Aspects*, New York: Oxford University Press.

Michael Holquist (1984), 'Prologue', in: Mikhail M. Bahktin, *Rabelais and His World*, Bloomington, IN: Indiana University Press.

Eduard van Holst Pellekaan (1991), 'Move on everybody: rave', in: *Haagse Post-De Tijd*, 7 June, Amsterdam.

Stewart Home (1989a), *Pure Mania*, Edinburgh: Polygon.

Stewart Home (1989b), 'Demolish serious culture!', in: *Smile*, No. 11, London.

Walter Hughes (1994), 'In the empire of the beat: discipline and disco', in: Andrew Ross and Tricia Rose, *Microphone Fiends: Youth Music and Youth Culture*, London and New York: Routledge.

Bernard Hulsman (1991), 'De meisjes blijven weg', in: *NRC-Handelsblad*, 22 November, Rotterdam.

Chris Humphreys (1990), 'Showing men the door', in: *Manchester Evening News*, 26 February, Manchester.

Laud Humphreys (1970), *Tearoom Trade*, London: Gerald Duckworth and Co. Ltd.

Josephine Hussey (1994), 'A law to make you raving mad', in: *Living Marxism*, July, London.

Vicky Hutchings (1994), 'Fight for the right to party', in: *New Statesman and Society*, 6 May, London.

Andreas Huyssen (1988a), 'The hidden dialectic: avantgarde — technology — mass culture', in: *After The Great Divide: modernism, mass culture and postmodernism*, Basingstoke and London: The Macmillan Press.

Andreas Huyssen (1988b), 'The vamp and the machine', in: *After The Great Divide: modernism, mass culture and postmodernism*, Basingstoke and London: The Macmillan Press.

Fredric Jameson (1984), 'Postmodernism, or the cultural logic of late capitalism', in: *New Left Review*, No. 146, July-August, London.

Ruurd Jellema (1991), 'MDMA in het laboratorium' in: Dirk Korf, Peter Blanken and Tom Nabben (ed.), *Een nieuwe wonderpil? Verspreiding, effecten en risico's van ecstasy gebruik in Amsterdam*, Amsterdam: Jellinek Centrum/IADA.

Radcliffe A. Joe (1980), *This Business of Disco*, Lakewood, NJ: Billboard Books/Watson-Gutpill Publications.

Alan Jones (1992), 'Indies Clean Up', in: *Record Mirror-Music Week*, 18 January, London.

Steve Jones (1992), *Authorship and Authenticity*, unpublished paper, Tulsa, OK: University of Tulsa.

Steve Jones (1993), 'Who fought the law? The American music industry and the global popular music market', in: Tony Bennett et al. (ed.), *Rock and Popular Music; politics, policies, institutions*, London and New York: Routledge.

Sjoerd de Jong (1992), 'House is sociale verniewing in praktijk', in: *NRC-Handelsblad*, 7 March, Rotterdam.

Sjoerd de Jong (1993), 'Evangelisch verzet tegen house-muziek', in: *NRC-Handelsblad*, 26 November, Rotterdam.

Chris de Jongh (1991), 'House legt de oergevoelens blood', in: *NRC-Handelsblad*, 6 June, Rotterdam.

Judge Jules (1988), sleeve note for: *Salsoul Classics*, CD version, Luton: Indigo Musik.

Holger Kalweit (1988), *Dreamtime and Inner Space*, Boston, MA: Shambhala Publications.

Bob Killbourn (1986), sleeve notes for: *The Best of Parliament*, London: Club/Phonogram.

Abigail King (1992), 'Sweets!', in: 'i-D Club Supplement', *i-D*, No. 100, January, London.

Stephen Kingston (1994), 'All aboard the freedom train', in: *24 Seven*, June, London.

Margalith Kleijwegt (1990), 'Op zoek naar de Nederlandse acid house-scene', in: *Vrij Nederland*, 17 February, Amsterdam.

Gordon Knott (1994), 'Monsieur Kervorkian', in: *DJ*, No. 111, 31 March-13 April, London.

Frankie Knuckles (1990), transcribed research interview conducted by Jon Savage, for: The Rhythm Divine [originally Abseil Productions], Kinesis Films, Channel 4.

Dirk Korf, Peter Blanken and Tom Nabben (1991), *Een nieuwe wonderpil? Verspreiding, effecten en risico's van ecstasy gebruik in Amsterdam*, Amsterdam: Jellinek Centrum/IADA.

Hein de Kort (1987), 'Klein maar dapper', in: *Oor*, 21 February, Amsterdam.

Bernard Krausse (1983), 'Electronic music', in: *Making Music*, edited by George Martin, Basingstoke: Pan Books.

Jurgen Laarman (1993), 'Alles naar de kl**te!', in: *DJ*, No. 81, 28 January-10 February, London.

Karin de Lange (1989), 'Acid house', in: *Club Veronica*, March, Hilversum.

Tony Langlois (1992), 'Can you feel it? DJs and house music culture in the UK', in: *Popular Music*, Vol. 11/2, Cambridge.

Dave Lee (1993), 'Disco Dave', in: 'Disco! DJ supplement', *DJ*, No. 84, 11-24 March, London.

Ian Levine (1990), transcribed research interview conducted by Jon Savage, for: The Rhythm Divine [originally Abseil Productions], Kinesis Films, Channel 4.

Ioan M. Lewis (1989), *Ecstatic Religion: a study of Shamanism and spirit possession*, London: Routledge.

Lifeline (1991), *The Peanut Pete Series*, Manchester: Lifeline, NW regional drug training unit.

Lifeline (1992), *Too Damn Hot!*, Manchester: Lifeline, NW regional drug training unit.

Lifeline (1993), *The Big Blue Book Of Dance Drugs*, Manchester: Lifeline, NW regional drug training unit.

Dominic Loehnis (1991), 'Young clamour to break into the dance fortress', in: *The Sunday Telegraph*, 4 August, London.

Richard Lowe and William Shaw (1993), *Travellers: voices of the new age nomads*, London: Fourth Estate Ltd.

Celia Lury (1993), *Cultural Rights: technology, legality and personality*, London and New York: Routledge.

Norman Mailer (1959), 'The white negro', in: *Advertisements for Myself*, London: Andre Deutsch.

Peter Manuel (1993), *Cassette Culture: popular music and technology in North India*, Chicago, IL and London: The University of Chicago Press.

Tony Marcus (1993), 'Summer of Chaos', in: *i-D*, No. 119, August, London.

Tony Marcus (1994), 'Groovy Trance', in: *Mixmag*, Vol. 2, No. 35, April, Slough.

Herbert Marcuse (1987), *Eros and Civilisation: a philosophical inquiry into Freud*, London: Ark Paperbacks/Routledge.

Terry Martin (1992), 'Knuckles' Chicago', in: *Crossfade*, No. 3, November, Chicago, Illinois.

Brad Maugham (1994), 'Junk!', in: *Boyz*, 2 April, London.

Jon McCready (1994), 'They called it HOT .. and it was '88', flyer blurb for: *Classics 88*, Fac 51 The Hacienda, March, Manchester.

Peter McDermott (1993), 'Grassed Up', in: *The Face*, No. 61, October, London.

Marshall McLuhan (1994), *Understanding Media: the extensions of man*, London and New York: Routledge.

Marshall McLuhan and Bruce R. Powers (1992), *The Global Village: transformations in world life and the media in the 21st century*, New York: Oxford University Press.

Angela McRobbie (1994), 'Shut up and dance: youth culture and the changing modes of femininity', in: *Postmodernism and popular culture*, London and New York, Routledge.

MDPI (1993), *Manchester Drugs Prevention Initiative: warning...hot!*, Manchester: Lifeline, NW regional drug training unit.

MDTIC (1992), *Keep Chillin': heatstroke and heat exhaustion*, Liverpool: Mersey Drug Training and Information Centre.

Antonio Melechi (1993), 'The Ecstasy of Disappearance', in: Steve Redhead (ed.), *Rave Off, Politics and Deviance in Contemporary Youth Culture*, Aldershot: Avebury.

Antonio Melechi and Steve Redhead (1988), 'The fall of the acid reign', in: *New Statesman and Society*, 23-30 December, London.

Richard Middleton (1990), *Studying Popular Music*, Milton Keynes and Philadelphia: Open University Press.

Elvis Mitchell (1990), *The Motown Album: the sound of young America — three decades of magic!*, London: Sarah Lazin

Books/Virgin Books.

Mixmag (1986), 'DMC's UK Dance Chart', in: *Mixmag*, No. 44, September, Slough.

Tom Moulton (1975), 'Disco Action', *Billboard*, No. 43, 10 February, Nashville, TN.

John Mowitt (1987), 'The sound of music in the era of its electronic reproducibility', in: Richard Loppert and Susan McClary (eds.), *Music and Society: the Politics of Composition, Performance and Reception*, Cambridge: Cambridge University Press.

Ronald Moy (1991), *Enginicians and Theft*, part of PhD thesis, Liverpool: Liverpool University.

Drs. J. Mulder (1993), *Met House naar een Andere Wereld*, Waddinxveen: Lumen Mundi.

Laura Mulvey (1989), *Visual and Other Pleasures*, London and Basingstoke: The Macmillan Press.

The Museum of Modern Art (ed.) (1934), *Machine Art*, Manchester, NH: Arno Press.

Peter Nasmyth (1985), 'Ecstasy: a yuppie way of knowledge', in: *The Face*, No. 66, October, London.

Frank Natale (1995), *Trance Dance: the dance of life*, Shaftesbury, Rockport, MA and Brisbane: Element Books.

Keith Negus (1992), *Producing Pop: culture and conflict in the popular music industry*, London, New York, Melbourne and Auckland: Edward Arnold.

Russell Newcombe (1991), *Raving and Dance Drugs: house music clubs and parties in North-West England*, Liverpool: Rave Research Bureau.

Willis Ninja (1994), 'Not a mutant turtle', in: Andrew Ross and Tricia

Rose (ed.), *Microphone Fiends: Youth Music and Youth Culture*, London and New York: Routledge.

Richard Norris (1990), 'Turning the tables on the record industry', in: *Select*, August, London.

Editorial: NRC-Handelsblad (1993), '"Leuzen" op house-feest taboe', in: *NRC-Handelsblad*, 5 December, Rotterdam.

Catriona O'Shaughernessy (1992), 'If you've got the music in you now's the time to get it out', in: 'Spring Student Special', *The Independent*, London.

Frank Owen, Simon Reynolds and Dylan Jones (1987), 'Now that's what I call music', in: *i-D*, No. 46, April, London.

Graeme Park and Tom Wainright (1993), 'Hacienda hassles', in: *DJ*, No. 96, London.

Sima Patel (1993), *Dance music, marketing and design*, unpublished BA dissertation, Stoke-on-Trent: Staffordshire University.

Editorial: Pauze (1988), *Pauze*, January, Amsterdam.

Dom Phillips (1992), 'Did "Charly" kill rave?', in: *Mixmag*, Vol. 2, No. 15, August, Slough.

Maria Pini (1993), *Rave, Dance and Women*, unpublished MA dissertation, London: Thames Valley University.

Sadie Plant (1992), *The Most Radical Gesture: the situationist international in a postmodern age*, London and New York: Routledge.

Sadie Plant (1993), 'Building The Hacienda', in: *Hybrid*, No. 1, February/March, London.

Steve Platt (1994), 'Editorial: criminal injustice', in: *New Statesman and Society*, 29 April, London.

Mark Poster (1990), *The Mode of Information*, Oxford: Polity Press.

Ray Pratt (1990), *Rhythm and Resistance: explorations in the political uses of popular music*, London: Praeger.

Erik Quint (1988), 'Een nieuwe subcultuur: acid house', in: *Rotterdams Nieuwsblad*, 21 November, Rotterdam.

Ravescene Magazeen (1992), *Call Yourself a Raver? Ravescene year book 1993*, London: Yage Corporation.

Steve Redhead (1990), *The End-Of-The-Century Party: youth and pop towards 2000*, Manchester and New York: Manchester University Press.

Steve Redhead (1991), 'Rave Off: youth, subculture and the law', in: *Social Studies Review*, Vol. 6, No. 3, Deddington.

Steve Redhead (ed.) (1993a), *Rave Off: Politics and Deviance in Contemporary Youth Culture*, Aldershot: Avebury.

Steve Redhead (1993b), 'The politics of ecstasy', in: Steve Redhead (ed.), *Rave Off: Politics and Deviance in Contemporary Youth Culture*, Aldershot: Avebury.

Steve Redhead (1995), *Unpopular Cultures*, Manchester and New York: Manchester University Press.

Steve Redhead and Hillegonda C. Rietveld (1992), 'Down at the club', in: Jon Savage (ed.), *The Hacienda Must Be Built*, Woodford Green: International Music Publications.

Simon Reynolds (1990a), 'Euro Body Music: Front 242', in: *Blissed Out*, London: Serpent's Tail.

Simon Reynolds (1990b), 'Mantra-onics', in: *Blissed Out*, London: Serpent's Tail.

Simon Reynolds (1990c), 'Where "now" lasts longer', in: *Blissed Out*, London: Serpent's Tail.

Hans Richter (1965), *Dada: art and anti art*, London: Thames and Hudson.

Hillegonda C. Rietveld (1992a), *The Hacienda Files*, Archiving project, Manchester: Manchester Institute for Popular Culture.

Hillegonda C. Rietveld (1992b), introduction and research for: *Popular Culture*, slide pack, No. DP2, Manchester: The Slide Library, Manchester Metropolitan University.[598]

Hillegonda C. Rietveld (1993), 'Living the Dream', in: Steve Redhead (ed.), *Rave Off, Politics and Deviance in Contemporary Youth Culture*, Aldershot: Avebury.

Gonnie Rietveld (1994), 'Work It/Mix It', in: *The Jockey Slut*, January/February, Manchester.

Hillegonda Rietveld (1995), *House music: the politics of a musical aesthetic*, PhD thesis, Manchester: Manchester Metropolitan University.

Hillegonda Rietveld (1996), 'Pure Bliss' (internet version) in: Lachlan Brown (ed.), *Difference Engine*, String 2 ('ecstasies of innovation') http://www/gold.ac.uk/difference/oz.html. London: Goldsmiths' College.

Cynthia Rose (1991), *Design After Dark*, London: Thames and Hudson.

Tricia Rose (1994), *Black Noise: rap music and black culture in contemporary America*, Hanover, NH: Wesleyan University Press/University Press of New England.

Gilbert Rouget (1985), *Music and Trance: a theory of the relations between music and possession*, Chicago and London: University of Chicago Press.

Rudy Rucker (1994), 'Wetware', in: *Live Robots*, New York: Avon Books.

---

[598] Slide sets @ £20 each, or £54 all 3. Set 1: *Flyers*; Set 2: *The Hacienda*; Set 3: *Posters*.

Neil Rushton (1982), 'Out on the floor', in: *The Face*, No. 29, September, London.

Kelly Rust (1996), *How Does Women's Experience of Gabba Differ from their Experience of Other Music Subcultures?*, unpublished BA dissertation, London: Goldsmiths' College, London University.

Edward W. Said (1985), *Orientalism*, London, New York, Victoria, Ontario and Auckland: Peregrine/Penguin Books.

Nicholas Saunders (1993), *E for Ecstasy*, London: Nicholas Saunders.

Nicholas Saunders (1995), *Ecstasy and the Dance Culture*, London: Nicholas Saunders.

Jon Savage (1983), introduction to: *Industrial Culture Handbook*, San Francisco, CA: RE/Search, No. 6-7.

Jon Savage (1988), 'The way we wore', in: *The Face*, No.93, February, London.

Jon Savage (1991), *England's Dreaming: anarchy, Sex Pistols, punk rock, and beyond*, New York, St. Martin's Press.

Jon Savage (1992), *The Hacienda Must Be Built*, Woodford Green: International Music Publications.

Jon Savage (1993), sleeve note for: *Cybotron interface: the roots of techno*, London: Southbound.

Jon Savage (1996), 'Machine Soul: a history of techno', in: *Time Travel*, London: Chatto and Windus.

Helene Schilders (1992), 'de jacht is geopend', in: *Revu*, 5 March, Amsterdam.

Thomas G. Schumacher (1995), '"This is a sampling sport": digital sampling, rap music and the law in cultural production', in: *Media, Culture and Society*, Sage, Vol. 17, London, Thousand Oaks and New Delhi.

237

John Shepherd (1991), *Music As Social Text*, Oxford: Polity Press.

Ronald K. Siegel (1989), *Intoxication: life in pursuit of artificial paradise*, London: Simon and Schuster.

Richard Smith (1992), 'going back to my roots', in: *Mixmag*, Vol. 2, No. 17, October, Slough.

Solomon H. Snyder (1986), *Drugs and the Brain*, New York, Scientific American Library.

Susan Sontag (1982), 'Notes on camp', in: *A Susan Sontag Reader*, London, New York, Victoria, Ontario and Auckland: Penguin Books.

Claudia Springer (1991), 'The pleasure of the interface', in: *Screen*, 32:3, autumn, Oxford.

Sam Steele (1994), 'No shit! this is D-jax Up beats', in: *The Jockey Slut*, May/June, Manchester.

Jay Stevens (1989), *Storming Heaven: LSD and the American dream*, London: Paladin/Grafton Books.

C.J. Stone (1996), *Fierce Dancing; adventures in the underground*, London: Faber and Faber.

Will Straw (1991), 'Systems of articulation, logics of change: communities and scenes in popular music', in: *Cultural Studies*, October, London.

David Swindles (1983), 'Turn on, tune in, sort it out', in: *The Observer Life*, 5 December, London.

Sheep T. (1993), 'The user interface', in: *Mediamatic*, 7:1, Amsterdam.

Phillip Tagg (1994), 'From refrain to rave: the decline of figure and the rise of ground', *Popular Music*, No. 13, Cambridge.

Rogan Taylor (1985), *The Death and Resurrection Show*, London: Antony Blond.

TBC (text) and Jim Browne (drawings) (1992), 'Moody DJ', in: *The London Illustrated Chortlers Companion*, No. 1-2, London.

Paul Theberge (1989), 'The Sound of Music: technological rationalisation and the production of popular music', in: *New Formations*, No. 7, Spring, London.

Paul Theberge (1993), 'Random access: music, technology, postmodernism', in: Simon Miller (ed.), *The Last Post*, Manchester and New York: Manchester University Press.

Anthony Thomas (1989), 'The house the kids built: the gay black imprint on American dance music', in: *Out/Look*, Summer, US. Also in: Corey K. Creekmur and Alexander Doty (1995), *Out in Culture: Gay, Lesbian and Queer Essays on Popular Culture*, London: Cassell.

Barry Thompson (1993), *The Spiritual Dimensions of Popular Music*, unpublished BA dissertation, Salford: Salford College University.

Sarah Thornton (1993), *From Record Hops to Raves: cultural studies of youth, music and media*, PhD thesis, Glasgow: John Logie Beard Centre, University of Strathclyde.

Sarah Thornton (1994), 'Moral panic, the media and British rave culture', in: Andrew Ross and Tricia Rose, *Microphone Fiends: Youth Music and Youth Culture*, New York and London: Routledge.

Sarah Thornton (1995), *Club Cultures: music, media and subcultural capital*, Cambridge: Polity Press.

The Timelords (1988), *The Manual*, Haverhill: KLF Publications/Panda Press.

C. Tisdall and A. Bozzolla (1977), *Futurism*, London: Thames and Hudson.

Alan Tomlinson (1990), 'Consumer culture and the aura of the commodity', in: Alan Tomlinson (ed.), *Consumption, Identity and Style: marketing, meanings and the packaging of pleasure*, London and New York: Routledge.

Pete Tong (1990), transcribed research interview conducted by Jon Savage, for: The Rhythm Divine [originally Abseil Productions], Kinesis Films, Channel 4.

David Toop (1984), *The Rap Attack: African jive to New York hip hop*, London and Leichhardt: Pluto Press.

David Toop (1992a), 'Throbbery with intent', in: *The Wire*, No. 98, April, London.

David Toop (1992b), 'Dub!', in: *Mixmag*, Vol. 2, No. 19, December, Slough.

David Toop (1995), *Ocean of Sound: aether talk, ambient sound and imaginary worlds*, London and New York: Serpent's Tail.

Simon Trask (1992), 'Touching bass', in: *Music Technology*, May, Ely, can also be found in 'Jazz Angels', in: Chris Kempster (ed.) (1997), *History of House*, London: Sanctuary Publishing.

Michael Tucker (1992), *Dreaming with Open Eyes*, London and San Francisco, CA: Aquarian/Harper.

Robert C. Tucker (ed.) (1978), *The Marx-Engels Reader*, New York: W.W. Norton.

Graeme Turner (1990), *British Cultural Studies: an introduction*, New York and London: Routledge.

Louise Veares and Richard Woods (1993), 'Entertainment', in: *Leisure Futures*, Vol. 3, London: The Henley Centre for Forecasting Ltd.

Gert van Veen (1988), 'Acid', in: *de Volkskrant*, 2 September, Amsterdam.

Gert van Veen (1989a), 'Loodrecht op de kille elektronica', in: *De Volkskrant*, 7 April, Amsterdam.

Gert van Veen (1989b), 'U hoort nog van ons', in: *De Volkskrant*, 29 July, Amsterdam.

Gert van Veen (1989c), 'Discjockey-gevecht in rumoerig Paradiso', in: *De Volkskrant*, 18 October, Amsterdam.

Gert van Veen (1992), 'De wil van de dansvloer', in: *De Volkskrant*, 20 August, Amsterdam.

Alain C. Verhave and Robbert P. ter Weijden (1991), *Amsterdam Housenation: de ontwikkeling van housemuziek en zijn publieksgroep, en de doorstroom van housemuziek tot mainstream popmuziek*, Amsterdam: self publication.

Paul Virilio (1991), *The Aesthetics of Disappearance*, Brooklyn, NY: Semiotext(e).

Fred de Vries (1991), 'House ebt weg: Roxy wendt reeds de steven', in: *Parool*, 12 August, Amsterdam.

Fred de Vries (1992), 'Een enkeltje magisch centrum', in: *NRC-Handelsblad*, 5 September, Rotterdam.

Nils L. Wallin (1991), *Biomusicology: neurophysiological, neuropsychological and evolutionary perspectives on the origins and purposes of music*, Stuyvesant, NY: Pendragon Press.

Barry Walters (1989), 'Burning down the house', in: *Spin*, June, Bellevue WA.

James Ware (1992), opinion in: *Music Week*, 25 January, London.

Arnold M. Washton (1989), *Cocaine Addiction*, London: W. W. Norton and Co.

Ian Waugh (1994), 'Wave for Windows: direct-to-disk recording system', in: *MT, the music technology magazine*, No. 91, May, Ely.

Editorial: Wave (1994), 'Ieder zijn eigen stam', in: *Wave*, No. 2, June, Zaventem and Amsterdam.

Allon White (1989), 'Hysteria and the end of carnival', in: *The Violence of Representation*, Nancy Armstrong and Leonard

Tennenhouse (ed.), London and New York: Routledge.

DJ White Delight (1993), 'Een rustig weekendje', in: *10 Dance*, No. 2, December, Hilversum.

DJ White Delight (1994), 'Op zoek naar de ware betekenis van Trance en Tribal', in: *10 Dance*, No. 5, March, Hilversum.

Paul Willis (1978), *Profane Culture*, London: Routledge and Kegan Paul.

Paul Willis (1990), *Common Culture*, Buckingham: Open University Press.

Mary Bittner Wiseman (1989), *The Ecstasies of Roland Barthes*, London and New York: Routledge.

Peter van Woensel Kooy (1989), 'Cultuur & Co', in: *Haagse Post*, 25 November, Amsterdam.

Niki de Wolf (1991), 'House verliest exclusiviteit', in: *Rotterdams Dagblad*, 24 October, Rotterdam.

Niki de Wolf (1992), '"Safe House Campaign" test XTC tijdens Euro Rave op zuiverheid', in: *Rotterdams Dagblad*, 3 September, Rotterdam.

Tom Wolfe (1989), *The Electric Kool-Aid Acid Test*, London, Moorebank and Auckland: Black Swan/Transworld Publishers.

Sol Yurick (1985), *Behold Metatron: the recording angel*, New York: Semiotext(e).

Audio material

Stu Allen, *Stu Allen Show*, Key 103, Manchester, 1991.

Marcel Bakker, interview with the author, Amsterdam, January, 1992.

Ardy Beesemer, interview with the author, Rotterdam, January, 1992.

Burt 'Non-Stop' Blanchard, interview with the author, Chicago, June, 1992.

Evie Camp, interview with the author, Chicago, June, 1992.

Sarah Champion, in conversation with the author, London, October, 1993.

Phil Cheeseman, interview with the author, London, November, 1993b.

Paul Cons, interview with the author, Manchester, February, 1991.

Tyree Cooper, interview with the author, Chicago, June, 1992.

on Dasilva, interview with the author, Manchester, May, 1992.

Mike E-Block, interview with the author, Manchester, May, 1994.

Fast Eddie, interview with the author, Chicago, June, 1992.

Kevin Elliott, interview with the author, Chicago, September, 1992.

Kevin Elliott, telephone discussion with the author, Manchester/Chicago, September, 1993.

Goa Gee, in conversation with the author, Goa, December 1996.

Andre Halmon, interview with the author, Brookfield, June, 1992.

Alan Haughton, in conversation with the author, Manchester, September, 1991.

Alan Haughton and Hillegonda Rietveld, discussion group 'Researching the Phenomena of Dance Drugs', at: Lifeline Conference, *The New Drugtakers — They Come in Search of Paradise*, NW regional drug training unit, Manchester, 1992.

Steve 'Silk' Hurley, interview with the author, Brookfield, June, 1992.

Linda Hyneman, interview with the author, London, April, 1995.

ITC: In The City, 'It ain't just the Bee Gees, is there money in dance?', a heated panel discussion between Keith Blackhurst (De-Construction) and Ian Levine (Motor City Records) with a 'guest appearance' by Pete Waterman (PWL) observed by the author, Manchester, September, 1992.

Maurice Joshua, interview with the author, Brookfield, June, 1992.

Princess Julia, interview with the author, London, November, 1993.

Peter Larwood, telephone interview with the author, Manchester, May, 1994.

Scott Lash, conversation with the author, Manchester, October, 1992.

Vince Lawrence, interview with the author, Chicago, June, 1992.

Rick Lenoir, interview with the author, Chicago, June, 1992.

Lu, conversation with the author, London, October, 1993.

Jazzy M, interview with the author, London, November, 1993.

Joe Marshall, in conversation with the author, Manchester, August, 1994.

Gary McLarnan, interview with the author, Manchester, September, 1990.

Mark Moore, interview with the author, London, November, 1993.

Mixmaster Morris, in conversation with the author, London, July, 1994.

Lutgard Mutsaers, in conversation with the author, Amsterdam, July, 1994.

NMS: New Music Seminar, 'Dance Independents', panel discussion recorded by the author, New York City, June, 1992a.

NMS: New Music Seminar, 'Sampling and Copyright', panel discussion recorded by the author, New York City, June, 1992b.

Justin O'Connor, conversation with the author, Manchester, March, 1993.

Graeme Park, interview with the author, New York City, June, 1992.

To Pereira, conversation with the author, Lisbon, August, 1993.

Mike Pickering, conversation with the author, New York City, September, 1983.

Bob Pieck and Rik Zwaan, interview with the author, Amsterdam, January, 1992.

DJ Pierre, interview with the author, New York City, June, 1992.

Hillegonda C. Rietveld, documentary tape, February, 1993.

Reinier Rietveld, in conversation with the author, Rotterdam, July, 1992.

Andrew J. Robinson, interview with the author, Manchester, March, 1993.

Frank Rodrigo, interview with the author, Brookfield, June, 1992.

Richard Rogers, conversation with the author, Chicago, June, 1992.

Jon Savage, in conversation with the author, Manchester, October, 1993c.

Larry Sherman, interview with the author, Chicago, June, 1992.

Earl Smith Jr. ('Spanky'), interview with the author, New York City, June, 1992.

Joe Smooth, interview with the author, Chicago, June, 1992.

E Smoove, interview with the author, Brookfield, June, 1992.

Rogan Taylor, telephone discussion with the author, Manchester/ Liverpool, May, 1994.

Alain C. Verhave, interview with the author, January, 1992.

Erik van Vliet, interview with the author, Rotterdam, June, 1992.

Gary Wallace, interview with the author, Chicago, June, 1992.

Pete Waterman, interview with the author, Manchester, September 1992.

Audio-visual material

Saturday Night Fever, Sony, 1977.

Paris Is Burning, ICA, 1991.

The Rhythm Divine, Kinesis Films/NBD Entertainment, Channel 4 1991.

Lyrics

Larry Heard and Chuck Roberts (1988), Fingers Inc. featuring Chuck Roberts, *Can You Feel It? (in our house)*, Desire Records, London and New York: Leo Song/Fiction Song.

Discography[599]

Adonis, *No Way Back*, US Trax, 1986.

---

[599] Unless indicated otherwise, all of these records are on vinyl 12" format.

Afrikaa Bambaataa and the Soul Sonic Force, *Planet Rock*, Polydor, 1982.

Aly-us, *Follow Me*, Strictly Rhythm, 1992.

Bam Bam, *Give It To Me*, Westbrook Records, 1988.

Bananarama, *Love in the first degree*, London Records, 1987.

Bang The Party, *Glad All Over*, Bostich, 1986.

Bang The Party, *Release Your Body*, Warriors Dance, 1987.

The Beach Boys, *Good Vibrations*, Capitol, 1966.

Kim Beacham, *Trouble*, East 111, 1992.

The Beatmasters with the Cookie Crew, *Rok da House*, Torso, 1988.

Biz Markie, *Alone Again*, on: *I Need A Haircut* (album), Cold Chillin', 1992.

Black Box, *Ride on Time*, Disco Magic/DeConstruction, 1989.

Black Uhuru, *Chill Out*, Island Records, 1982.

Black Uhuru, *The Dub Factor*, Island Records, 1983.

Brand New Heavies, *Brand New Heavies* (album), Delicious Vinyl, 1990.

Miquel Brown, *So Many Men So Little Time*, Record Shack, 1983.

Tyrone Brunson, *The Smurf*, on: *Classic Electro Volume 1* (album), MC mastercuts, 1994.

Cabaret Voltaire, *Mix Up*, 1979.

Cabaret Voltaire, *The Crackdown* (album), Some Bizarre/Virgin Records, 1983.

Cabaret Voltaire, *The Dream Ticket*, Some Bizarre/Virgin Records, 1983.

Capella, *U & Me* (Techno and Champagne-version), Internal Dance, 1994.

Mariah Carey, *Dreamlover*, Columbia, 1993.

Shawn Christopher, *Don't Loose The Magic*, Arista, 1992.

Cold Cut, *Doctoring the House*, Ahead Of Your Time, 1988.

Cubic 22, *Night In Motion*, Big Time International, 1991.

Cyberia, *Albatross*, Hypercycle/Virgin, 1992.

Cybotron, *Interface, the roots of techno* (album), South Bound, 1993.

DAF (Deutsch-Amerikanischer Freundschaft), *Alles Ist Gut*, Virgin, 1981.

DAF, *Der Mussolini*, Virgin, 1981.

DAF, *Fur Immer*, Virgin, 1982.

Hazel Dean, *Searchin'*, Proto, 1984.

Degrees Of Motion, *Shine On*, Esquire Records, 1992.

Demo with the basic sequenced instrumental loop for *Holding Out*, 1992.

Depeche Mode, *Speak and Spell* (album), Mute Records, 1981.

Depeche Mode, *See You*, Mute, 1982.

Dexy's Midnight Runners, *Search for the young soul rebels* (album), EMI, 1980.

Digital Boy, *Gimme A Fat Beat*, Flying Records, 1991.

D-Mob, *We call it Acieed*, FFRR, 1988.

Double Exposure, *Ten Percent*, Salsoul, 1976.

Double Exposure/Walter Gibbons, *Ten Percent*, on: *Salsoul Classics* (album), This Compilation/Indigo Music, 1989.

Double Exposure/Masters At Work, *Ten Percent*, on: *Salsoul Synergy* (album), Double J Records, 1992.

D-Shake, *YAAAAH!*, Go Bang, 1990.

D Train, *Keep On*, Prelude (around 1981).

e-zee possee, *everything starts with an "e"*, More Protein, 1989.

Einsturzende Neubauten, *Kollaps*, Zick Zack, 1981.

Brian Eno, *Music For Films* (album), Polydor, 1978.

Euromasters, *Alles Naar De Kl**te*, Rotterdam Records, 1992.

Euromasters, *Rotterdam Ech Wel/Amsterdam Waar Lech Dat Dan?*, Rotterdam Records, 1992.

Fad Gadget, *Ricky's Hand/Handshake*, Mute Records, 1980.

Farley 'Jackmaster' Funk feat. Daryl Pandy, *Love Can't Turn Around*, DJ International, 1986.

Fast Eddie, *Yo Yo Get Funky*, DJ International, 1988.

Fingers Inc., *Feelin' Sleazy*, on: *Another Side* (album), Jack Trax, 1988.

Fingers Inc. featuring Chuck Roberts, *Can You Feel It? (in our house)*, Desire 1988 (also available on: Various, *In The Key Of E*, Desire, 1988).

Mr Fingers, *Mystery of Love*, Jack Trax, 1988.

First Choice, *On & On*, Salsoul, 1979.

First Choice, *Let No Man Putasunder*, Salsoul, 1983.

4 House, *Mr. Kirk's Nightmare*, Reinforced Records, 1991.

Front 242, *Body To Body*, Red Rhino Europe, 1981/New Dance, 1982.

Taana Gardner, *Heartbeat*, West End, 1980.

Marvin Gaye, *Sexual Healing*, CBS, 1992.

Goldie, *Timeless*, FFRR, 1995.

The Green Man, *Shut Up and Dance*, Shut Up and Dance Records, 1992.

A Guy Called Gerald, *Voodoo Ray*, Rham, 1988.

Hashim, *Al-Naafiysh*, Cutting Records, 1982.

Lolleatta Holloway, *Love Sensation*, Salsoul, 1980.

Holy Noise, *The Noise*, Hithouse Records, 1991.

Holy Noise featuring Global Insert Project, *James Brown Is Still Alive!*, ARS Records, 1991.

House of Gypsies, *Somba*, Freeze Records, 1992.

The Human League, *Reproduction* (album), Virgin Records, 1979.

The Human League, *Travelogue* (album), Virgin Records, 1980.

Human Resource, *The Complete Dominator*, R&S, 1991.

Humanoid, *Stakker Humanoid*, Westside, 1989.

Steve 'Silk' Hurley, *Jack Your Body*, US Underground, 1986.

impLog, *Holland Tunnel Dive/Broadway*, Infidelity, 1980.

Indeep, *Last Night A DJ Saved My Life*, Sounds of New York Records, 1983.

Inner City, *Big Fun*, Ten Records, 1988.

Candy J, *Shoulda Known Better*, Vinyl Solution, 1993.

Jack and Jill, *Work It Girlfriend*, Strictly Rhythm, 1993.

Janet Jackson, *Throb (David Morales Legendary Dub)*, Virgin, 1994.

Michael Jackson, *Billy Jean*, Epic, 1983.

Marshall Jefferson, *The House Anthem*, Trax Records, 1986.

Loose Jointz, *All Over My Face*, West End, 1980.

BP Johnson, *I Believe In The Power*, Stealth Records, 1992.

Klein & MBO, *Dirty Talk*, Baby Records, 1982.

Kraftwerk, *Autobahn* (album), Phillips, 1974.

Kraftwerk, *Trans Europe Express* (album), EMI, 1977.

Kraftwerk, *Computer World* (album), EMI, 1981.

Kraftwerk, *Techno Pop*, Capitol, 1983.

LA Style, *James Brown Is Dead*, Bounce, 1991.

Laibach, *The Occupied 1985 Europe Tour* (album), Side Effects Records, 1986.

Annie Lennox, *Little Bird* (Todd Terry remix), RCA, 1993.

LFO, *LFO*, Warp, 1991.

Liasons Dangereuses, *Los Ninos Del Parque*, Roadrunner, 1981.

Lil Louis, *French Kiss*, FFRR, 1989.

LNR, *Let's Work It To The Bone*, Night Club, 1988.

LNR, *Bubbles*, Night Club, 1991.

Man Parrish, *Hip Hop, Be Bop (Don't Stop)*, on: *Classic Electro Volume 1* (album), MC mastercuts, 1994.

Manix, *Head In The Clouds*, on: *Illegal Rave III* (double album), Strictly Underground, 1994.

Mantronix, *Who Is It?*, Ten Records, 1987.

M/A/R/R/S, *Pump Up The Volume*, 4AD, 1987.

Mercedes, *Living For The Moment*, Vinyl Solution, 1994.

Midnight Sunrise, *On The House*, Nightmare Records, 1986.

Kylie Minogue, *I Should Be So Lucky*, PWL, 1988.

Model 500, *No UFO's*, Metroplex, 1985.

More Kante, *Ye Ke Ye Ke*, Barcley Records, 1987 (licensed for Britain by London Records).

Giorgio Moroder and Donna Summer, *Love To Love You Baby*, Casablanca, 1975.

M-People, *Northern Soul* (album), DeConstruction, 1992.

Neuro, *Mama*, R&S, 1993.

New Order, *Blue Monday*, Factory Records, 1983.

The Normal, *TVOD/warm leatherette*, Mute Records, 1978.

Gary Numan, *Cars*, Beggars Banquet, 1978.

Orbital, *Chime*, FFRR, 1990.

Gilbert O'Sullivan, *Alone Again (Naturally)*, MAM, 1972.

Paragliders, *Paraglide EP*, Superstition Records, 1993.

Parliament, *The Best of Parliament* (album), Club/Phonogram, 1986.

Pascal's Bongo Massive, *Pere Cochon*, Tomato Records, 1994.

Peech Boys, *Don't Make Me Wait*, Island Record, 1983.

Pet Shop Boys, *It's All Right*, Parlophone, 1989.

Phase II, *Reaching*, Movin' Records/Republic Records, 1988.

Phuture, *Acid Tracks/Your Only Friend*, Trax, 1987.

Jamie Principle, *Baby Wants to Ride*, Trax Records, 1984.

The Prodigy, *Charly*, XL-Recordings, 1991.

Quando Quango, *Go Exciting*, Factory Records, 1982.

Quando Quango, *Love Tempo*, Factory Records, 1983.

Quando Quango, *Atom Rock*, Factory Records, 1984.

Quando Quango, *Genius*, Factory Records, 1985.

Rage Against The Machine, *Rage Against The Machine* (album), Epic, 1992.

Ravel, *Bolero* (version by Halle Orchestra), EMI, 1979.

Raze, *Jack the Groove*, Champion, 1986.

Sharon Red, *Beat The Street*, Prelude, 1982.

The Residents, *Diskomo/Goosebump*, Ralph Records, 1980.

Rhythim Is Rhythim, *Strings of Life, Kaos*/Model 500, *Off To Battle* (EP), Jack Trax, 1987.

Rhythim Is Rhythim, *It Is What It Is*, Transmat, 1988.

Richard Rogers, *All I Want*, Sam Records, 1992.

Hillegonda Rietveld and Andrew Robinson demo, 1989.

Hillegonda Rietveld and Denise Johnson, *Save Me*, demo 1989.

Hillegonda Rietveld and Sonya, *Opening Up*, demo 1998.

Rotterdam Termination Souce, *Poing/Feyenoord Reactivate*, Rotterdam Records, 1992.

Royal House, *Can You Party*, Torso, 1988.

Jesse Saunders, *On & On*, Trax Records, 1983.

Search, *Holding Out*, Robsrecords, 1993.

Search, *Holding Out* (regular version), Robsrecords, 1993.

Search, *Holding Out* (dance version 117), Robsrecords, 1993.

Search, *Holding Out* (unreleased funky Kincy version), 1992.

Search, *Holding Out* (unreleased teaser version), 1992.

Seduction, *Seduction*, Break Out, A & M records, 1988.

Senser, *Stacked Up*, Ultimate, 1994.

S-Express, *Theme from S-Express*, Torso/Rhythm King, 1988.

Shades of Rhythm, *Extacy*, ZTT, 1991.

JM Silk, *Shadows of Your Love*, DJ International, 1986.

JM Silk, *I Can't Turn Around*, RCA/Victor, 1986.

Joyce Sims, *All and All*, Sleeping Bag, 1986.

Sister Sledge, *Lost In Music* (Sure is Pure remix), Atlantic, 1993.

Joe Smooth, *Promised Land*, DJ International, 1987.

Sonic Surfers, *Beat of Zen*, Fifth World, 1991.

Sperminator, *No Women Allowed*, Rotterdam Records, 1992.

State 808, *Pacific*, Eastern Bloc, 1989.

Suicide, *Dream Baby Dream*, ZE Records, 1979.

T-Coy, *Carino*, DeConstruction, 1987.

Technotronic, *Pump it Up*, ARS Records, 1989.

Ten City, *Devotion*, WEA, 1987.

Todd Terry, *Sound Design*, TNT, 1992.

Evelyn Thomas, *High Energy*, Nightmare Records, 1984.

Evelyn Thomas, *High Energy ('90 remix)*, Passion, 1990.

T99, *Anasthesia*, Who's That Beat Records, 1991.

Liz Torres, *When You Hold Me/What You Make Me Feel*, on: Liz Torres featuring Master C&J, *Can't Get Enough* (album), Jack Trax, 1987.

The Trammps, *Disco Inferno*, Atlantic Records, 1977.

Transglobal Underground, *Earth Tribe/Slowfinger*, Nation Records, 1994.

Triple M Bass, *Worse 'Em*, Profile, 1986.

King Tubby, *August Pablo meets Rockers uptown* (album), Yard Music, 1976.

2 Unlimited, *No Limits*, Bite, 1993.

Tyree, *Lonely (No More)*, DJ International, 1990.

Urban Dance Squad, *The Bureaucrat of Flaccostreet*, Ariola, 1991.

Various, *Ambient House* (album), DFC, 1991.

Various, *Artificial Intelligence Part I & II* (album series), Warp Records, 1993/94.

Various, *Beat This: Rhythm King* (double album), Stylus Music, 1989.

Various, *Bleeps International* (album), Fast Forward Records, 1991.

Various, *Classic Electro Vol. 1* (double album), MC Mastercuts, 1994.

Various, *Classic House Vol. 1* (double album), MC Mastercuts, 1994.

Various, *The Deepest Shades of Techno* (album), Reflect, 1994.

Various, *The Drum Album* (album), Drum Records, 1994.

Various, *Electronic Body Music* (album), Play It Again Sam Records, 1988.

Various, *Food for Woofers: Car Hifi Demo* (CD), FFW, 1992.

Various, *Happy Trax, Vol. 1-3* (series of EPs), Happy Records, 1992/93.

Various, *The House Sound of ...*, Vol. 1 to 5 (series of albums), FFRR, 1986/89.

Various, *The House Sound of Chicago, Vol. 3, Acid House* (album), FFRR, 1987.

Various, *The House Sound of London, Vol. 4* (album), FFRR, 1988.

Various, *Illegal Rave III* (double album), Strictly Underground, 1994.

Various, *In The Key Of E* (album), Desire, 1988.

Various, *Jack Trax series* (albums and 12" limited edition re-releases of Chicago and Detroit material), Jack Trax/Indigo Music, 1987/89.

Various, *None of these are love songs* (triple album), Caustic Vision, 1994.

Various, *Rob Olson's Chicago Jack Beat, Vol. 1* (album), Rhythm King, 1986.

Various, *Salsoul Classics* (four album box), Indigo Musik, 1989.

Various, *Saturday Night Fever* (double album), RSO, 1977.

Various, *The Secret Life of Trance* (double album), Rising High, 1993.

Various, *Soul Beats No. 1 & 2* (EP series), Simply Soul, 1992/93.

Various, *Strictly Rhythm* (double album), Strictly Rhythm Records, 1991.

Various, *Strictly Rhythm Tracks 92* (album), Strictly Rhythm Records, 1992.

Various, *Strictly Underground II* (double album), Strictly Underground, 1994.

Various, *Techno Grooves* (EP), Mach 5, Stealth Records, 1992.

Various, *This is Strictly Rhythm: Vol. 3* (double album), Strictly Rhythm Records, 1993.

Various, *Warehouse Raves*, Rumour Records, 1994.

Various, *The West End Story* (album series), West End, 1994.

Various, *XL-Recordings; The Second Chapter, Hardcore European Dance Music* (double album), XL-Recordings, 1991.

Sven Vath, *Ritual of Life*, Q Records, 1992.

Virgo, *Virgo Project*, Trax Records, 1985.

Sterling Void and Paris Brightledge, *It's Alright*, DJ International, 1987.

Whodini, *Magic Wand*, on: *Classic Electro Volume 1* (double album), MC mastercuts, 1994.

Yazz and the Plastic Population, *Only Way Is Up*, Big Life, 1988.

Yello, *I Love You*, Stiff, 1985.

Z Factor, *Fantasy*, Mitchball, 1983.

Z Factor, *I Like To Do It In A Fast Car*, Mitchball, 1983.

Part VI
Appendices

A Hillegonda re-enters the studio

This appendix is an extract from a tape transcription, which shows that this research is not that of an outsider. It was during the course of doing research interviews for this project that I started to realise, with some bewilderment, how much I was actually part of the events which led to the articulation of house music. Instead of walking into strange territory, I ended up being welcomed like a lost member of the family. The following interview extracts are only an example of this attitude, which was repeated in different manners in the various encounters I had with producers, DJs and journalists. Because of this the access to research material was relatively easier for me than for someone who had freshly entered this field of research.

The tape documentary follows a part of my conversation with Chicago dance music producer Vince Lawrence, who suggested during the interview visit that we should make a record together. In order to stay in control of the subsequent process of marketing, I chose to release the record in England. Support came from Rob Gretton in Manchester, England, who used to be director of my old record label Factory Records and who had set up his own record label, Robsrecords. In this manner an international collaboration was set up, which is not unusual within the area of dance music and which shows that geographical boundaries are not always applicable in defining a musical genre. Rather, the realm of house music is part of one of the many global villages which make up contemporary world culture. However, it has to be stressed that the choice of sounds and of rhythm patterns are recognisably African-American, while the Americans who visited the Chicago studio when we were working on the track felt that the track[600] had a European flavour in its melody structure and in its minimalism of instrumentation: a global village which behaves like a musical scene [Straw, 1991] breeds hybrids of many kinds.

Transcription

Commentator: Hillegonda Rietveld.

Interview material from Chicago: Burt 'Non-Stop' Blanchard; DJ.
Vince Lawrence; producer.
Hillegonda Rietveld; PhD student and musician.
Richard Rogers; singer.

Commentator: This is the story about the making of the dance song *Holding Out*, by a project called Search. The record came about as a part of research I have done for the Manchester Institute for Popular Culture and also for a project I am doing on house music and in the course of that I interviewed Vince Lawrence of Go Bang Productions. Since I couldn't find any better way of describing the record that we finally made I'll give you quotes of what Vince says about the music he makes.

Vince: "Right now everything that I'm working on is really slow and musical and jazzy, you know, house music to fuck by (laughs) you know that's what everybody is calling this shit."

Richard: giggles.

Commentator: "That last giggle was Richard Rogers one of the singers on *Holding Out*. This was how I was introduced to him — he ran off."

Vince: "You should talk to Richard, 'cause Marshall Jefferson produced some stuff for Richard that's gonna be like house music classics."

Richard: "(He knows) everything about me, everything. I'm right back" (laughs and leaves).

Vince: "Richard can sing."

Commentator: "Yes, Richard can sing as you can hear later on. But how do they actually go about making records in Chicago? Well, this

---

[600] See Chapter 3.

was the first invitation. Just listen to how the interview develops."

[Interviewer (Hillegonda Rietveld) and interviewee (Vince Lawrence) had started a discussion about the music scene and the cultural 'generations' of musicians that follow in each others footsteps. According to Vince, who started making records in 1982, there have been five waves of new musicians since him.]

Vince: "It's funny it makes me feel like an old assed codger, man."
Hillegonda: "It makes me feel old as well, actually. I mean, yeah, I had my first 808 in 1982."
Vince: "Woh, yeah! So you know what time it is."
Hillegonda: "That's why I'm doing this project now because I used to make, like, dance music — not house music but, you know, I had my 808 and experimented in my own way making dance music."
Vince: "What sort of stuff did you make?"
Hillegonda: "Well, the band at the time was called Quando Quango ..."
Vince: "Wait a minute, Quando Quango? Didn't they make *Love Tempo* (sings)?"
Hillegonda: "Yeah, that's our tune."
Vince: "Oh, man!!!!! God!! Freak out!!! Well, see you inspired, like you're part of the inspiration for all this shit, man! Oh man, that was my cut. I know guys that would freak to meet you, and you're interviewing me! Bogus! (laughs) We should just go make a tune or something. Skip the bullshit!"
Hillegonda: "Oh yeah!" (laughs)
Vince: "So how long are you here for? A week?"
Hillegonda: "Yeah, I'm going to New York on Friday week."
Vince: "Yeah? Are you coming back to Chicago?"
Hillegonda: "Nah, that's it."
Vince: "Let's cut some tunes before you go then."
Hillegonda: "Yeah, I'd like to."
Vince: "We could cut something tomorrow and have it out by Tuesday."
Hillegonda: "Yeah, that's the way it works." (laughs)
Vince: "I have a deal that like simplifies everything. It's like because we're working together you'd be attached directly to my involvement with all the other guys that I know. So it's like I may have to cut a

deal with a pressing plant[601] to press it and distribute it but you get half of what ever I get."

Commentator: "Well, as you can hear, I was major shy there and was just trying to keep my cool so I was just saying: 'yeah, yeah, yeah, I could play that.'" The conversation continued:

Vince: "Say, who did that bass line (of *Love Tempo*)?"

Hillegonda: "I did."

Vince: "Oh, fuck. Shiiiit." (giggles)

Hillegonda: "I just had it playing for like month after month and I sort of thought, oh, I like this bass line."

The conversation which follows is with Chicago DJ Burt 'Non-Stop' Blanchard, who, in the run of my interview with him about Chicago house music, turned out to be fan of Quando Quango as well. We were both amazed:

Hillegonda: "(We made) a track called *Love Tempo* and apparently that did alright."

Burt: "Wait a minute! No!!! No (fucking) way. No, you did not play with that band. No way."

Hillegonda: "I made that music."

Burt: "And Atomic Rock?"

Hillegonda: "*Atom Rock*, yeah?"

Burt: "Atomic, *Atom Rock*."

Hillegonda: "We were just like figuring out this technology."

Burt: "No way!"

Hillegonda: "Yeah." (giggles)

Burt: "What, *Love Tempo* was one of the first import 12" I bought when I first started DJ-ing seriously and we were just collecting music and ... I can't believe it."

Hillegonda: "Well, I can't believe it myself because I never knew. I mean, I wish someone would have told me. I would have come over to Chicago. I mean, any excuse (to come over)."

Burt: "Oh, man! You wouldn't believe."

Hillegonda: "We've been playing in New York, but never here."

Burt: "I still play that record and people still scream."

---

[601] This turns out to be Larry Sherman's plant. See Chapter 3.

B   Dance music compilations[602]

Compilations are useful in order to get an overview of certain musical genres and categories. This list attempts to trace a development of house music via disco music. Some other related musical forms are also represented and have been listed according to country of release. The fact that British releases are over represented in this list is partly because most of the research for this thesis has been undertaken in Britain and partly because in England house music and related musical forms were embraced more on a wholesale basis than anywhere else.

This list does not pretend to be complete. Due to the popularity of dance music, which is usually released on relatively expensive 12" vinyl disks, dance music compilations have become an economically successful format and so the amount of dance music compilations is huge. It is outside the scope of this book to attempt to trace every one of these; a sample is sufficient. Having said so, I am quite certain that the most important house music compilations, which were released around 1988, are present in this list.

Disco

Saturday Night Fever, RSO, 1977.

---

[602] In order of musical category and (to show examples of dance music which were inspired by the 'house explosion') geographical place of release; sub ordered on year of release and, following that, in alphabetical order.

Salsoul Classics, Indigo Music, 1989.

Garage

The Garage Sound of Deepest New York, Republic Records, 1988.

Garage Classique, 4th & Broadway, 1989.

The Garage Sound; the third generation, Republic Records, 1991.

House

Jack Trax, album 1-6, Jack Trax/Indigo music, 1987.

House Beats 1, Warrior Records, 1987.

The House Sound (of Chicago), FFRR, 1986.

The House Sound (of Chicago); Vol. II, FFRR, 1987.

The House Sound (of Chicago); Vol. III: Acid Tracks, FFRR, 1987.

The History of the House Sound of Chicago, BCM Records, 1988.

The House of Hits, DJ International/Westside Records, 1988.

Westside House Music (Box Set), Westside Records, 1988.

Ultimate House, Champion Records, 1988.

Urban Acid, GRC Records, 1988.

The Best of Hip House, Street Sounds/DJ International, 1989.

Hip House, K-Tel, 1989.

Ware's The House, Stylus Music, 1989.

The House Sound of the Underground (the storm before the calm),

FFRR, 1991.

Classic House, MC Master Cuts, 1994.

US club

Strictly Rhythm, Strictly Rhythm Records, 1991.

Strictly Rhythm Tracks 92, Strictly Rhythm Records, 1992.

Happy Trax Vol. 1-3, Happy Records, date unknown (1993?).

Soul Beats No. 1 & 2, Simply Soul, date unknown (1993?).

This is Strictly Rhythm: Vol. 3, Strictly Rhythm Records, 1993.

UK dance

The House Sound (of London): Vol. IV, FFRR, 1988.

In The Key Of E, Desire, 1988.

North, Deconstruction, 1988.

Beat This: Rhythm King, Stylus Music, 1989.

Smash Hits Rave!, Dover/Chrysalis Records, 1990.

Bleeps International, Fast Forward Records, 1991.

UK DJ's Rhythms from Within, Champion Records, 1991.

XL Recordings — The Second Chapter: Hardcore European Dance Music, XL Records, 1991.

Dub House Disco (This is what Guerilla is about), Guerilla, 1992.

Two Clouds Above Nine: 10 original tracks from the Grove, London,

Tomato Records, 1992.

In: House Music, A&M/P&M, 1993.

Obsessive House Culture, Obsessive Records, date unknown.

Tony Humphries (Comp.), Ministry of Sound — the Sessions, Vol. 1, MOS Recordings, 1993.

The Secret Life of Trance, Rising High Records, 1993.

Transcend, Rumour Records, date unknown.

Trance Europe Express, Vol. 1 (dist.) BMG, 1993.

Trance Europe Express, Vol. 2 (dist.) BMG, 1994.

Artificial Intelligence part I, Warp Records, 1993/94.

Artificial Intelligence part II, Warp Records, 1993/94.

Strictly Underground; the Compilation II, Strictly Underground, 1994.

None Of These Are Love Songs, Caustic Vision, 1994.

German trance

Dance Yourself To Death, Black Out/Boy Records, 1992.

Italian house

The House Sound (of Europe), Vol. V, FFRR, 1989.

C Specialist press

The following magazines and small press have been used as research material for this book:

American titles (1992/93)

Billboard — the authoritative weekly of the US music business.
Chicago Music Magazine — local music magazine from Chicago with dance column.
Crossfade — Chicago zine for the house fan of the 90s.
Rolling Stone — leading rock magazine with a rock attitude towards dance club and digitally recorded music.
Spin — music monthly.
Streetsound — 'North America's International DJ Authority'.
Underground News! — New York and Chicago collaboration on dance club music.
Under One Sky — Brooklyn based techno/rave zine.
US Rave — regular paper for fans of Euro styled raves.

British titles (1991/94)

Ace Of Clubs — dance club zine.
The Big Issue — general what's on; with dance music and club reviews.
Blues and Soul — 'black' popular musical genres.
Boyz — free weekly for gay club culture.

Boy's Own — elite rave zine from the first hour with footy attitude.
Champion — rave/techno zine with a football fan attitude; funny.
City Life — Manchester's what's on; with dance music and club reviews.
Deadline — underground cartoon zine with info on dance culture.
Disco Mirror — trade magazine for club owners and promoters.
DJ — leading dance club and music magazine for DJs.
Drum — dance music magazine.
Ear To The Ground — rave zine for the 'acid ted'.
Echoes — 'black' popular musical genres.
Encyclopaedia Psychedelia International — an early Frazer Clark 'new zippy' zine.
Eternity — underground dance zine.
The Face — leading style magazine on the 'edge' of culture.
Generator — dance club/rave zine.
The Herb Garden — cynical dance club zine with punk attitude.
i-D — leading magazine on new cultural phenomena.
The Jockey Slut — 'disco pogo for punks in pumps'; intelligent articles.
Joy of Life — 'the lifestyle magazine for ravers'.
Melody Maker — rock/indie music paper; includes some 'dance'.
Mixmag — leading dance club and music magazine.
Mixmag Update — weekly club news, charts and record reviews for DJs.
Music Technology — leading magazine for studio musicians.
Music Week — weekly UK music business news; *Record Mirror*.
The Nerve — dance club zine with attitude (check 'Moody DJ').
NME — indie/punk music paper with a dance groove section.
Northern Light — dance club zine for the North.
Pod — DIY zine for road protests, sound systems, squats, etc.
Ravescene Magazeen — forthnightly rave zine for the more or less legal UK rave scene.
Record Mirror — dance music specialist magazine; inside *Music Week*.
Remix — Irish dance info zine for DJs.
Sky Magazine — pop magazine which tells you more.
Street — advertising freebie with stuff on dance music.
Sub — Mancunian student zine.
Time Out — London's what's on; with dance music and club reviews.
Touch — dance music zine.

24 Seven — death cults and dance music; bizarre bitterness?
24-7 — predecessor of *24 Seven*; rave and club music.
Wire — the educated person's pop magazine.
Zippy Times — a Fraser Clark offshoot (see: London club night 'Megatripolis').

Dutch titles (1991/94)

Bassic Groove — leading 'Modern dance and lifestyle magazine'.
Circuit — Rotterdam's what's on; with dance music and club reviews.
City Life — Amsterdam's English what's on incorporating club zine *Wild!*.
Dance Update — dance music, party and club reviews.
Fret — free pop, rock and dance music magazine.
Hi Tech Music — claims to 'set standards for music, technology and the studio of today'.
Midi Magazine — reviews and articles related to digital music technology.
Music Maker — reviews and articles related to electronic music technology.
Nieuwe Revu — general interest magazine; discusses dance related issues.
Oor — national rock music paper with a dance groove section.
Sextrema magazine — dance club and party magazine.
10 Dance — leading dance music magazine for the Benelux.
Wild! — was the first British styled dance party zine in the Netherlands; ended up inside *City Life*.

D   Disco DJs

Although many DJs have been described in the previous chapters, some of the earlier disco DJs should be placed in a historical perspective which seems to run from Francis Grosso to the 'Fathers of House' and beyond. Perhaps as persons they may not matter, since without the availability of new technologies as well as a specific cultural context they would not exist. If there had not been a Frankie Knuckles, there would still have been a Marshall Jefferson in Chicago during the 80s and without David Mancuso there would most likely still have been a Larry Levan in 70s New York. Many DJs talk of how they were at 'the right place at the right time' when they 'kind of rolled into the job' [Princess Julia, 1993]. For instance, Larry Levan was a lighting man at the Continental Baths in New York when there was no DJ one night. His boss told him to fill the gap, even though it meant he had to borrow his friend's records to do it [Harvey, 1983]. A similar story comes from English garage DJ Graeme Park, whose boss at the record shop where he worked opened a club (appropriately) called the Garage in Nottingham but had no DJ for the opening night and so convinced Graeme to do it 'temporarily' [Park, 1992]. Graeme became a celebrated DJ who presided over the Haçienda in Manchester on Saturday nights and who was voted 'DJ of the year' both in 1991 and 1992. It is a particular kind of historical writing which wants to find its 'authentic' heroes and for every hero, a person may argue that there are many others who are, justifiably or not, more important. Yet at the same time, apart from being handy landmarks in a rather chaotic cultural phenomenon, these people have been revered as true seminal heroes by armies of audiences as well as by generations of DJs which followed. Some of these were

273

mentioned in the previous chapters concerning house music. However, disco existed before house music, so I want to give some appendix space to some of the heroes of yesteryear. At times, my heroes are the Nuyorican production remix team, Masters at Work, 'Little' Lovie Vega and Kenny 'Dope' Gonzalez.

After Walter Grosso from the Sanctuary, Walter Gibbons stands out due to an innovating DJ and remix style. Starting his remix work in the mid-70s, he made creative use of newly available technologies at that time. The employment of reverbs and effects in his DJ mixes and his knack of recreating songs for use in dance clubs put him in the vanguard of a new generation of disco DJs and remixers who would create tracks specially for their own clubs and who are still revered as founders of house music in the popular club press. Some of these have become canonical giants like Frankie Knuckles of the Warehouse in Chicago in the late 70s and early 80s and Larry Levan of Paradise Garage in New York in the same period.[603] A DJ who is often mentioned as a major influence by other New York DJs is David Mancuso of the Loft, who had a very eclectic style and a critical ear for sound systems. He was renowned for his ideas of what a club should sound like and the type of audience it should draw. His club was very exclusive; entry was by invitation only. He did not favour mixing and had a policy whereby a record should be played from beginning to end, presumably he thought the artist 'intended' it that way. He did not only play disco, but also European imports and rock, thereby 'opening up' the ears of other innovators. Another DJ from that era who is often mentioned with reverence by most current house DJs to whom I have spoken is Tony Humphries who DJed at the exclusively African-American club the Zanzibar in Newark into the early 1980s. During the 1980s and early 1990s his legendary radio hot mix shows on New York's Kiss FM have inspired the mixing style of many dance club DJs all over the world through pirated radio tapes of his show.[604] Most of the influential DJs have been part of the dance underground which, in DJ Francois Kervorkian's words, can be described in a kind of sweeping manner as being 'black, gay, afterhours — (where) the beat was like a hammer' [Harvey, 1983], which continued regardless of the opinion by the rest of the world on the subject of dance club music.

---

[603] See Chapter 2.

[604] There was great excitement in the British club world when Humphries took on a residency for 3 months at London's Ministry of Sound.

E   La Gonda

As a result of the knowledge which was gathered during my many years of working in the Haçienda club in Manchester as well as during the specific period of my PhD research, I was able to become a house DJ, which gave me an insight into the experience of a house DJ's act in various locations such as bars, private parties, dance clubs, after hours clubs and 'gay' men clubs in both England and the Netherlands, as well as a huge lesbian club in the centre of London and a large house party, attended by more than 5000 dancers, in the countryside of Belgium.

Initially this involved rehearsing several sets of record sequences, putting some of those on tape, sending the recorded mixes out to organisers, using every social contact available and 'blagging' my way into prestigious venues and events as well as onto various promotional mailing lists which provided me with some free up-to-date dance recordings. The relative success I had as a house DJ is an indication that the research material I had gathered was accurate. I have to admit that I more or less threw myself in at the deep end, which meant that I had to learn very quickly about how to relate to a wide variety of audiences; I had to drop the idea of a rehearsed set in order to adjust to the mood of the night and I had to bring as many 'reserve' records as I could carry without immediately causing damage to my body frame with the 'deadly' weight of vinyl. My personal taste has always veered towards the funkier side of house music, which meant that I bought a lot of American imports. I prefer syncopated bass lines and productions which hit me in the gut. After a while I was able to guess where the compromise between me and a certain audience would be, so I could afford to venture out to a venue with less records.

My approach seems to have worked; I have had excellent reactions and was tempted to become a professional DJ. After all, to use Nietzschian terminology, Dyonisian cultural practice can give the type of instant gratification which Apollonian theoretical practice can only provide on a delayed and long term basis; compare Freud's pleasure principle versus the death principle [Marcuse, 1987]. However, I do hope that this book has not swayed too much towards the death principle, in other words, killing a living culture, by pinning it down in a static non-contradictory manner. Rather, I hope this text contributes to the lively debate which surrounds and underpins contemporary dance culture, in the way that a DJ takes part in the creation of forever changing dance music forms.